NATIVE PLANTS

for High-Elevation
Western Gardens

NATIVE PLANTS
for High-Elevation
Western Gardens

**Janice Busco
and Nancy R. Morin**

Photographs by Gene Balzer

FULCRUM PUBLISHING
GOLDEN, COLORADO

PUBLISHED IN PARTNERSHIP
WITH THE ARBORETUM AT FLAGSTAFF

Library of Congress Cataloging-in-Publication Data

Busco, Janice.
  Native plants for high-elevation western gardens / Janice Busco and
Nancy R. Morin ; photographs by Gene Balzer.
      p. cm.
Includes bibliographical references and index.
  ISBN 1-55591-475-6 (pbk. : alk. paper)
  1. Alpine garden plants—West (U.S.) 2. Native plants for
cultivation—West (U.S.) I. Morin, Nancy R. II. Balzer, Gene. III.
Title.
SB421.B87 2003
635.9'528'0978—dc21
                        2002152977

Editorial: Ellen Wheat, Alice Copp Smith, Daniel Forrest-Bank
Design: Constance Bollen, cb graphics
Cover and back cover photographs: Gene Balzer, except where noted above.

Printed in China
0 9 8 7 6 5 4 3 2 1

Fulcrum Publishing
16100 Table Mountain Parkway, Suite 300
Golden, Colorado 80403
(800) 992-2908 • (303) 277-1623
www.fulcrum-books.com

ACKNOWLEDGMENTS

We are grateful for the vision and foresight with which Frances McAllister founded The Arboretum at Flagstaff and for her unfailing and generous support through its first twenty years. For over a decade, staff and volunteers at The Arboretum at Flagstaff have contributed their expertise and observations to the database underlying the species descriptions provided in this book, much of that time under the supervision of Joyce Maschinski, including Wayne and Judy Hite, Ken Asplund, Bob Wilson, Hattie Braun, Joanne Baggs, and June Beasley. We thank Rose Houk for her fine editing of the manuscript. We thank Cheryl Casey, Mar-Elise Hill, and Derek Nelson for locating suitable plants for the photographs and assisting photographer Gene Balzer. We are especially grateful to the Stanley Smith Horticultural Trust and to the National Fish and Wildlife Foundation for their generous financial support of this project.

CONTENTS

PLANTING AND MAINTAINING
THE NATIVE GARDEN

NATIVE PLANT
SPECIES

Allium cernuum

THE JOY OF GROWING NATIVE PLANTS

❖

Gardeners choose to grow native plants for many reasons. Often their desire springs from the wish to use less of everything—water, energy, pesticides, fertilizer, labor. It's true that, once established, many native plants demand little coddling and need little maintenance. For many gardeners, however, the reasons are more aesthetic and intuitive than practical. The sheer excitement and pleasure of getting to know native plants and bringing them into the garden is beyond description—the joy of seeing penstemons and gilias in pink and red, daisies and sunflowers with their cheery yellows, and coneflowers in soft purple, abuzz with butterflies and hummingbirds dipping in for their payoffs of nectar. It is a true reward to plant just the right shrub that will actually thrive in a particular shaded spot, to choose a gorgeous native grass for a dry, sunny meadow, or to find a ground cover that will spread and ask little attention. With a base of knowledge and a sense of cooperation with nature, nurturing native plants can bring much more gratification than growing standard nursery fare.

When we bring native plants into our gardens, we are often witnesses to delightful interactions between the plants and their pollinators. Hummingbirds, bee flies, bees, hawk moths, and butterflies are all frequent visitors to the native garden. And although few natives are as large-flowered or showy as their commercially bred counterparts, they are beautiful in their own right for their subtle textures, forms, fragrances, and colors. Plantings of native species can re-create the harmonious communities seen in nature, where these plants grow naturally together because they are adapted to the same climate, soils, topography, altitude, and available water. In a garden they create a sense of place. They are aesthetically pleasing because they look right together.

Intimately linked with this sense of place is an even more compelling reason to use native plants in the garden. Unlike exotic plants, which may spread uncontrollably once introduced, most native plants maintain an interactive and beneficial relationship with the other plants and animals in their environment. Most native plant communities are diverse in species makeup and structure and thus provide food and shelter for a wide range of other organisms. They live in true community—supporting neighboring life forms as diverse as mammals, birds, butterflies and other insects, fungi, bacteria, and nematodes, and even acting as nurse plants for one another. Adapted to local conditions, they thrive within natural limits of water and soil fertility and tolerate natural levels of insect populations and pathogens.

THE ARBORETUM AT FLAGSTAFF

◆

The Arboretum at Flagstaff, at an elevation of 7,150 feet, focuses on native plants and plant habitats of the Colorado Plateau. Founded in 1981 by gardener and local philanthropist Mrs. Frances McAllister, it is located 8 miles southwest of Flagstaff, Arizona. Its 10 acres of gardens, situated within 200 acres of natural area, provide a wonderful introduction to native plants of the Colorado Plateau. As at many public botanical gardens and arboreta, visitors can see mature plants grown in a variety of appropriate conditions and garden designs. During the past ten years Arboretum staff have been testing native plants in various garden settings to determine their cultivation requirements and suitability. The Arboretum also conducts research on endangered southwestern plants and is a member of the Center for Plant Conservation, a consortium of botanical gardens and arboreta committed to the conservation of plants in the United States.

Mountain regions in the West host a diversity of plant communities: high desert, grassland, chaparral, pinyon-juniper woodland, ponderosa pine forest, spruce-fir, and subalpine and alpine tundra. This book focuses on high-elevation areas where these plant communities are found. In northern Arizona the elevations covered are 6,000 feet and above. Further north the same plant communities occur at somewhat lower elevations. For instance, treeline—the elevation above which trees do not occur—is at 12,460 feet on the San Francisco Peaks outside of Flagstaff, Arizona, but only 8,530 feet in Glacier Park, Montana. The plants discussed in this book are native to—found naturally in—these areas. Some species are widespread in the wild, while others may be very locally distributed, but all will grow well in gardens in our region if given proper care.

Perhaps one of the most important reasons to grow native plants is that they are adapted to the wild extremes and variations of climate, both seasonal and daily, which are the hallmarks of the western mountains and high plains. Our region is characterized by intense sun and wide temperature fluctuations. At higher elevations, winters are long and below-zero temperatures are not unusual. Depending on snow accumulation, springtime can be first soggy with snow melt and later dry with bright sun and howling winds, or simply dry, sunny, windy, and cold at night. From mid-May to mid-June—the time of year most people want to plant—it's often dry and windy and not conducive to planting. Between July and September plants thrive with the arrival of afternoon rains, or monsoons. In the Rocky Mountains from about Salt Lake City south to central Arizona and New Mexico, about half of the year's usable precipitation comes in summer in short, intense, afternoon deluges. Winter snow, although plentiful, sublimates quickly in the dry air. Still, rainfall varies from year to year in both amount and intensity. Autumn can be much like spring—sunny and dry, or drizzly and dark—before fading into winter. In Flagstaff, the growing season can range from 68 days to 147 days, with an average of 103 days.

The textured patchwork of plant communities as they spread, merge, and change tells us the story of our home: where the water flows, where the soils are heavy, where the wind and sun conspire to parch the land, where we have disturbed the earth, where cows and sheep have fed, where elk have stood. When we use native plants in natural combinations, they link us even more closely to our sense of place. Residents of Flagstaff, for example, will know different plants from those familiar to people in Santa Fe or Denver; on a still more local level around Flagstaff, plants found in Walnut Canyon are different from the plants of Hart Prairie or Doney Park. Flagstaff is in the midst of the world's largest ponderosa pine/Arizona fescue forest. The grasslands are populated by hundreds of species of native grasses and are graced throughout the growing season with a myriad procession of colorful wildflowers.

But even if a particular plant is locally native, there is no guarantee it will succeed in our gardens. For best results, we need to select plants from habitats that match the specific locations in our gardens where we'll be planting them. The most critical factors in this selection are soil characteristics, available moisture, and available sunlight. Soil characteristics depend in part on the actual material and in part on texture. The Colorado Plateau has had a complex geological history and hosts a wide range of soil types. Much of the area is of volcanic origin. At one time, part of it lay beneath an internal sea. Rivers have cut across plateaus and deposited sediments. Forested areas often have rather thin soils, whereas grasslands occupy deeper soils. The kinds of materials to be expected include clay, cinder, sandstone, limestone, and loam, intermixed to various degrees with sand, gravel, or cobbles. Gardeners in this region often have to struggle with very heavy clay soils or with lots of rocks. Available water will depend in large part on the kind of soil and whether there is any top-dressing to reduce evaporation. It is common to have one part of a garden that drains very rapidly while another part has standing water for days at a time. Available sunlight will depend on whether structures or existing trees shade the area during part or all of the day.

BOTANICAL GARDENS AND ARBORETA IN HIGH-ELEVATION WESTERN REGIONS

Botanical gardens and arboreta are great places to learn more about the plants that will do well in an area. Many of them have annual plant sales as well.

ARIZONA

The Arboretum at Flagstaff
4001 South Woody
Mountain Road
Flagstaff, AZ 86001
928-774-1442
www.thearb.org

COLORADO

Betty Ford Alpine Gardens
Vail Alpine Garden
Foundation
183 Gore Creek Drive
Vail, CO 81657
970-476-0103
www.bettyfordalpinegardens.org

Colorado Springs Horticulture
Art Society Garden
P. O. Box 7706
Colorado Springs, CO 80933
719-475-0250

Denver Botanic Gardens
1005 York Street
Denver, CO 80206
720-865-3500
www.botanicgardens.org

Hudson Gardens
6115 South Santa Fe Drive
Littleton, CO 80120
303-797-8565
970-245-9030
www.hudsongardens.org

Western Colorado
Botanical Garden
641 Struthers Avenue
Grand Junction, CO 81501
www.wcbotanic.org

IDAHO

Idaho Botanical Garden
2355 North Penitentiary Road
Boise, ID 83712
208-343-8649
www.idahobotanicalgarden.org

Sawtooth
Botanical Garden
3 Gimlet Road
Ketchum, ID 83340
208-726-9358
www.sbgarden.org

NEVADA

Desert Demonstration
Gardens
3701 West Alta Drive
Las Vegas, NV 89107
702-258-3205

University of Nevada–
Las Vegas
4505 Maryland Parkway
Las Vegas, NV 89154-1013
702-895-3182

NEW MEXICO

Rio Grande Botanic Garden
Albuquerque Bioparks
2601 Central Avenue N.W.
Albuquerque, NM 87104
505-764-6200
www.cabq.gov.biopark/garden/

Santa Fe
Botanical Gardens
6401 Richards Avenue
Santa Fe, NM 87502-3343
505-428-1684

UTAH

Red Butte Botanic Garden
and Arboretum
300 Wakara Way
Salt Lake City, UT 84108
801-581-4747
www.redbuttegarden.org

WYOMING

Cheyenne
Botanic Gardens
710 South Lions Park Drive
Cheyenne, WY 82001
307-637-6458
www.botanic.org

More information on botanical gardens and arboreta in the United States and Canada can be found on the American Association of Botanical Gardens and Arboreta website, aabga.org.

Temperature, especially the extremes of temperature, is another factor that determines where plants can or cannot grow. The United States Department of Agriculture's plant hardiness zone system, used in this book, is an essential tool in plant selection. These zones are based upon average minimum temperature range. Plants are classified under the coldest zone in which they normally succeed. This book describes plants suitable for use in hardiness zones 1 through 6, which range from a minimum of -50°F (zone 1) to 0°F (zone 6). The table on page xiv, "Plant Zones of the High-Elevation West," shows some native plants typical of each of these six zones. Although plants native to the warmer zones are not likely to survive the harshest winters in colder zones, it is usually possible to bring plants from colder zones into warmer climates, provided their need for winter chilling is met.

In the first chapters of this book we give some basic information on how to garden successfully in western high-elevation regions, with particular application to native plants. We discuss how to evaluate your site (and modify it if necessary); how to make the most of that most precious resource, water; how to prepare the site and control weeds; how and where to obtain native plants and seeds; how to plant; how to nurture your plants through their first critical season; and how to maintain your native garden and keep it healthy.

The largest section of the book, the Species Descriptions, gives detailed information on more than 150 species of native plants suitable for our region. Along with the hardiness zone for each species, individual accounts include the plant's native range, outstanding features, size, shape, flower color and form, season of bloom, cultural requirements, and landscape uses. We also indicate which pollinators and other creatures each plant attracts. Where historical and modern uses of a plant are known, they are also noted.

Native plants reward us with a wealth of experience, information, and joy. When we learn to grow them from seed or cuttings, we build a body of knowledge that can help restore declining populations, or simply be shared with our friends and neighbors so that they, too, can learn the value and beauty of this botanical wealth. When we bring native plants into cultivation in our gardens, when we preserve or reintroduce them to natural areas on our land, when we take the time to learn their names and their histories, when we recognize them for their imposing diversity, they connect us to the richness of this region of the Earth. Enjoying these plants in our own gardens can deepen our appreciation of the inherent worth of natural communities—on the Colorado Plateau, in other regions of the West, and wherever we may live or travel.

PLANT ZONES
OF THE HIGH-ELEVATION WEST*

ZONE/MINIMUM TEMPERATURE RANGE/ELEVATION	HABITATS	TYPICAL PLANTS
Zone 1 Temperature: Below -50°F Elevation: Very high	Arctic, alpine, and subalpine habitats including Rocky Mountain alpine tundra, Rocky Mountain subalpine conifer forest, subalpine grassland, high-elevation montane meadows	*Populus tremuloides* (quaking aspen), *Geum triflorum* (old man's whiskers), *Arenaria fendleri* (Fendler's sandwort), *Hymenoxys hoopesii* (western sneezeweed), *Primula parryi* (Parry's primrose)
Zone 2 Temperature: -50° to -40°F Elevation: Very high to high	Alpine and subalpine habitats Subalpine conifer forest, Rocky Mountain conifer forest, high-elevation montane meadows, mixed conifer forest	*Potentilla fruticosa* (shrubby cinquefoil), *Campanula rotundifolia* (harebells), *Artemisia frigida* (fringed sagebrush), *Penstemon strictus* (Rocky Mountain penstemon), *Delphinium geraniifolium* (geranium-leaf larkspur), *Penstemon whippleanus* (Whipple's penstemon)
Zone 3 Temperature: -40° to -30°F Elevation: High	Subalpine habitats including mixed conifer forest, open parks, and meadows	*Juniperus communis* (common juniper), *Antennaria rosulata* (Kaibab pussytoes), *Erigeron flagellaris* (whiplash daisy), *Ipomopsis aggregata* (scarlet gilia), *Lupinus argenteus* (silvery lupine), *Geranium richardsonii* (Richardson's geranium)
Zone 4 Temperature: -30° to -20°F Elevation: High to middle	Mid-elevation mountain meadows; colder zones of ponderosa pine forest	*Parthenocissus inserta* (western Virginia creeper), *Agave parryi* var. *parryi* (Parry's agave), *Eriogonum racemosum* (redroot buckwheat), *Calylophus hartwegii* subsp. *fendleri* (Fendler's sundrops), *Callirhoe involucrata* (wine cups), *Penstemon palmeri* (scented penstemon)
Zone 5 Temperature: -20° to -10°F Elevation: Middle	Moderate zones and warm exposures in ponderosa pine forest; pinyon-juniper woodland; riparian woodland; open, mid-elevation grasslands	*Agastache cana* (double bubble mint), *Achnatherum hymenoides* (Indian ricegrass), *Zinnia grandiflora* (prairie zinnia), *Epilobium canum* subsp. *latifolium* (hardy hummingbird trumpet), *Anemopsis californica* (yerba mansa)
Zone 6 Temperature: -10° to 0°F Elevation: Middle to lower	Mild zones and hottest exposures in ponderosa pine forest; pinyon-juniper woodland; high desert grassland; oak woodland; mid-elevation riparian woodland; chaparral	*Arctostaphylos pungens* (pointleaf manzanita), *Acer macrophyllum* (bigleaf maple), *Baileya multiradiata* (desert marigold)

*Based on minimum temperature range, from the U.S. Department of Agriculture's Plant Hardiness Zone System

USDA PLANT HARDINESS ZONE MAP

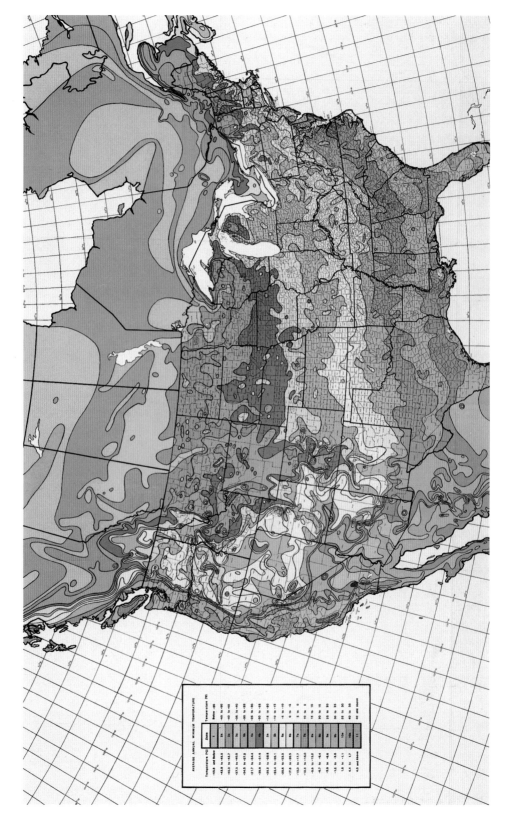

Planting and Maintaining the Native Garden

❖

Hymenoxys subintegra

Senecio wootonii

TAKING STOCK

Get to Know Your Site

Before you begin gardening with native plants, you will need to take some methodical steps to ensure long-term success. First, spend time—ideally, an entire year—getting to know the natural features of the site where you will be putting the plants. Become familiar with the plants already existing on the site, those that grow naturally nearby or that were there historically, and the animals, from insects to mammals, that visit them. Inventory the site's natural features: soils, slopes, aspect (north- or south-facing, for example), topography, drainage, and amount of sun or shade. Make special note of any microclimates—areas that are warmer or colder, wetter or drier, than the rest of the site.

This getting-acquainted period is also a good time to visit botanical gardens, nearby wild areas, and established local landscapes (parks, neighborhoods) to learn more about what you like and what will grow well in your garden. The time you take getting to know your location will save you many costly mistakes in plant selection and placement.

Your Goals and Your Capacities

A realistic assessment of your needs and desires for the site is important. Beauty, function, and utility often go hand in hand. What are you trying to accomplish in your landscape? Perhaps you are at the edge of a natural area and you want your garden to provide additional needed resources to species stressed by encroaching development. Is there a particular bird, insect, or other animal you are trying to accommodate? Often, it will be necessary to provide water, habitat, and food for desired species to attract them to your garden. Or perhaps you have simply seen native plants that you liked on local hikes or outings, and you would like the pleasure of seeing them daily in your own garden.

How do you plan to care for your garden? How much maintenance time can you realistically invest? Select plants on the basis of your actual situation, rather than some idealized picture of what you will provide.

Make the Most of Water

How Much Water Will Your Native Plants Need?

The next critical need to consider is available water. Native plants do well on natural water alone only when they are naturally adapted to the moisture regimens they will receive. In the Species Descriptions section of this book, we classify the water needs of plants according to the system in the table below, "Categories of Water Use." The first column lists the categories we use in the species descriptions under the heading "Water use." The second column specifies the frequency of watering that will be required for that category of water use. The third column indicates how wet or dry the soil should be, and the fourth column gives examples of plants that require that particular watering regime.

CATEGORIES OF WATER USE

CATEGORY	FREQUENCY OF WATERING	WHAT SOIL MOISTURE SHOULD BE	PLANTS THAT DO WELL
Very little	No supplemental water once established	Excessively dry and well drained	Yucca baccata Agave parryi Datura wrightii
Low	Only occasional water once established. May need water once a month during dry season.	Dry	Gaillardia pulchella Mirabilis multiflora Macromeria viridiflora
Low to moderate	Infrequent water. Water once or twice a month during dry season.	Dry	Heuchera rubescens Helianthella quinquenervis Penstemon barbatus
Moderate	Infrequent but regular water. Water several times a month during dry season.	Frequently moist	Potentilla thurberi
Moderate to high	Regular water. Water once a week during dry season.	Moist	Mimulus guttatus
High	Very frequent water, or plant where soil is naturally moist.	Always moist to saturated	Lobelia cardinalis

These water requirements are based on the needs of mature plants once they are established. Being "established" means that plants have had sufficient time and growth to become acclimatized to the planting site and that their roots have extended far enough into the surrounding soil to encounter soil moisture. Generally, native plants become pretty well established within three years.

Be wary of claims that native plants need little or no water. In their zeal to encourage the use of native plants, promoters will sometimes exaggerate their drought tolerance. When a plant is described as being suitable for a range of conditions, it may indeed survive at one extreme but will often look better with judiciously timed watering. Many native plants survive drought by going into a resting state known as dormancy; in this state they may cease growing above ground although their roots may still be active. This may not be what you want in the garden. Most drought-induced dormancy can be curtailed by just a few well-timed deep waterings.

Work with Nature to Increase and Conserve Water

To get the best out of native plants in the garden with minimal use of water, always try to work with nature. Rain barrels, cisterns, and rain-fed water-capture systems can extend natural precipitation. For thousands of years, humans have encouraged plant growth with water-harvesting techniques that capture surface flow, prevent runoff, and direct rainfall to locations where it can best be used by plants. Water-harvesting techniques can be as simple as planting in natural depressions or as sophisticated as creating depressions and sinks to retain water, devising intricate systems of water channeling, and contouring slopes to catch and slow runoff.

Use rocks and mulches to conserve and collect water. In nature, many plants establish and thrive only under the care of "nurse" rocks that offer protection from cold and wind and hold water and warmth. Apply summer mulches once soil is wet (either from summer rains or from watering); apply winter mulches once soil is frozen, to prevent frost and ice heaving. To prevent rotting of plant crowns and stems, keep mulch several inches away from crowns and main branches; be sure to place mulch under shoots and branches, not on top of them.

Plant a few well-placed, fast-growing plants to modify your site conditions. Although fast-growing plants often need a good deal of regular water to become established, they will quickly create shade and humidity (which will eventually reduce water needs), serve as windbreaks, and help create a habitat in which other desired species can become established. Where water is limited, temporary structures and shelters can help plants get established in the face of high winds, bright sun, and low humidity.

Ipomopsis arizonica

PREPARING YOUR SITE

In gardening with natives, proper site preparation is one of the most important determinants of your success. How you choose to prepare your site depends on its history of use, its current condition, and how you plan to manage and maintain it after planting.

Soils

Almost all Colorado Plateau soils lack organic matter and are either coarse-textured and excessively drained (sands and cinders) or fine-textured (wind-blown soils and clays). Adding organic matter helps open up fine-textured and compacted soils, allowing water to enter them. It will also help hold moisture in coarse, highly drained soils. If you are aiming for rich, loose, garden-bed conditions, or if very fast growth of native perennials is a necessity, adding up to a third of the soil volume of composted organic matter is recommended. If you are trying to restore, renovate, or enhance a natural area by planting adapted native species, it is best to plant directly in unamended soil. To avoid creating a discontinuity between potting mixes and native soils (which would inhibit the flow of water to the root ball), gently shake potting mixture off the root ball and fill the planting hole with loosened native soil. If you are planning to have a completely unirrigated garden or to do only minimal hand-watering, unamended soils will often perform better in the long run.

If your soil has suffered from construction damage or compaction, you can take steps to reverse the damage. Highly compacted soils should be dug to a depth of one to two feet when dry or only slightly moist to allow plant roots to penetrate. Soils that have been deluged with cement, paints, or building chemicals often become highly alkaline; a soil test to determine pH level can often help you to determine whether you can simply choose plants that tolerate alkaline soil, whether you'll need to adjust the pH by chemical means, or whether you might have to remove and replace soil.

Some soils are rocky, but unless you are planting turf or a ground cover that needs a level surface, rocks can be an asset in your garden, holding moisture and heat. Leave them in place, unless they make planting impossible.

Weed Control

One of the most important principles of low-maintenance gardening is to avoid doing anything that will result in ongoing work in the garden. Whenever possible, avoid introducing weeds as you prepare your site. Weeds usually come into the garden in one of two ways—either they find a foothold in disturbed areas and spread, or they are introduced intentionally by gardeners unaware of how quickly and prolifically they will spread. Vinca, English ivy, and honeysuckles are excellent examples of plants commonly used in gardens that can quickly take over an area. Prevent unnecessary soil disturbance by limiting your digging and tilling to the smallest areas possible. Whenever you're preparing to work in the garden or moving from a weedy to a nonweedy area, take the time to clean dirt from shoes and equipment with a blasting stream of water or a scrub brush so that you won't transport weeds or weed seeds from place to place.

If you are planning a construction project, take steps to protect soils from damage. Fence off areas to be protected, and tell all workers on the site that soil protection is a high priority. Be careful to avoid unnecessary walking, driving, and moving equipment across soils, especially if they are wet, which is when they are particularly vulnerable to compaction and weed invasion. Many weeds have evolved to thrive in areas that have been heavily trodden, either by people or by animals. Their seeds can successfully germinate in soils too tough for more desirable native plants, and many are able to spread by runners that can even break through concrete. Soil disturbance around construction areas often begins the process by which a natural landscape becomes degraded and subsequently broken down into smaller and smaller pieces of habitat. These fragmented areas are then unable to support wildlife and the natural plant communities that were formerly present.

If no plants whatsoever (desired or otherwise) are growing in the area you want to plant, check the land's past use. If it was treated with preemergent broad-spectrum herbicides (which prevent seed germination) or soil sterilizers, you'll need to add activated charcoal to the soil, or remove and replace it. If you're going to bring soil or soil amendments onto a site, make every effort to obtain materials that are free of weed seeds. Once these materials are in place, monitor the area closely and remove any weeds that germinate before they infest the site.

Always begin planting with a weed-free area. Before planting, survey for weeds, remove them completely including roots, water the area to germinate any weed seeds in the ground, and then remove the new crop as soon as it sprouts. Manual weed control is often the best course (it's good exercise too!) and can provide good results. Many people prefer chemical weed control because it is easy and does not require intense physical labor. Most chemicals,

Geranium viscosissimum

however, are not beneficial to the environment, so consider their benefits and liabilities carefully before using them. If you are removing an old lawn, or removing weeds from a large, nonrocky area, rototilling followed by removing all tops and roots can ease the task of hand weeding.

Soil solarization is a nonchemical technique that utilizes the sun's heat to kill weeds and weed seeds already present in the soil. (It will kill weed seeds and seeds of desirable native plants alike, though, so use this method only in areas where weeds are dominant.) You'll need to do it in spring or early summer, when skies are clear and the sun will heat the soil enough to kill weeds and weed seeds.

First soak the ground thoroughly to a depth of at least a foot to encourage active plant growth and even distribution of heat throughout the soil. Then place clear plastic over the entire area to be treated and tightly seal all the edges to the ground by securing them with concrete blocks or rocks or burying them in the earth. Now let the sun do its work. It usually takes several weeks for a succession of seeds to germinate and die; check regularly to make sure that the edges of the plastic stay tightly sealed and soil remains moist. Once solarization is complete, remove the plastic and thoroughly water soil to bring up any remaining weed seeds. (It is often necessary to hand-weed seedlings of clover, pea, and other legumes after solarization because hot soil temperatures stimulate their germination.)

Physical barriers are often employed to control weeds in the landscape. Landscape cloth, also known as weed cloth, is a woven fabric that allows water and air to penetrate but prevents growth of seedlings in the soil beneath the fabric by blocking out light. It can be useful, particularly when you are planting in weed-infested areas. Plants are placed in holes cut into the landscape cloth, followed by a thin layer of soil or mulch over the cloth. (Any weeds that do germinate in that layer are easily removed.) One disadvantage of weed cloth is that it will prevent self-seeding of desirable native species. An even worse product for landscape use with native plants is black plastic; because it is impermeable to air and water, it can cause disease or even kill the plants.

Controlled burns can be used in the restoration of forests, meadows, and prairies. Fire favors some species (often native) over others, returns carbon and nitrogen to the nutrient cycle, and can stimulate germination of seeds long dormant in the soil. Consult with your local fire department for guidelines for controlled burning.

Be sure to understand the life cycle of plants you will be introducing to an area. Plants known to be weedy should not be planted where they can spread to natural areas. Check with your local University Extension office, weed council, or botanical garden or arboretum for information on potential weeds. Waterways and moist areas are especially vulnerable to weed invasion. If a new plant proves to be too successful in your garden, prolifically self-seeding and crowding out other species, quickly remove it from the garden before it becomes an established pest.

Diversity

Genetic diversity is nature's way of ensuring survival for many species. Species diversity in the landscape creates a hedge against disease, and diversity in the garden assures that a single event like a late-season frost will not affect the entire garden. Diversity of plant size and type also allows a variety of bird, animal, and insect species to find the food, shelter, and habitat they need in the garden. By taking advantage of existing microclimates in your garden—including exposure, slope, moisture, and soils—you can often broaden the range of available plant species.

For garden beauty and wildlife value, select a succession of long-blooming, resource-rich plants. Including plants with a diversity of bloom time, as well as those with edible fruits and seeds, ensures that your garden will have flowers, pollen, and food for animals throughout the growing season.

You can use a different aspect of diversity to create over time the site conditions you want, introducing plants in several stages. For instance, if you are planting shade trees but the site is currently in full sun, you will need to create shade before you can grow shade-loving perennials. To achieve this, you can set up temporary structures to protect shade-requiring plants while overstory plants are growing. Or consider a temporary planting of sun-loving species that can be moved to another sunny location once the shade-creating canopy begins to fill in. Trees and shrubs can change the microclimates after only a few years. To perpetuate a planting of sun-loving perennials, it may become necessary to prune or thin branches of overstory species. Early successional species (plants that colonize disturbed areas first) are fast-growing, easy-to-establish colonizers with the ability to reproduce quickly. Along with mulches and an active weed control program, they can be used to keep weedy species in check while other, slower-growing plants gain a foothold.

Oenothera macrocarpa

GETTING THE PLANTS
YOU WANT

◆

Types of Plant Material

Once you have chosen the species you want to plant in your garden, the next step is to decide which forms of plant material are right for your project. You may have several options: nursery-grown container plants of various sizes, from plugs to large specimens; bare-root plants; plants or seedlings collected in nature, sometimes called wildlings; or seed.

Container plants are easy to transport and easy to care for before planting. They are readily available throughout the growing season. Their cost per unit is often higher than that of bare-root plants, but with proper planting and care their survival rate is also likely to be higher. Container plants are usually grown in lightweight, soil-less potting mixes, which can dry out quickly, so they must be kept watered before and after planting.

Bare-root specimens of some native plants are available from nurseries in spring. These can be an inexpensive alternative to container plants, but they are often difficult to plant successfully in the fluctuating temperatures and dry, windy conditions typical of the Colorado Plateau in springtime. If you do decide on bare-root plants, it's vital to keep their roots moist throughout all phases of handling and planting. Protect them from sun and drying air, soak them thoroughly before putting them into the ground, plant them into already moistened soil, and water them in thoroughly. After planting, they are likely to require daily (or even twice-daily) watering for several weeks to several months as they become established.

Many plants spread by aboveground and belowground runners, by offsets, or by multiple shoots emerging from the ground; these can be dug, the offsets or multiple shoots divided, and transplanted for propagation.

Growing natives from seed is one of the easiest and most inexpensive ways to obtain plants for your garden. Seeds can be planted directly into the ground or started in a protected location under controlled conditions. If you need a large number of native plants, seeds provide an economical way to obtain them. In addition, seeds of local plants of known origin can be collected from local populations. Growing plants from seed is the one best way to assure the presence of genetic diversity in a batch of plants of the same species. Establishing plants from seeds can be challenging, but it offers one major benefit: The plants have a range of natural variability and genetic diversity that makes them more adaptable to local conditions.

Sources of Native Plants

It's important to establish the original source of native plants you buy to make sure they will work in your environment. Specialized local native plant nurseries are usually your best choice. Nonspecialty nurseries often stock a number of native plants, but because these typically come from a wide geographical range, they may not be grown from parent material as drought-tolerant or as well adapted to local conditions as specimens of the same species that originate locally or even regionally. Many nursery-grown specimens have been inadvertently selected to grow in lusher, moister conditions than their wild counterparts. For instance, a Douglas fir tree grown from seed collected in the humid, moist Pacific Northwest cannot tolerate the bright sun and strong winds of the Colorado Plateau, whereas one from seed collected at high elevations of the Plateau will, once established, better tolerate open conditions with wind, spring drought, and intense sunlight.

As soon as you know which species you want to plant, check to make sure they're available. Many times, a gardener's good intentions to plant appropriate natives are thwarted by finding that his or her first choices are unobtainable. Without advance planning, the gardener often settles for last-minute substitutions of commonly available but less desirable native plants or even non-native species.

Although many native species are easy to obtain, if you need to purchase them in quantity you may need to have a local nursery grow them. Many nurseries will contract-grow plants on request. It's important to give the nursery sufficient lead time—usually one season for perennials and fast-growing woody species, more for slower-growing woody species and slow-growing perennials.

There are many excellent mail-order sources of native plants and seeds, though mail-order plants are typically available in rather small sizes. Sometimes the only way to obtain less commonly available species is by purchasing seed and growing them yourself. When ordering by mail, try to purchase from sources nearest to you, and inquire about the origin of the plants or seeds. Make it a point not to buy any native plant material obtained at the expense of wild populations. Some nurseries do advertise that they have propagated the plants they sell.

On the other hand, if you visit a nursery and notice that the roots of a native plant seem to have been compressed into its pot, that the soil in the pot differs from that around the roots, or that the leaves are skewed and irregular, chances are good that the plant was wild collected. Be especially wary of sales of native bulbs. Any wild collecting, whether of seed, cuttings, or entire plants, must be done ethically and effectively. It may be possible to collect native plants from habitats similar to your garden, but before you remove any plants or seeds from the wild, be sure you have the permission of the landowner, or a valid permit from the governing agency. Avoid collecting any rare or locally scarce, sensitive species. Be familiar with the plants you are collecting, their growth habits, and in particular the depth, size, and other characteristics of their root systems. As much as possible, avoid site disturbance, and restore soil conditions so that you don't encourage weeds to spread into the collection area. Fill in any holes you create, tamp soils back into place firmly, and leave no trace of your activities. Always bring water along on collecting trips, and water the gathered plants as soon as possible.

Salvage collection from areas about to be developed is another good and inexpensive alternative for obtaining native plants from local sources. If you know that a site is slated for development, talk to the developer or property owner to obtain permission to collect plants before the site is graded and plants are lost.

Erigeron speciosus

PLANTING

◆

When to Plant

Once you have prepared your soil, decided on your plants, and acquired them, it's time to plant! At high elevations, you can plant anytime from when the soils thaw in spring until they freeze in autumn. But the best time to plant is monsoon season, generally July and August. During summer rains, soils are moist, and both rainfall and humidity help plants to establish themselves without shock or trauma. If you have to plant during a dry spell, be ready to irrigate. You may need to water up to twice a day in springtime during periods of bright sun and high winds.

Bare-root plants are usually planted as soon as the ground thaws, which in Flagstaff may not be until late May. If you are not able to give them adequate irrigation during this demanding time, consider temporarily planting them in a prepared bed or container where you can more easily care for them. Once monsoons bring more favorable conditions, transplant them to their permanent garden location.

Planting early in the morning or late in the afternoon minimizes the chance that roots will be injured by heat and sun. When preparing for planting, don't lay plants out any sooner than is absolutely necessary. If you do set out container plants next to their planting locations, be sure the containers are standing upright so that the sun won't beat on the sides, cooking the roots and killing the plants.

Dig the Planting Holes

The holes you dig will depend on the size of the plant's root ball; on whether you are planting a tree, shrub, or perennial; and on whether you are planting a garden, enhancing a natural area, or restoring a habitat. The hole should be deep enough to accommodate the entire depth of plant roots without crowding. If soil is compacted, loosen it to a depth twice

17

Linum lewisii

that of the root ball. One way to ensure that water will be available for deep plant roots is to fill the hole to the top with water the day before planting, allow it to drain, fill it a second time, and let it drain again. If drainage is very slow—that is, if water remains standing in the hole after twenty-four hours—either choose a plant that tolerates standing water and poor drainage or choose a different planting location.

Get the Plants Ready

Handling transplants correctly before planting is critical in successful transplanting. Keep container plants in a cool, partially shaded location until they are planted out, and water them thoroughly just before planting. Double-watering, a technique nurseries use, is the best way to make sure that the soil is saturated and that the water penetrates the entire root ball. Gently fill the container to the top, allow water to drain, and repeat until water flows easily from the pot's drainage holes.

Bare-root plants should be unwrapped and placed in a bucket of warm water the night before planting to take in as much water as possible; do not remove them from the water until just before you place them directly in their premoistened planting holes.

Plants and cuttings that have been collected in the wild should be kept in a cool, protected place until planting. Make sure that their soil is moist but not soggy, and that roots are able to breathe.

Space Plants Carefully

With short growing seasons and low nighttime temperatures year-round, plants can grow slowly on the Colorado Plateau. Resist the temptation to place plants close together for quick cover. Overcrowding will lead to poor air circulation, disease and insect problems, competition for nutrients, and reduced plant vigor. Place plants that will be a permanent part of your landscaping far enough apart so that they can achieve their mature size. Temporary plantings of fast-growing annuals and short-lived perennials, decorative mulches, and ground covers can all serve to attractively fill in the spaces between permanent plants while they reach full stature.

Fertilize

It is not necessary to fertilize native plants in "natural" situations; most are adapted to lean native soils. In landscape situations, native plants can be fertilized to encourage strong root growth, but too much fertilizer, especially a fertilizer high in nitrogen, is likely to produce lush, soft top growth that is susceptible to drought, disease, and insects.

The formulation numbers on the package (for example, 10-8-5) indicate the proportions of nitrogen, phosphorus, and potassium, respectively, that the fertilizer contains. Choose organic or balanced fertilizers over those with higher proportions of nitrogen. A 14-14-14 formulation is preferable to a 20-0-0. At planting time you may want to incorporate an organic or a slow-release fertilizer by mixing it thoroughly into the backfill. Unlike a fertilizer applied as a top-dressing, fertilizers applied directly to the root zone (which may be planting tablets, slow-release fertilizers, or water-soluble fertilizers) nourish plants without contributing to weed growth in the garden.

Encourage Soil Mycorrhizae

Mycorrhizae are structures on the roots of plants that are formed through a beneficial association between the roots and certain soil fungi. The fungi help plants efficiently use soil moisture and take up nutrients, particularly phosphorus. The presence of mycorrhizae is particularly helpful in plantings that will not receive continuous irrigation. To encourage mycorrhizal relationships in your garden, you can purchase commercially available mycorrhizal-forming fungal spores and incorporate them into garden soils by watering them directly into the plant's root zone, or you can incorporate soil or soil debris from the vicinity of similar native plant species into your garden at the time of planting.

Water Well

To best ensure successful planting, provide plenty of water during all stages of planting. Again, make sure the plant has been kept moist so that it is not dehydrated or water-stressed. At planting time, water the root ball thoroughly and water-in the planting hole. Then place the root ball in the planting hole, being sure to keep the crown (the point at which the aboveground part of the plant joins the root) at the same soil level it was before planting. Gently refill the planting hole with excavated soil plus any fertilizers or amendments, making sure they are mixed in thoroughly prior to backfilling the hole. Continue to hold the plant in place with one hand and gently fill with the other. Once the hole is filled, tamp down the soil gently with your feet or the handle of a shovel or broom. (Soil should be firm but not densely packed, so that water and air can move in and out.) Once planting is complete, gently water-in the planting hole, being careful not to wash away soil. Let the water percolate down into the soil, and repeat this process several times. This thorough method of watering forces pockets of air out of the soil and fills soil pores with water, ensuring that the plant will immediately get all the water it needs. The plant should remain upright after watering. If the soil caves in or the plant begins to sink or fall over, gently hold up the top of the plant and place more soil firmly around it, making sure to maintain the relationship between the crown of the plant and the level of the soil.

Take Special Care in the First Season

The first season after transplant is critical. Water generously to speed establishment. The root ball of a new transplant should never be allowed to dry out. (Cacti are an exception. They can rot easily, so hold off on watering them for one to two weeks after planting.) All new plantings should be mulched—to keep water in the ground, and in the case of fall plantings to prevent alternating thaws and freezes from heaving plants out of the ground. Watch soil moisture carefully; check it at least once daily for several months.

Once roots have grown out into the surrounding soil, you can slowly wean plants to the degree of irrigation they'll eventually receive. Check soil moisture by sticking a finger down two to three inches into the root ball; it should be moist to the touch. If you're not confident of your ability to assess soil moisture, consider purchasing a moisture meter and keep all new transplants within the green zone on the meter. Keep in mind that in warm, dry weather soils can dry out very quickly.

Protect from Predators, Pests, and Weeds

Grasshoppers, earwigs, deer, elk, rabbits, gophers, and weeds can all take their toll on young plants, as can competition from weeds. Monitor plants for predator and pest damage, and remove any encroaching weeds promptly. If you have questions about plant or insect identification, a visit to a local herbarium or botanical garden can help you recognize noxious weeds and differentiate between beneficial and harmful insects. University Extension services can also be very helpful.

Grasshoppers are a major problem in some areas. Nolo bait can be used to reduce their populations; be sure to buy it early in the spring and follow label directions carefully because it must be applied during the right stage of the grasshoppers' development. Hand removal is another way to help keep grasshopper populations down. Encouraging birds to visit your garden by providing shallow clean water for bathing and drinking also helps. Cages of fine mesh can protect young transplants from grasshoppers (make sure you're not enclosing any young grasshoppers in the cage along with the plants). Plants will be less vulnerable later in the season, when they have more top growth, other nearby plants are vigorously growing, and grasshopper numbers have diminished. Some experienced western gardeners provide a sacrifice bed or garden for grasshoppers (and deer), planted far away from new transplants. Grasshoppers seem to favor large-leaved species such as hollyhocks, while most deer are wild about pansies.

In areas with deer, elk, and rabbits, fencing is the best guarantee of plant survival. If you won't be able to fence these animals out of your garden, try to select either plants that they won't eat or plants that are adapted to seasonal grazing. Whenever possible, protect young plants until they are established to maximize their chances of success.

Heliomeris multiflora

STARTING FROM SEED

◆

Seeding Directly

Depending on the species to be grown and on-site conditions, seeds can either be sown directly into the ground or started in seed flats or containers. Direct seeding is effective for seeds that germinate easily, and it can be employed with many native grasses and wildflowers. Few seedlings can withstand competition from weeds, so try to germinate and remove weed seed before seeding the natives; remove all underground parts of rhizomatous weeds and till under all young weed seedlings before they can set seed. If you have a very large area to seed, it is usually best to seed a small portion first, control weeds and get native seedlings well established, and then gradually expand your seeding area.

The most common way to seed wildflowers and meadows is hand, or broadcast, seeding. First loosen the soil and roughen the surface; then spread seed at the desired density. Mixing it with sand or some other carrier will help you distribute it more evenly. Plants will be spindly and lack vigor if they are crowded, so follow recommended seeding rates carefully. After broadcasting, rake seed into soil and cover to a depth of a quarter-inch to a half-inch; then walk over it or use a roller to firm it in place. To prevent erosion and help keep moisture in, the soil surface should be contoured or roughened again by raking or stamping into furrows to create depressions that will hold water.

To protect the seeded area, use fencing to keep out rabbits and other hungry creatures. Watch out for gophers, which can wipe out an entire wildflower meadow in a matter of weeks. To protect seed from birds, rodents, insects, and winds, and to maintain moisture as seeds germinate, apply a mulch—pine needles, compost, or composted manure. Native hay of wildflowers and grasses also makes an excellent mulch. Other possibilities include landscape cloth and Reemay™. Mulches of pine needles, cloth, or hay should be removed approximately two to three weeks after the seeds have germinated,

Hymenoxys richardsonii

before the seedlings elongate from lack of light. Whatever your mulch, be sure it is free of weed seeds. As always, keep an eye out for weeds and remove them before they outcompete young seedlings.

Seed drilling, a technique developed in agriculture, can be used to seed large areas quickly. A seed drill is pulled behind a tractor, making holes at a set depth and placing a seed in each hole.

Hydroseeding is the application of seed in a slurry of mulch and water; usually it is employed on slopes and roadside areas. For this technique to be successful, seed must remain moist once germination begins. On the Colorado Plateau, this means that hydroseeded plantings must be irrigated regularly.

The two best times for direct seeding in the high-elevation West are at the start of the monsoon season and at the end of summer. Many seeds sown in spring or early summer will germinate with summer monsoons, but some native seeds require a period of winter chilling to break dormancy, so they won't germinate until the next spring. Many native species, such as beeweed (*Cleome serrulata*) and coneflowers (*Echinacea* spp.), germinate best when they are sown directly outdoors and exposed to natural temperature fluctuations. Seeds need constant moisture to germinate and grow, so if monsoons fail to materialize you will need to water regularly.

Seeding in Containers

Although direct seeding works well for many natives, there are situations in which you might want to consider container seeding. Plants are seeded into containers when a high rate of success is needed or when protection from the elements and predators is necessary. In addition, many Plateau species require controlled seed treatments, such as cold stratification or temperature fluctuation, that mimic conditions in nature. One excellent reference on the subject is *Collecting, Processing, and Germinating Seeds of Wildland Plants* by James A. and Cheryl G. Young

Campanula parryi

KEEPING YOUR PLANTS ALIVE AND HEALTHY

❖

Monitor Your Plants

The first key to establishing plants successfully is to give them adequate water. Once plants harden off and begin to show vigorous growth and reduced need for water, they should be weaned by slowly cutting back on the frequency of watering. Established plants should always be watered deeply and thoroughly, but less often. The second key is to visit your plants on a regular schedule and monitor them closely. In addition to checking whether they need water, look to see whether they are being crowded by weeds, whether pests are injuring them, and whether they are becoming weedy or creating any problems within or outside the landscape. (As they mature, you might also check to confirm that they are actually the plants you thought you were planting.) Here is a sample checklist to help you be more systematic about this task:

Daily and Weekly Monitoring Checklist for Plant Establishment—Sample Journal Entry

SPECIES	DATE PLANTED	DATES WATERED	PESTS/ TREATMENT	PROBLEMS?	ACTION TAKEN
Scarlet globemallow	6/28/02	6/28, 6/29, 6/30	Aphids— washed off	Coming up in the lawn;	Remove?

Maintain Your Native Planting

Like all plants, natives require some maintenance to keep them in best form. Routine maintenance should include watering as necessary; weeding regularly (in particular, early in the season with the first flush of weedy growth, and again soon after the onset of summer rains); and pruning to control shape, increase vigor, and encourage fruiting and seed production. Deadheading (removing faded flowers) will encourage repeat bloom. It can also be used to neaten plants at the end of the season, but keep in mind that many seed heads provide late-season interest and supply seeds for overwintering birds and animals. Removing injured or insect-infested plant parts will not only help to control diseases and pests but also keep the garden looking tidy. Native plants of our region do best with plenty of air circulation; be sure to thin and prune them whenever they become overly crowded.

SEASONAL MAINTENANCE PLAN

Spring	Remove dead top growth. Control early weeds.
Summer	Fertilize. Plant. Monitor. Weed.
Fall/winter	Water. Mulch.
As needed	Control insects. Prune. Divide. Move plants.

Winter Preparation

Most native gardens will benefit from preparation for the winter. If autumn is dry, a few well-timed waterings will help plants get ready to survive winter. Mulches, applied once the ground is frozen, will help maintain a constant soil temperature. Any plants that are marginally cold hardy for your site should be covered with a light mulch of pine needles or protected with a loose covering of cut juniper boughs.

Troubleshooting

Although some problems with native plants may need expert diagnosis, most are simpler to analyze. Here are a few of the most common.

Common Plant Problems

PROBABLE CAUSE	SYMPTOMS
Lack of water	Plants droop. In many drought-tolerant species, the older leaves will first yellow and then drop as plants channel moisture to actively growing newer leaves
Too much water	Entire plant yellows and droops
Lack of light	Rangy plant growth, no flowering
Nitrogen deficiency	Entire plant is pale or yellow
Insect damage	Spots, holes, chewed areas, actual insects
Disease	Drooping in spite of adequate water; die-off of one species; one-sided drooping or die-off
Chemical or environmental problems	Die-off of all species

Sometimes, despite our best efforts, we find we have placed a plant in the wrong place. All plants take a little time to become established in the garden. However, any plant that fails to thrive while other species in the planting are doing well should be removed or relocated to a better spot in the garden. If a plant is constantly plagued by heavy insect infestation, fails to bloom or set fruit, or becomes weedy, spreading excessively and crowding out other plants or spreading seeds beyond the garden, it's time to relocate the plant or remove it entirely.

Published information is limited on all but the most common native plants in the varied situations and microhabitats found in high elevations of the West. The experience you garner—your successes, problems, and solutions—is valuable. Local native plant societies often welcome input at meetings and articles for publications in newsletters. Extension agents and staff at botanic and public gardens can put your knowledge to use for the good of the community. Joining and participating in local garden clubs, sharing plants and information with school groups, and opening your native garden for occasional public visitation are all ways to share your success and encourage others to give native plants a try.

NATIVE PLANT
SPECIES

Datura wrightii

Bouteloua gracilis

INTRODUCTION

◆

The species described in the following pages are mostly herbaceous perennials. Some are woody at the base or are small shrubs, a few are vines, and a few are grasses and sedges. Because of harsh winter conditions and the short growing season, most high-elevation native plants have underground parts that can overwinter. Their buds form close to the ground, often in the preceding season, allowing the plant to bloom quickly once conditions are right.

We have not included many trees, and very few annuals. In any particular high-elevation area, the native tree and shrub diversity is not great, but those species are readily available from local nurseries.

Species are arranged alphabetically by scientific name, followed by common name. Although common names are more familiar to many people, a given species many have many common names, and sometimes the same common name can refer to several very different species. (You'll find both the Latin names and the common names in the index at the back of the book.) Knowing the scientific name is the most reliable way to be sure you're buying the plant you want, and most nurseries include it on the label. As new knowledge has become available, some scientific names have been changed; to help readers find a plant they might know by an older scientific name, we show these older names in parentheses.

Knowing that a species belongs to a particular plant family can be a very useful bit of information. You'll begin to recognize some family traits as you read the descriptions. For instance, plants in the mint family, *Lamiaceae*, often have fragrant foliage.

We also indicate the native range for each species. Some plants have a very broad geographic distribution in the wild. For instance, western yarrow (*Achillea millefolium* var. *occidentalis*) occurs throughout the Northern Hemisphere, including the mountain ranges of the western United States.Other plants have a relatively narrow native range. Double

Ipomopsis x *tenuituba*

bubble mint (*Agastache cana*), for example, is native only to New Mexico and western Texas, although it can be grown elsewhere in the high-elevation West.

Along with the height, width, and hardiness zone for each plant, you'll find a straight-forward description of the plant's shape, foliage, flowers, seed pods, and such. To help ensure a procession of flowering in your garden from early spring until the snow flies, check the heading "Season of bloom."

One of the wonderful things about gardeners is their ability to visualize what will be! To supplement the color photos, "Outstanding features" will help you envisage what each plant's shining characteristics will be once it is in your garden.

Under "Culture," you'll find what kind of soil and exposure each plant wants, how much water it needs, how to propagate it, and what kind of maintenance you'll need to give it. We also suggest how the plant might be used in the landscape. For many gardeners, attracting butterflies is a top priority, so for each plant we've noted which pollinators visit it and what mammals are likely to browse it (and sometimes even which wildlife species find it distasteful). A paragraph at the end of each plant description gives even more information, such as the names of good companion plants that will help you create striking color combinations in your garden.

Achillea millefolium var. *occidentalis*

Achillea millefolium var. occidentalis
(Achillea millefolium var. lanulosum, A. lanulosum)

WESTERN YARROW
SUNFLOWER FAMILY (*ASTERACEAE*)
HERBACEOUS PERENNIAL
HEIGHT: 6–24 INCHES
WIDTH: SPREADING
ZONE 3

CHARACTERISTICS: Spreading, ground-hugging perennial with fragrant, fernlike, finely divided, bright green leaves; large, flat-topped clusters of small white daisylike flowers with yellow centers.

NATIVE RANGE: Northern Hemisphere

SEASON OF BLOOM: All summer

OUTSTANDING FEATURES: Long blooming season. Can be cut for fresh arrangements or for drying. Can be mown and used as a turf substitute.

CULTURE

Soil: Any

Exposure: Sun to light shade

Water use: Low to moderate

Propagation: Seed, division

Care and maintenance: Deadhead in fall. To maintain as a turf substitute, mow periodically.

LANDSCAPE USES: Ground cover, turf substitute (can take moderate traffic), meadow, leachfield, erosion control

WILDLIFE ATTRACTED: Butterflies and bees

HISTORICAL AND MODERN USES: Leaves brewed as a medicinal tea for female disorders, used to stop bleeding, and used by Navajos to treat saddle sores on their animals; dye plant (stems, leaves, and flowers produce yellow, gold, or green colors).

Like many easy-to-grow plants, yarrow has strong potential for weediness and should be planted only where it is welcome to grow and spread. When used as a turf substitute, it should be treated in much the same way as grass, with careful soil preparation including amendment with organic matter, and seeded at the rate of 1 ounce per 3,000 square feet.

Achillea millefolium var. *occidentalis*

Seeds require constant moisture until they germinate and become established. Yarrow is drought-tolerant but will look better with regular water. It will take moderate or even heavy traffic but needs time to recover from the latter. Though yarrow cultivars of many colors are available, they are hybrids between non-native species. Yarrow has an extensive and ancient history of medicinal use. Its genus name comes from Achilles, who is said to have discovered the plant's healing powers for treating his soldiers. Pollen remains of yarrows have been found in Neanderthal caves in Iraq.

Achnatherum hymenoides, showing fall color

Achnatherum hymenoides (Oryzopsis hymenoides)

INDIAN RICEGRASS
GRASS FAMILY (*POACEAE*)
PERENNIAL BUNCHGRASS
HEIGHT: 2 FEET
WIDTH: 2 FEET
ZONE 5

CHARACTERISTICS: Green spikelets of rounded florets borne in large, diffuse, open panicles held above the blades, their color maturing to straw; blades erect, narrow, and inrolled.

OUTSTANDING FEATURES: Beautiful cool-season native bunchgrass with attractive, showy panicles that look great moving in the wind; very drought-tolerant.

NATIVE RANGE: Western North America and the Plains, in a wide variety of habitats. Common on the Colorado Plateau in dry, open woods, on sandy plains, and on native grasslands at elevations below 7,000 feet.

SEASON OF BLOOM: Late spring

CULTURE

Soil: Well-drained

Exposure: Full sun, warm site

Water use: Very low to low

Propagation: Seed

Care and maintenance: Very low, but because it is short lived, needs to be reseeded regularly to maintain a continuous population.

LANDSCAPE USES: Butterfly garden, dry garden, dry meadow, erosion control, range plant

WILDLIFE ATTRACTED: Although wind-pollinated, provides habitat and food for birds, insects, and mammals.

HISTORICAL AND MODERN USES: Cool-season edible grain, traditional Native American spring food

Native people still harvest the edible seeds of this dry-loving, cool-season grass, which are then roasted and cooked as a delicious mush. Indian ricegrass does best in warm, windswept areas. After seeds set, they are retained in showy straw-colored panicles that are beautiful moving in the wind. Indian ricegrass will look great planted with dry-loving grasses, flowers, and woody plants including cowboy's delight (*Sphaeralcea coccinea*), sand sagebrush (*Artemisia filifolia*), fringed sage (*Artemisia frigida*) four-wing saltbush (*Atriplex canescens*), Mormon tea (*Ephedra nevadensis*), desert olive (*Forestiera neomexicana*), common cliffrose (*Purshia stansburiana*), prickly poppy (*Argemone* spp.), sacred datura (*Datura wrightii*), redroot buckwheat (*Eriogonum racemosum*), blackfoot daisy (*Melampodium leucanthum*), showy four-o'clock (*Mirabilis multiflora*), dry-loving evening primroses (*Oenothera* spp.), Lambert's locoweed (*Oxytropis lambertii*), phlox penstemon (*Penstemon ambiguus*), rosemary mint (*Poliomintha incana*), paperflower (*Psilostrophe* spp.), prince's plume (*Stanleya pinnata*), prairie zinnia (*Zinnia grandiflora*), buffalograss (*Buchloe dactyloides*), Plains lovegrass (*Eragrostis intermedia*), purple and poverty three-awn (*Aristida purpurea* var. *purpurea* and *A. divaricata*), and dropseeds (*Sporobolus* spp.).

Agastache cana

Agastache cana

DOUBLE BUBBLE MINT, MOSQUITO PLANT
MINT FAMILY (*LAMIACEAE*)
HERBACEOUS PERENNIAL
HEIGHT: 2 TO 3 FEET
WIDTH: 3 FEET
ZONE 5

CHARACTERISTICS: Bushy, upright habit; square stems; medium-textured, shiny gray-green leaves; hot-pink, two-lipped, fragrant, tubular flowers on 2- to 3-foot stalks.

NATIVE RANGE: New Mexico and Western Texas; rare in its native range but available in the nursery trade, where it has been grown as an ornamental plant for many years.

SEASON OF BLOOM: Late summer and early autumn

OUTSTANDING FEATURES: Long-blooming, easy-to-grow plant that attracts hummingbirds, butterflies, and bees. Striking hot-pink flowers on tall, stout flower spikes above deliciously scented leaves with scalloped edges.

CULTURE

Soil: Warm, well-drained

Exposure: Full sun, reflected light

Water use: Low

Propagation: Seed, cuttings

Care and maintenance: Let seeds mature and fall to naturalize; deadhead after seed falls.

LANDSCAPE USES: Fragrance garden, dry garden, hummingbird and butterfly plant

WILDLIFE ATTRACTED: Hummingbirds, butterflies, bees

HISTORICAL AND MODERN USES: Beverage, medicinal tea and sachet, insect repellent, bee plant

This delightfully fragrant plant thrives on sun, warmth, and low water. Like all the members of the mint family, it has square stems. As its common name "double bubble mint" suggests, this plant smells good enough to eat, and it can be used in teas and sachets. Place it where you can brush against the leaves to release the scent and where you can observe frequent visits from hummingbirds and butterflies. Double bubble mint needs a sunny location, especially when planted in cooler areas; reflected heat and light will boost growth and bloom. In cooler areas with heavy, moist soils, two varieties of a related species do well: mountain hyssop (*Agastache pallidiflora* subsp. *pallidiflora* var. *pallidiflora*) and giant hyssop (*A. pallidiflora* subsp. *pallidiflora* var. *greenei*). Both of these gently scented species hail from subalpine plant communities, are extremely tolerant of heavy soils and "wet feet," and will do well in periodically saturated, cold microclimates. Mountain hyssop's flowers are white; flowers of giant hyssop are a showy purple-pink.

Agave parryi

Agave parryi subsp. *parryi* (*A. parryi* var. *couesii*)

PARRY'S AGAVE
AGAVE FAMILY (*AGAVACEAE*)
SUCCULENT PERENNIAL
HEIGHT: BASAL ROSETTE OF LEAVES 12 INCHES,
FLOWER SPIKE 6–8 FEET
WIDTH: 18 INCHES
ZONE 4

CHARACTERISTICS: Large basal rosette of thick, blue-gray leaves armed with spines; tall upright flower spike consisting of many flowers in a tall panicle atop a 6- to 8-foot stem. Individual flowers have six petal-like structures fused into a tube. Bat-pollinated southern populations bear yellow blooms; in the north, flowers are tinged with red to attract hummingbirds.

NATIVE RANGE: Arizona, New Mexico, and northern Chihuahua, Mexico; in northern Arizona, found at elevations of 4,500 to 8,000 feet. Its natural northern limit in central

Arizona is the Mogollon Rim; studies have shown that the distribution above the rim is the result of prehistoric introduction.

SEASON OF BLOOM: June to August; plants bloom only once, when approximately 25 years old.

OUTSTANDING FEATURES: Beautiful architecture, striking in the landscape; very drought-tolerant.

CULTURE

Soil: Well-drained, rocky, coarse-textured

Exposure: Full sun to light shade

Water use: Very low to low

Propagation: Seed or offsets

Care and maintenance: Remove offshoots and transplant in early summer.

LANDSCAPE USES: High-elevation desert landscaping, dry garden, container plant, accent plant

WILDLIFE ATTRACTED: Hummingbirds in northern populations, bats in southern populations

HISTORICAL AND MODERN USES: Used by nearly every historical Indian group in Arizona for food (flowers and roasted hearts), fibers, soap, fermented beverages, medicine, smoking, ceremonial objects, and musical instruments. Hearts of the agave were roasted in pits and eaten by many native peoples. It is a source of wax, and provides dietary calcium.

Parry's agave is named for Charles C. Parry, a prolific plant collector in North America in the mid-1800s. Like all agaves, it is monocarpic—that is, the plant will die once it has bloomed and set seeds. (Agaves are known as "century plants" because they live for many years before blooming.) Fear not; before blooming, it will send out many pups, or offshoots. Detach the pups from the parent plant and transplant, and each one will grow quickly. Parry's agave makes a good companion plant to yuccas (*Yucca* spp.), beargrass (*Nolina microcarpa*), cacti, Indian ricegrass (*Achnatherum hymenoides*), and other dry grasses. It is one of the most cold hardy species in the agave family, but check the plant's geographic origin when you purchase it; southern populations will not tolerate the extreme cold of the Colorado Plateau and places farther north.

Allium cernuum flower head

Allium cernuum

PINK NODDING ONION
LILY FAMILY (*LILIACEAE*)
HERBACEOUS BULB-FORMING PERENNIAL
HEIGHT: 8 INCHES
WIDTH: 4–6 INCHES
ZONE 4

CHARACTERISTICS: Fine-textured, upright, clumping, bulb-forming perennial with shiny, grasslike leaves; nodding, showy clusters of small, bell-shaped, clear pink flowers with six petal-like tepals.

NATIVE RANGE: North America; commonly found throughout moist, montane zones of the Southwest at elevations of 5,000 to 8,500 feet.

SEASON OF BLOOM: Late summer

OUTSTANDING FEATURES: A dainty plant with umbels of many nodding pink flowers at the top of a leafless stem; both leaves and flowers edible; multiplies rapidly.

CULTURE

Soil: Moist

Exposure: Sun to light shade

Water use: Moderate to high

Propagation: Bulbs, seed, divisions

Care and maintenance: Very low. Let seed drop to naturalize. Divide clumps as needed for increase.

LANDSCAPE USES: Edging plant, container plant, rock garden, moist wildflower meadow, butterfly garden, edible garden, naturalizing in moist places

WILDLIFE ATTRACTED: Butterflies

HISTORICAL AND MODERN USES: Edible leaves, blossoms, and bulbs; many medicinal uses including as a diuretic and to relieve flatulence.

All portions of this plant have traditionally been used as a food source by indigenous people. In modern use, flowers serve as a sweet garnish in salads or soups. The crushed leaves have a pungent, oniony smell and can be eaten like chives. Nodding onion multiplies rapidly in the garden. Plant in combination with other small, fine-textured, moisture-loving perennials, including native violets (*Viola canadensis* and *V. adunca*), mountain lobelia (*Lobelia anatina*), Whipple's penstemon (*Penstemon whippleanus*), harebells (*Campanula rotundifolia*), and Idaho fescue (*Festuca idahoensis*). Nodding onion can also be planted in front of taller plants with similar cultural needs, such as alkali pink (*Sidalcea neomexicana*), golden columbine (*Aquilegia chrysantha*), Rocky Mountain columbine (*Aquilegia caerulea*), Parry's primrose (*Primula parryi*), cardinal flower (*Lobelia cardinalis*), Richardson's geranium (*Geranium richardsonii*), geranium-leaf larkspur (*Delphinium geraniifolium*), and meadow grasses—alpine timothy (*Phleum alpinum*), tufted hairgrass (*Deschampsia caespitosa*), and ticklegrass (*Agrostis scabra*). A related species, *Allium geyeri*, has a coarser texture, gray-green leaves, and upright umbels of white to pale pink flowers; it is native to high-elevation meadows and is hardy to zone 2.

Allium cernuum

Anaphalis margaritacea

Anaphalis margaritacea
(Gnaphalium margaritaceum)

PEARLY EVERLASTING
SUNFLOWER FAMILY (*ASTERACEAE*)
HERBACEOUS PERENNIAL
HEIGHT: 2 FEET
WIDTH: 2 FEET
ZONE 2

CHARACTERISTICS: Upright form; woolly stems, silver leaves; dense terminal clusters of golden, everlasting flowers with silver bracts.

NATIVE RANGE: North America, Europe, and Asia; on the Colorado Plateau, along roadsides, in open woodlands and forests, near streams and in canyons, at elevations of 4,500 to 8,500 feet.

SEASON OF BLOOM: Late summer

OUTSTANDING FEATURES: Easy to grow; silver leaves make excellent contrast with green-leaved plants; clusters of golden everlasting flowers are surrounded by rounded, silvery bracts the color of pearls.

CULTURE

Soil: Any; will tolerate heavy soil

Exposure: Sun to light shade

Water use: Low to moderate

Propagation: Seed, root divisions

Care and maintenance: Very low; cut dead stems to ground in fall for tidiness if desired

LANDSCAPE USES: Wildflower meadow, silver color accent, dry garden, butterfly garden, front of border, ground cover for small areas, erosion control, stabilizer for road cuts and disturbed areas.

WILDLIFE ATTRACTED: Butterflies and bees

HISTORICAL AND MODERN USES: Flowers and foliage used in fresh or dried arrangements and wreaths. Leaves are edible. Native American medicinal uses include reducing inflammation of membranes and healing wounds.

An easy garden plant that colonizes, spreading by underground rootstocks, making it an excellent candidate for planting in disturbed areas such as road cuts and construction disturbances. At The Arboretum at Flagstaff, pearly everlasting can be seen in the Entrance Garden, where it grows in the foreground with Arizona honeysuckle (*Lonicera arizonica*) and western blue flag (*Iris missouriensis*) and beside the vibrant multicolored foliage of mountain sorrel (*Oxyria digyna*). Like all silver-leaved plants, it provides an excellent contrast to green-leaved plants and plants with purple, red, and yellow fall color such as agrimony (*Agrimonia striata*), native geraniums (*Geranium* spp.), dogbane (*Apocynum cannabinum*), and bee balm (*Monarda fistulosa* var. *menthaefolia*).

Anaphalis margaritacea

Anemone multifida

Anemone multifida
(Anemone globosa)

CUTLEAF ANEMONE, GLOBEFLOWER
BUTTERCUP FAMILY (*RANUNCULACEAE*)
HERBACEOUS PERENNIAL
HEIGHT: 1 FOOT
WIDTH: 6 INCHES
ZONE 2

CHARACTERISTICS: Upright, clumping perennial with many finely divided leaves above a woody basal stem. Flowers borne on hairy stems in umbels of two to three 1-inch flowers that lack petals. Their showy petaloid sepals can be purple, maroon, reddish, yellow, cream, or bicolored and surround a green receptacle covered with many yellow stamens and pistils.

NATIVE RANGE: North America, in alpine and subalpine habitats

SEASON OF BLOOM: Early summer

OUTSTANDING FEATURES: Early bloom; long-lasting flowers, which may range in color from creamy ivory to purple or maroon; flowers mature into beautiful, long, silky seed heads that glimmer in the sunlight.

CULTURE

Soil: Moist during active growth

Exposure: Full sun to partial shade

Water use: Moderate

Propagation: Seed or division

Care and maintenance: Very low

LANDSCAPE USES: Rock garden, perennial garden

WILDLIFE ATTRACTED: Bees, syrphid flies

HISTORICAL AND MODERN USES: Insect repellent (plant is toxic; contact with sap may irritate skin)

As with all anemones, aggregations of many plumed seeds persist after bloom, providing an interesting accent. Breathtakingly beautiful when planted where the many hairs on stems, leaves, and seeds will be backlit by the sun. Cutleaf anemones are treasured for their early, symmetrical bloom and cut foliage. An even earlier spring bloomer of rounded, compact habit is the pasque-flower (*Anemone patens,* syn. *Pulsatilla patens* var. *multifida*), which bears large, single, purple, cylindrical flowers and has hairy leaves and persistent feathery seed heads. Another, the long-head thimbleweed (*Anemone cylindrica*), is native to canyons and has cream-colored, five-part flowers borne singly atop upright stems, followed by cottony achenes (dry, one-seeded fruits) held in a thimble-shaped receptacle.

Anemone cylindrica

Anemopsis californica

Anemopsis californica

YERBA MANSA, LIZARD TAIL
LIZARD TAIL FAMILY (SAURURACEAE)
HERBACEOUS PERENNIAL
HEIGHT: 18 INCHES
WIDTH: 2 FEET, SPREADING
ZONES 4 TO 6

CHARACTERISTICS: Oblong leaves form upright, low rosettes; plant spreads by trailing aboveground red runners and belowground rhizomes. "Flower" is actually a showy compound inflorescence, made up of reflexed, white, petal-like bracts at the base of an upright conelike aggregate of tiny light green flowers.

NATIVE RANGE: Western United States from Oregon and California east to Nebraska and Texas; common in lowland meadows and wet alkaline places.

SEASON OF BLOOM: Early summer

OUTSTANDING FEATURES: Beautiful, unique, cone-shaped inflorescences above fragrant medicinal leaves; alkaline-tolerant; can be used as a ground cover that will take light traffic and occasional high mowing.

CULTURE

Soil: Neutral or alkaline; seasonally moist

Exposure: Sun or light shade

Water use: Moderate

Propagation: Seed or offsets

Care and maintenance: In the garden, water regularly; mulch in colder zones (5 and 6).

LANDSCAPE USES: Ground cover or low-traffic turf substitute, front of border, accent plant, container garden, medicinal garden. Plant at edges of ponds, streams and water features, and in seasonally moist meadows.

HISTORICAL AND MODERN USES: Roots of this cure-all are used in a decoction to treat ulcers, indigestion, and lung complaints; leaves used as a poultice for rheumatism and swelling; all parts dried and powdered for use as a disinfectant.

Yerba mansa occurs naturally in moist and seasonally moist places. It will tolerate saturated soils and spring drought. In zones 5 and 6, it will benefit from seasonal protection or a sheltered microclimate; in zones 4 and colder it can be kept as a container plant with winter protection or moved indoors for the cold season. Yerba mansa has been planted as an alkaline-tolerant turf substitute that will take periodic high mowing. All parts of the plant, including seeds, are fragrant and used medicinally. In the landscape, yerba mansa does well with other plants of similar moisture needs including scarlet monkeyflower (*Mimulus cardinalis*), yellow-stream monkeyflower (*M. guttatus*), alkali pink (*Sidalcea neomexicana*), native violets (*Viola* spp.), rushes (*Juncus* spp.), and sedges (*Carex* spp.). In areas of adequate warmth and moisture, it quickly spreads to form a fragrant, coarse-textured, flowering ground cover.

Antennaria parvifolia

Antennaria parvifolia
(Antennaria aprica)

LITTLELEAF PUSSYTOES
SUNFLOWER FAMILY (*ASTERACEAE*)
HERBACEOUS PERENNIAL
HEIGHT: 3 INCHES
WIDTH: SPREADING
ZONE 4

CHARACTERISTICS: Silvery leaves form ground-hugging mat only 3 inches tall. Spreads by underground stems. White rayless flowers the size of your pinkie fingernail, soft to touch, in fruit form small, cottony pads like cats' toes that give the plant its common name.

NATIVE RANGE: Western North America; in ponderosa pine forests, mixed conifer forests, and mountainous areas, at elevations from 5,000 to 12,000 feet.

SEASON OF BLOOM: Late spring and early summer

OUTSTANDING FEATURES: An excellent small-area ground cover, providing a wonderful splash of rough-textured gray that complements shrubs and wildflowers in the garden. Moderately drought-tolerant.

CULTURE

Soil: Tolerates either clay or well-drained soils

Exposure: Partial shade to full shade

Water use: Low to moderate

Propagation: Division, cuttings, seed

CARE AND MAINTENANCE: Keep free of debris and pine needles. In dry years, an early summer deep watering will encourage rapid, healthy growth.

LANDSCAPE USES: Ground cover, can take light foot traffic. Ideal between flagstones or pavers or planted among rocks.

WILDLIFE ATTRACTED: Butterflies and bees

HISTORICAL AND MODERN USES: Used by Native Americans as a blood medicine and in ceremonies.

Littleleaf pussytoes is an excellent small-area ground cover in shade and filtered light. Interplant with spring bulbs and low-growing native wildflowers. Great for naturalizing with native grasses such as Arizona fescue (*Festuca arizonica*), blue grama (*Bouteloua gracilis*), and little bluestem (*Schizachyrium scoparium*) in openings among ponderosa pine trees. Another shade-loving pussytoes, white-margin pussytoes (*Antennaria marginata*), has fat lancelike leaves with shiny green upper surfaces and white undersides. Small white flowers on short stems bloom from May to June. Its angular rosettes provide a geometric pattern in the garden, where it prefers filtered light or shade and slightly more moisture than that required by *A. parvifolia*. It naturally grows in alpine and subalpine habitats and in shady, moist canyons where it receives moderate moisture. Planted with *A. parvifolia*, it creates an interesting mosaic of green and silver.

Antennaria rosea

Antennaria rosea
(Antennaria dioica var. rosea)

Rosy pussytoes
Sunflower family (*Asteraceae*)
Herbaceous perennial
Height: 4 inches
Width: Spreading
Zone 4

CHARACTERISTICS: Low-growing silver carpet with upright stems and flowers. Rayless flowers, borne on short upright stems above the leaves and shoots, are rose pink to deep maroon in bud, aging to a cat's paw of fluffy silver seeds.

NATIVE RANGE: North America, broadly distributed from Alaska south to the western United States; believed to have arisen through hybridization.

SEASON OF BLOOM: Early summer

OUTSTANDING FEATURES: Lovely, felt-leaved, silver, year-round ground cover with tiny, beautiful rose-colored flowers. Early blooming, drought-tolerant.

CULTURE

Soil: Will tolerate either heavy or well-drained soils

Exposure: Full sun to partial shade

Water use: Low

Propagation: Division, cuttings, seed

Care and maintenance: Very low. Prune off any dead growth after winter dormancy.

LANDSCAPE USES: Ground cover, silver color accent, dry garden or rock garden, container garden.

WILDLIFE ATTRACTED: Butterflies, bees. Rabbit resistant.

HISTORICAL AND MODERN USES: Native Americans used this plant as an eyewash.

With a more upright form than others of its genus, rosy pussytoes can be used as an edging plant to provide a contrasting color accent to green-leaved perennials or as an early-blooming filler in an herb or butterfly garden. Though all pussytoes provide year-round ground cover, this one boasts the most colorful flowers, ranging from rosy pink to a deep maroon in bud. Because of its drought tolerance, rosy pussytoes makes an excellent candidate for the dry garden or among rocks in excessively drained soils. For a miniature rock garden in a dish, try planting rosy pussytoes with Fendler's sandwort (*Arenaria fendleri*), wild candytuft (*Thlaspi montanum* var. *fendleri*), and a native stonecrop such as red pod stonecrop (*Rhodiola rhodantha*), ledge stonecrop (*Rhodiola integrifolia* subsp. *integrifolia*), or spearleaf stonecrop (*Sedum lanceolatum*).

Antennaria rosulata

Antennaria rosulata
(Antennaria bakeri, A. sierra-blancae)

KAIBAB PUSSYTOES
SUNFLOWER FAMILY (*ASTERACEAE*)
HERBACEOUS PERENNIAL
HEIGHT: 1 INCH
WIDTH: SPREADING
ZONE 3

CHARACTERISTICS: Very fine-textured rosettes of silvery leaves less than a half-inch long, in dense mats; tiny, pinkish, rayless flowers in aggregates resembling cat paws.

SEASON OF BLOOM: Early summer

OUTSTANDING FEATURES: The lowest growing and finest textured of the pussytoes. Its tiny silver leaves and delicate, faintly pink "pussytoes" blooms are charming. Incredibly hardy to cold and wind, and virtually maintenance free.

NATIVE RANGE: Arizona, Colorado, New Mexico, and Utah, in alpine meadows

CULTURE

Soil: Will grow in areas of spring saturation

Exposure: Full sun

Water use: Low to moderate

Propagation: Division, cuttings, seed

Care and maintenance: Very low

LANDSCAPE USES: Ground cover in sunny areas and in seasonally moist meadows; turf substitute (will tolerate light foot traffic); great in rock gardens.

WILDLIFE ATTRACTED: Butterflies and bees

HISTORICAL AND MODERN USES: Used by Native Americans as a pediatric aid and as a hunting medicine.

Littleleaf pussytoes (*A. parvifolia*) does best with filtered light, whereas Kaibab pussytoes (*A. rosulata*) thrives in full sun. One of the finest textured and lowest growing high-elevation plants available for the garden, it works admirably when used to soften the edges of planters and stonework.

Aquilegia caerulea

Aquilegia caerulea

ROCKY MOUNTAIN COLUMBINE
BUTTERCUP FAMILY (*RANUNCULACEAE*)
HERBACEOUS PERENNIAL
HEIGHT: 2 FEET
WIDTH: 2 FEET
ZONE 3

CHARACTERISTICS: Upright perennial with divided leaves that resemble maidenhair fern. Terminal racemes of large flowers on upright stems have pale blue to blue sepals and petals colored like the sepals with blades often white, the petals bearing long, slender spurs.

NATIVE RANGE: Rocky Mountain states, South Dakota, and Nevada, in subalpine and alpine habitats

SEASON OF BLOOM: Late spring to midsummer, with repeat bloom throughout the season

OUTSTANDING FEATURES: Everybody's favorite, Rocky Mountain columbine bears large blue and white flowers with long graceful spurs on upright stems above attractive ferny leaves. Reliable, early and repeat bloom. Very easy to grow and very rewarding!

CULTURE

Soil: Any

Exposure: Shade to sun

Water use: Low to high, depending on exposure

Propagation: Seed, division

Care and maintenance: To encourage repeat flowering, remove spent blooms before seed is set and water regularly; keep irrigation water off leaves to prevent powdery mildew.

LANDSCAPE USES: Perennial garden, shade garden, naturalizing, hummingbird garden. Said to be rabbit resistant.

WILDLIFE ATTRACTED: Hummingbirds

HISTORICAL AND MODERN USES: None. All parts of this plant are poisonous.

Flower color of Rocky Mountain columbine ranges from entirely pale blue to purple or darker blue with white. Alpine plants are commonly dwarfed, while those growing in

Aquilegia caerulea

lower elevations are larger. Like all columbines, this species readily seeds itself. Columbines also hybridize easily; to prevent crossing, only one species should be planted in a garden. Rocky Mountain columbine does well when planted in moist soils beneath aspens and red-twig dogwood; it does equally well in freely draining soils on slopes and in rich organic soils in sunny garden beds. The flowers contrast well when planted next to the glossy, deep green leaves of mountain lover (*Paxistima myrsinites*) or the dark green leaves of creeping barberry (*Mahonia repens*). They are beautiful in combination with early-blooming asters and fleabanes, western blue flag (*Iris missouriensis*), mountain bluebells (*Mertensia ciliata*), and Flagstaff bluebells (*M. franciscana*).

Aquilegia chrysantha

Aquilegia chrysantha

GOLDEN COLUMBINE
BUTTERCUP FAMILY (*RANUNCULACEAE*)
HERBACEOUS PERENNIAL
HEIGHT: 2 FEET
WIDTH: 2 FEET
ZONE 3

CHARACTERISTICS: Upright mound of bright green divided leaves; many large flowers, with yellow sepals and spurred yellow petals.

NATIVE RANGE: Utah and Colorado to Mexico, in moist habitats at elevations of 3,000 to 11,000 feet

SEASON OF BLOOM: Early summer, with repeat bloom in late summer

OUTSTANDING FEATURES: A profusion of early, clear-yellow flowers with long spurs; attractive, bright green divided leaves; repeat bloom; tough and drought-tolerant in shade.

CULTURE

Soil: Any

Exposure: Sun to shade

Water use: Low to moderate depending on exposure

Propagation: Seed, division

Care and maintenance: For repeat bloom, remove spent flowers and water regularly.

LANDSCAPE USES: Perennial garden, shade garden, hummingbird garden, naturalizing

WILDLIFE ATTRACTED: Hummingbirds, butterflies. Rabbit resistant.

HISTORICAL AND MODERN USES: None. All parts of this plant are poisonous.

In the wild, these freely blooming perennials are found in many habitats, from the understory beneath stands of mixed conifer and aspen groves, where they grow with native ferns and Canada violets, to streamside areas in the Sonoran Desert, where they form showy masses in moist areas. For all their appearance of delicacy, golden columbines are extremely tough and drought-tolerant when given protection from bright sun. Beautiful when planted with Whipple's penstemon (*Penstemon whippleanus*) and alpine timothy (*Phleum alpinum*).

Aquilegia chrysantha

Aquilegia desertorum

Aquilegia desertorum

DESERT COLUMBINE, RED COLUMBINE
BUTTERCUP FAMILY (*RANUNCULACEAE*)
HERBACEOUS PERENNIAL
HEIGHT: 2 FEET
WIDTH: 2 FEET
ZONE 3

CHARACTERISTICS: Compact mound of gray, pubescent, divided leaves; nodding flowers with red petaloid sepals and yellow petals.

NATIVE RANGE: Utah, rare in northern Arizona and New Mexico; on limestone outcrops and canyon slopes in ponderosa pine forests

SEASON OF BLOOM: Late spring to early autumn

OUTSTANDING FEATURES: A showy garden beauty that's drought-tolerant, long-blooming, easy to propagate, and a magnet for hummingbirds.

CULTURE

Soil: Will tolerate heavy, rocky, and limestone soil

Exposure: Shade to sun

Water use: Low to moderate

Propagation: Seed; naturalizes

Care and maintenance: Remove spent flowers for continued bloom.

LANDSCAPE USES: Accent, border, container, hummingbird garden, rock garden

WILDLIFE ATTRACTED: Hummingbirds

HISTORICAL AND MODERN USES: None. All parts of this plant are poisonous.

This long-blooming perennial bears an all-summer-long supply of showy, nodding, red flowers with five petal-like sepals and five red-spurred, red petals from late spring until early autumn. Flowers are borne above a mound of compact, gray, hairy foliage, with leaves divided into leaflets that resemble maidenhair fern. Two closely related species, barrel columbine (*Aquilegia triternata*) and Rocky Mountain red columbine (*A. elegantula*), are sometimes available in the nursery trade. Barrel columbine is a more upright plant, to 3 feet tall, with longer petal blades than *A. desertorum*, and spurs equal in length to the petals. Rocky Mountain red columbine, naturally occurring at elevations of up to 9,000 feet in southwest Colorado, southeastern Utah, and northern Mexico, is similar in size to *A. desertorum*, with smooth green leaves, yellow-tipped red sepals, and yellow petals. If different species are growing near one another, all columbines will hybridize easily. To maintain plants true to species, plant only one species of columbine in your garden, or remove chance seedlings.

Aquilegia desertorum

Aralia racemosa

Aralia racemosa subsp. *bicrenata*

AMERICAN SPIKENARD
GINSENG FAMILY (*ARALIACEAE*)
HERBACEOUS PERENNIAL
HEIGHT: 4 ¹/₂ FEET
WIDTH: 4 FEET
ZONE 4

CHARACTERISTICS: Upright, arching, coarse-textured, rhizomatous perennial with large, pinnately compound, bright green leaves; delicate white flowers in large, open panicles of many umbels mature into round, blue-black berries.

NATIVE RANGE: Colorado Plateau and Mexico

SEASON OF BLOOM: Early summer

OUTSTANDING FEATURES: Beautiful, coarse-textured foliage plant with white flowers followed by juicy, edible berries. Large leaves turn bright yellow in fall for a beautiful color accent in the garden.

CULTURE

Soil: Rich and moderately moist

Exposure: Shade to partial sun

Water use: Moderate

Propagation: Seed

Care and maintenance: Leaves die back to the ground in winter; remove dead growth in spring. Mulch to keep soil moist.

LANDSCAPE USES: Shade garden, fern substitute, coarse-textured background plant; fall color accent.

WILDLIFE ATTRACTED: Birds eat berries.

HISTORICAL AND MODERN USES: Used as a blood purifier. Edible leaves, stems, and roots; berries used for jam, jelly, or marmalade.

American spikenard occurs only in shaded areas along moist drainages and in sandy crevices in Colorado Plateau woodlands. It thrives in moist, organic soil, but its large rootstock allows surprising drought tolerance in dry years. Plant it in low spots where water will collect naturally. Good among rocks near water features. A great companion to ferns, shade plants, and other plants that do well with moderate water, such as bee balm (*Monarda fistulosa* var. *menthaefolia*), willow (*Salix* spp.), agrimony (*Agrimonia striata*), Gambel oak (*Quercus gambelii*), and native grasses.

Aralia racemosa

Arctostaphylos uva-ursi

Arctostaphylos uva-ursi

BEARBERRY, KINNIKINNICK
HEATH FAMILY (*ERICACEAE*)
WOODY PERENNIAL
HEIGHT: 6–12 INCHES
WIDTH: 3 FEET
ZONE 3

CHARACTERISTICS: Trailing evergreen ground cover forms a spreading prostrate mat of small, shiny, dark green leaves. Many light-pink, waxy, urn-shaped flowers followed by small red fruits.

NATIVE RANGE: Northern Hemisphere; on the Colorado Plateau, a component of the mixed conifer understory at elevations between 8,500 and 9,500 feet

SEASON OF BLOOM: Late spring to early summer

OUTSTANDING FEATURES: Easy care, neat appearance. Attractive, shiny leaves and pale-pink urn-shaped flowers. Leaves may show purple fall color in colder areas.

Excellent wildlife habitat plant; small red fruits are attractive to many birds and mammals.

CULTURE

Soil: Any. Will do well with some organic matter.

Exposure: Sun to light shade

Water use: Low to moderate

Propagation: Cuttings, layering

Care and maintenance: Remove dead branch tips after spring thaw. Brush away needles and debris.

LANDSCAPE USES: An evergreen ground cover that lends year-round structure and interest in the garden. Plant for early bloom and for edible fruit and flowers; good under oaks, in shade gardens, in mass plantings, on slopes for erosion control. Adaptable to commercial plantings, medians and parking strips, and containers.

WILDLIFE ATTRACTED: Birds, bees, hummingbirds, large and small mammals

HISTORICAL AND MODERN USES: Ingredient in smoking mixture; leaves used in teas; berries ground into meal, used in drinks, or for jams and jellies.

Bearberry is a charming, low-growing plant that is extraordinarily drought-tolerant in protected locations, though it requires more moisture in areas of bright reflected sun. It needs protection from harsh sun in high-elevation and interior areas and does best when given a northern exposure, morning sun, or filtered light. Popular cultivars are regional selections, many from eastern North America or coastal California. For planting at high elevations, be sure to select plants propagated from western interior regions. The common name for other *Arctostaphylos* species is "manzanita," which in Spanish means "little apples," referring to the small, applelike fruits. Related native species are greenleaf manzanita (*A. patula*), a 3- to 5-foot-tall shrub from open coniferous forests with an upright growth habit and beautiful, smooth tan bark; hardy manzanita (*A. nevadensis*), a mounding evergreen ground cover (18 inches high and 5 feet wide) with 3-inch olive-green leaves and pink flowers; and Colorado manzanita (*A.* x *coloradoensis*), a naturally occurring hybrid from the Rocky Mountains that is similar in form to hardy manzanita. Two other shrub manzanitas are pointleaf manzanita (*A. pungens*), a dense, 3-foot-tall shrub native to chaparral and dry hillsides in the ponderosa pine belt, and Pringle's manzanita (*A. pringlei*), a tall shrub (to 6 feet) with rounded leaves that is often found in chaparral growing with pointleaf manzanita. Shrub manzanitas are renowned for their smooth red bark and branches. They should be pruned when young to develop an open structure, since they tolerate pruning of mature branches poorly.

Arenaria fendleri

Arenaria fendleri

FENDLER'S SANDWORT
PINK FAMILY (*CARYOPHYLLACEAE*)
WOODY PERENNIAL
HEIGHT: 3–12 INCHES
WIDTH: 1 FOOT
ALL ZONES

CHARACTERISTICS: Compact, cushion-forming, ground-hugging mat with upright stems; small, white, five-petaled, star-shaped flowers with yellow centers in open clusters atop upright, grasslike stalks.

NATIVE RANGE: Arizona to west Texas and Wyoming; on the Colorado Plateau, at elevations between 4,000 and 12,000 feet, commonly in pine forests and open meadows to alpine tundra.

SEASON OF BLOOM: Late summer; long-blooming

OUTSTANDING FEATURES: Fine-textured, slender, sharp, bright-green, grasslike leaves; many starlike flowers in summer; long bloom period.

CULTURE

Soil: Requires good drainage; will grow in areas of spring saturation

Exposure: Full sun

Water use: Low to moderate

Propagation: Division, seed, cuttings

Care and maintenance: Very low

LANDSCAPE USES: Edging plant or low border, small-area ground cover, butterfly garden, rock garden, container plant. Good planted among grasses in wildflower meadow.

WILDLIFE ATTRACTED: Butterflies

HISTORICAL AND MODERN USES: The powdered root is used as a kind of snuff to induce sneezing.

When not in bloom, Fendler's sandwort resembles a fine-textured, low-growing, bright green grass. It provides an excellent color contrast when planted beside gray-leaved plants. In rock gardens it will go well with buckwheats (*Eriogonum* spp.), woolly cinque-

Arenaria fendleri

foil (*Potentilla hippiana*), columbines (*Aquilegia* spp.), stonecrops (*Sedum* spp., *Rhodiola* spp.), wandbloom penstemon (*Penstemon virgatus*), Whipple's penstemon (*P. whippleanus*), Rydberg's penstemon (*P. rydbergii*), and mat penstemon (*P. linari-oides*). It also grows well in combination with other open-meadow species including native grasses, mountain parsley (*Pseudo-cymopterus montanus*), and harebells (*Campanula rotundifolia*).

Argemone pleiacantha

Argemone pleiacantha

SOUTHWESTERN PRICKLY POPPY
POPPY FAMILY (*PAPAVERACEAE*)
HERBACEOUS PERENNIAL
HEIGHT: 2 FEET
WIDTH: 3 FEET
ZONE 3

CHARACTERISTICS: Upright perennial; giant white flowers, with crinkled petals and bright orange centers made up of many stamens, borne atop upright stems above blue-gray, deeply lobed, prickly leaves that clasp the stem. Fruit is a prickly, oblong capsule 1 ½ inches long that disperses seed through a circular pore on its upper surface.

NATIVE RANGE: Wyoming and South Dakota, south to Texas and Mexico, in open places including fields, roadsides, mesas, and washes at elevations of 1,400 to 8,000 feet.

SEASON OF BLOOM: All summer

OUTSTANDING FEATURES: This prickly perennial wildflower bears some of the showiest blooms on the Colorado Plateau: extraordinary, 4-inch, white, crinkled blossoms with bright orange centers. Thrives on bright sun, heat, and drought; flowers all summer.

CULTURE

Soil: Well-drained, warm

Exposure: Full sun

Water use: Very low to low

Propagation: Seed; naturalizes

Care and maintenance: Pinch back growing tips to encourage fullness and increase number of flowers. Remove flowers before seed set for longer bloom.

LANDSCAPE USES: Naturalizing, dry wildflower meadow, dry garden, white garden, blue-gray color accent, barrier planting

WILDLIFE ATTRACTED: Mourning doves, which eat the seeds

HISTORICAL AND MODERN USES: None. All parts of this plant are poisonous.

Southwestern prickly poppy provides spectacular bloom in the toughest places and will naturalize in disturbed areas and road cuts. Its large, showy flowers can bloom from late spring throughout the summer. For best results, give this tough beauty all the reflected heat, sun, and good drainage you can muster. Great when seeded or planted with California poppies (*Eschscholzia* spp.), lupines (*Lupinus* spp.), desert marigold (*Baileya multiradiata*), beardtongues including phlox penstemon (*Penstemon ambiguus*) and Wasatch beardtongue (*P. cyananthus*), desert bluebells (*Phacelia campanularia*), purplemat (*Nama demissum*), pale evening primrose (*Oenothera pallida* subsp. *pallida*), and other carefree, sun-loving wildflowers. For use as a fresh cut flower, place stalk in warm water to hydrate, then make a fresh cut and hold this over a match or flame to seal the stem. Prickly poppy flowers can also be preserved dry with silica gel. Like all members of the poppy family, southwestern prickly poppy has milky sap; though the sap of many species is white, the sap of this species is yellow. The abundance of this plant on large areas of rangeland indicates overgrazing.

Argemone pleiacantha

Artemisia frigida

Artemisia frigida

FRINGED SAGEBRUSH
SUNFLOWER FAMILY (*ASTERACEAE*)
EVERGREEN SUBSHRUB
HEIGHT: 1–2 FEET
WIDTH: 2 FEET
ZONE 2

CHARACTERISTICS: Fine-textured perennial subshrub with narrow, divided, gray leaves. Compact growth in early season, more upright from late season into fall, when it extends upright flowering stems clothed in many small, rayless, golden flowers in 3- to 6-inch panicles.

NATIVE RANGE: Alaska to northern Arizona, New Mexico, and Texas, in dry stony soils; also found in Siberia

SEASON OF BLOOM: All summer, persisting into fall

OUTSTANDING FEATURES: Attractive silvery foliage; exceptional drought tolerance and cold tolerance; ease of care

CULTURE

Soil: Well-drained

Exposure: Sun

Water use: Low

Propagation: Seed, division, cuttings

Care and maintenance: Very low. Remove dead stems in fall or spring. Cut back every few years to renew growth in spring.

LANDSCAPE USES: Ground cover, border or foundation planting, dry garden, silver garden, rock garden, color accent, fragrance garden, nurse plant, erosion control, container plant

WILDLIFE ATTRACTED: Valued as forage for various wild animals, such as deer, and for sheep; may attract butterflies

HISTORICAL AND MODERN USES: Many Native American medicinal uses include incense, insect repellent, seasoning, and toothache remedy. Cut flowers used for dried arrangements and wreaths.

Fringed sagebrush is a durable, neat, and easy-to-grow evergreen ("evergray"?) subshrub. It gives year-round definition to garden beds and is often used as an edging in herb gardens. This sagebrush is often found on windswept ridge crests and will grow well in areas of high wind, although it may be dwarfed. It will act as a low windbreak and can be used as a nurse plant to shelter other native plants in the landscape while they become established. Related species include prairie sagebrush (*Artemisia ludoviciana*), common throughout the Colorado Plateau; big sage (*A. tridentata*), best known for its strong fragrance and architectural beauty; and sand sagebrush (*A. filifolia*), an upright silver shrub with threadlike leaves. For a drought-tolerant silver garden, plant fringed sagebrush with other artemisias; four-wing saltbush (*Atriplex canescens*); sages such as cooking sage (*Salvia officinalis*), purple sage (*S. dorrii*), and big-flowered azure blue sage (*S. azurea* var. *grandiflora*); redroot buckwheat (*Eriogonum racemosum*); winterfat (*Krascheninnikovia lanata*); evening primrose (*Oenothera* spp.); and Fendler's sundrops (*Calylophus hartwegii* subsp. *fendleri*). All the artemisias can be used as a contrasting backdrop to wildflowers of yellow, orange, and red hues, and offer a pleasing complement to autumn leaves. They can be grown successfully in dry gardens with native cacti and succulents including agaves, beargrass (*Nolina* spp.), and yuccas. To set off a great fall color display, plant with colorful native grasses including little bluestem (*Schizachyrium scoparium*), cane bluestem (*Bothriochloa barbinodis*), silver beardgrass (*Andropogon saccharoides* var. *torreyana*), side-oats grama (*Bouteloua gracilis*), and switchgrass (*Panicum virgatum*).

Asclepias speciosa

Asclepias speciosa

SHOWY MILKWEED
MILKWEED FAMILY (*ASCLEPIADACEAE*)
HERBACEOUS PERENNIAL
HEIGHT: 3 $\frac{1}{2}$ FEET
WIDTH: SPREADING
ZONE 3

CHARACTERISTICS: Upright, coarse-textured perennial with light gray-green, oblong to lance-shaped leaves, smooth above and white-hairy below, on stout stems; spreads by underground runners. Many unusual 1-inch, starry, pink to rose-lavender flowers in large clusters at the top of each shoot in midsummer; flowers have five rose-purple sepals, five lavender-pink petals bent backward, and five lavender-pink horned hoods.

NATIVE RANGE: Western North America (also, rarely, in Iowa) in open coniferous forests, along roadsides, and in seasonally moist areas

SEASON OF BLOOM: Early to midsummer; long-blooming

OUTSTANDING FEATURES: A dramatic perennial with large clusters of unusual, star-shaped, pink to rose-lavender horned and hooded flowers that provide nectar to butterflies. Flowers develop into interesting hornlike seed pods filled with small seeds dispersed on the wind by attached fluff. Spreads readily; very drought-tolerant once established.

CULTURE

Soil: Seasonally moist, although plant will tolerate drought once established

Exposure: Full sun to light shade

Water use: Moderate

Propagation: Seed, division

Care and maintenance: Cut back stems at end of season.

LANDSCAPE USES: Accent plant, container plant, butterfly plant, wild meadow or streambed, naturalizing

WILDLIFE ATTRACTED: Butterflies and bee flies. Poisonous to livestock.

HISTORICAL AND MODERN USES: Milky sap used as chewing gum; edible flowers, fruits, leaves, stems, and roots; tender stems sometimes used as a potherb.

Showy milkweed is a distinctive native plant with interesting form, flower, seed pods, and leaf color. Flowers are followed by white-woolly, 4-inch-long, inflated pods that open to allow the wind to disperse their fluff-bearing seeds. When deciding where to plant showy milkweed, consider its spreading growth habit; it can be weedy if planted in the wrong location. If you want to control its growth while still enjoying its beauty, grow it in a large, deep container. (Be sure to water throughly, then wait to water again until the potting soil is dry to touch several inches below the soil surface.) Showy milkweed will bloom earlier

Asclepias speciosa

than butterfly weed (*A. tuberosa*) if the two are grown in the same location; having both in the garden will provide a succession of interesting, butterfly-attracting blooms. Another intriguing milkweed is antelope horns (*A. asperula*), a denizen of sunny, dry, rocky, open areas. Antelope horns has large, fragrant, maroon-and-green flowers in dense 3-inch-wide umbels, followed by the long, thick pointed pods that give this drought-loving perennial its common name. Hardy to zone 5, it requires good drainage and grows best when planted on rocky slopes or in open flat areas with full sun.

Asclepias tuberosa

Asclepias tuberosa

BUTTERFLY MILKWEED
MILKWEED FAMILY (*ASCLEPIADACEAE*)
HERBACEOUS PERENNIAL
HEIGHT: 8 INCHES
WIDTH: 20 INCHES
ZONE 4

CHARACTERISTICS: Upright perennial with bright green stems and symmetrical opposite leaves. Many five-sepaled, five-petaled, fragrant, waxy orange to yellow flowers in dense, flat-topped, 3-inch clusters at every branch tip.

NATIVE RANGE: Throughout the United States except in the Northwest. On the Colorado Plateau, often found growing in moist canyons from pinyon–juniper to mixed conifer forest.

SEASON OF BLOOM: Midsummer, long-blooming

OUTSTANDING FEATURES: Highly desired by the many butterfly species that frequent the showy yellow to orange flowers; enduring bloom, neat bright green foliage, interesting seed pods; proven ease as a garden specimen.

CULTURE

Soil: Well-drained

Exposure: Full sun

Water use: Low to moderate

Propagation: Seed, cuttings

Care and maintenance: Pruning first flowers in summer prolongs flowering season and gives plant a bushier form.

LANDSCAPE USES: Dry garden, butterfly garden, cutting garden (use seed pods in dried arrangements)

WILDLIFE ATTRACTED: Butterflies, honeybees, hummingbirds

HISTORICAL AND MODERN USES: Edible flowers, fruits, leaves, stems, and roots. Rhizome chewed as a folk remedy for pleurisy and other lung diseases. Contact with plant may cause dermatitis.

Butterfly milkweed has earned a long-honored place in gardens because of its prodigious bloom and ease of growth. Often featured in sunny, dry, southwestern-style, xerophytic gardens, this versatile perennial can also be planted with canyon dwellers such as bee balm (*Monarda fistulosa* var. *menthaefolia*), bracken fern (*Pteridium aquilinum*), tasselflower brickellbush (*Brickellia grandiflora*), taperleaf (*Pericome caudata*), pearlseed (*Macromeria viridiflora*), and native thistles (*Cirsium wheeleri, C. arizonica*) for a butterfly-inviting natural garden that will also offer hospitality to other wildlife including birds and bees. The fused petals of butterfly weed form a crown with five projecting horns; between the horns is sticky pollen, which attaches to the feet of butterflies and other insects when they visit the fragrant flower. Butterfly weed should be protected from extremes of cold; mulch it or plant it in a sheltered microclimate.

Asclepias tuberosa

Astragalus mollissimus

Astragalus mollissimus
(Astragalus thompsoniae,
A. mollissimus var. thompsoniae, A. syrticolus)

WOOLLY LOCOWEED
PEA FAMILY (*FABACEAE*)
HERBACEOUS PERENNIAL
HEIGHT: 1 FOOT
WIDTH: 2 FEET, WILL SPREAD
ZONE 4

CHARACTERISTICS: Low-growing, stemless, clumping perennial with soft, woolly, upright gray pinnate leaves made up of many rounded leaflets attached to a purple-tinged midrib. Pink-purple pea flowers in early summer, followed by beaked ovoid pods covered with dense, shaggy, unmatted hairs.

NATIVE RANGE: Southwest United States and western plains in desert shrub, grasslands, and openings in pinyon–juniper and pine forests from 3,300 to 7,000 feet

SEASON OF BLOOM: Early summer

OUTSTANDING FEATURES: Drought-tolerant; attractive, soft, silver-gray leaves; pretty pink-purple pea flowers followed by interesting beaked seed pods; early bloom.

CULTURE

Soil: Well-drained

Exposure: Full sun to light shade

Water use: Very low to low

Propagation: Seed, division

Care and maintenance: Very low. Divide periodically.

LANDSCAPE USES: Dry garden, dry pine forest, rockery, silver foliage accent, border, butterfly garden

WILDLIFE ATTRACTED: Butterflies

HISTORICAL AND MODERN USES: Traditional uses include use in ceremonies and as an emetic. Pods used in dried arrangements or on wreaths. The entire genus *Astragalus* is known to be toxic to livestock if eaten.

The purple-pink flowers of this locoweed emit a heavy, sweet odor. Woolly locoweed is similar in color, size, and flower color to Lambert's locoweed (*Oxytropis lambertii*), and the two make excellent garden companions. Plant them with purple three-awn (*Aristida purpurea* var. *purpurea*) for a striking combination of color and texture.

Astragalus mollissimus

Athyrium filix-femina

Athyrium filix-femina subsp. *cyclosporum*

LADY FERN, SUBARCTIC LADY FERN
WOOD FERN FAMILY (*DRYOPTERIDACEAE*)
DECIDUOUS RHIZOMATOUS FERN
HEIGHT: 3 FEET
WIDTH: 3 FEET
ZONE 3

CHARACTERISTICS: Light green, pinnately cleft fronds form an upright, arching, vaselike tuft. Like all ferns, lady fern bears no flowers; plants reproduce by spores borne in dark brown, curved sori on the undersides of the fronds.

NATIVE RANGE: Worldwide in cooler climates, in shaded areas and rich soils

SEASON OF BLOOM: Spores in summer

OUTSTANDING FEATURES: A cold-hardy, rhizomatous native fern for shade gardens, with an elegant and imposing form. Lacy 3-foot fronds unfurl a pale green and turn darker as the season progresses.

CULTURE

Soil: Moist, enriched with organic matter

Exposure: Light sun to shade

Water use: Moderate to high

Propagation: Spores, division, rhizomes

Care and maintenance: Remove dead fronds; water regularly.

LANDSCAPE USES: Shade garden, fern garden, bower, canyon garden, northern slope or rockery, container or interior plant

Lady fern is a stately and beautiful plant for a shady border, natural garden, or woodland setting. It should be protected from strong winds and intense sun. The plant's arching form can be used to direct the eye upward, or to soften the edges of garden walls and hardscapes. In a woodland garden, lady fern can be combined with compatible perennial plants of similar form and stature such as pearlseed (*Macromeria viridiflora*), taperleaf (*Pericome caudata*), and American spikenard (*Aralia racemosa* subsp. *bicrenata*); it will grow well with New Mexican raspberry (*Rubus neomexicanus*) and native currants and gooseberries (*Ribes* spp.). When it is planted with agrimony (*Agrimonia striata*), snowberry (*Symphoricarpos* spp.), western Virginia creeper (*Parthenocissus inserta*), white virgin's bower (*Clematis ligusticifolia*), and creeping barberry (*Mahonia repens*), the result is a beautiful show of color in any woodland garden.

Berlandiera lyrata

Berlandiera lyrata

CHOCOLATE FLOWER, LYRE-LEAF GREENEYES
SUNFLOWER FAMILY (*ASTERACEAE*)
HERBACEOUS PERENNIAL
HEIGHT: 15 INCHES
WIDTH: 18 INCHES
ZONE 4

CHARACTERISTICS: Flat, spreading leaves with shallowly lobed edges mound below flowers on 2- to 3-foot stems. Inflorescence a light yellow daisy with green center and an outer ring of maroon; petals (ray flowers) have maroon markings on the undersides. Solitary flowers are fragrant and long blooming.

NATIVE RANGE: Western plains in the United States to northern Mexico, in dry rocky soils

SEASON OF BLOOM: Late summer

OUTSTANDING FEATURES: Drought tolerance, profuse bloom throughout the season, delightful chocolate scent, and edible, bright green, lyre-shaped leaves.

CULTURE

Soil: Well-drained; tolerates most soils

Exposure: Full sun

Water use: Very low

Propagation: Seed (direct-sow outdoors for best germination)

Care and maintenance: Very low. Let seed drop to ground to naturalize.

LANDSCAPE USES: Dry garden, rock garden, fragrance garden, butterflies, slope, small-area ground cover, dry meadow

WILDLIFE ATTRACTED: Butterflies. Reported to be deer resistant.

HISTORICAL AND MODERN USES: Edible leaves

As its common name implies, the fragrant flowers of this plant give off a hint of chocolate. Beautiful with other low-growing plants from the western plains including prairie grasses. A partial list of compatible species includes blue grama (*Bouteloua gracilis*), side-oats grama (*B. curtipendula*), little bluestem (*Schizachyrium scoparium*), galleta grass (*Pleuraphis jamesii*), buffalograss (*Buchloe dactyloides*), locoweeds (*Astragalus mollissimus* and *Oxytropis lambertii*), prairie clover (*Dalea purpurea*), wine cups (*Callirhoe involucrata*), cowboy's delight (*Sphaeralcea coccinea*), evening primrose (*Oenothera pallida* subsp. *pallida* and *O. pallida.* subsp. *runcinata*), old man's whiskers (*Geum triflorum*), and purplemat (*Nama hispidum*). Chocolate flowers are not only very tolerant of but downright welcoming to wind, heat, and harsh reflected sunlight. In cooler areas, a rock mulch or surface layer of cinder or crushed granite will help give them the warmth they need to thrive.

Blepharoneuron tricholepis

Blepharoneuron tricholepis

PINE DROPSEED, HAIRY DROPSEED
GRASS FAMILY (*POACEAE*)
PERENNIAL BUNCHGRASS
HEIGHT: 2 ¹/₂ FEET
WIDTH: 2 ¹/₂ FEET
ZONE 3

CHARACTERISTICS: Upright, arching, circular bunchgrass of medium texture. Florets borne in slender, loosely flowered panicles, green aging to straw as the rounded seeds ripen. Dried inflorescences remain on the plant throughout the fall and into winter.

NATIVE RANGE: Southwestern United States and Mexico, in dry or moist open woods from 2,500 to 10,000 feet

SEASON OF BLOOM: July through October

OUTSTANDING FEATURES: Warm-season bunchgrass; florets in slender panicles remain on the plants for fall interest and provide food and cover for birds, butterflies, and small mammals.

CULTURE

Soil: Any

Exposure: Sun to light shade

Water use: Low to moderate

Propagation: Seed, division

Care and maintenance: Very low. Where high level of maintenance is appropriate, gently pull off dried blades in spring.

LANDSCAPE USES: Accent plant, dry garden, wildflower meadow, naturalizing, butterfly and wildlife plant, ground cover (low traffic), native pasture (eaten green, not dry)

WILDLIFE ATTRACTED: Wind-pollinated, but seeds are an excellent fall bird and wildlife food source, and plant provides shelter for many vertebrate and invertebrate species including butterflies.

HISTORICAL AND MODERN USES: Edible seed parched and made into mush or bread; native pasture

Pine dropseed is a warm-season bunchgrass native to clearings and open pine forests. Like other bunchgrasses, it makes an excellent filler in gardens and provides a sense of motion as wind rustles the leaves and flowers. It tolerates some shade; try planting it with Arizona fescue (*Festuca arizonica*), muttongrass (*Poa fendleriana*), puccoon (*Lithospermum multiflorum*), and mountain parsley (*Pseudocymopterus montanus*). In open meadows and clearings, it adds textural richness and provides wildlife habitat.

Bouteloua gracilis

Bouteloua gracilis

BLUE GRAMA
GRASS FAMILY (*POACEAE*)
SOD-FORMING GRASS
HEIGHT: 6–12 INCHES
WIDTH: SPREADING
ZONE 3

CHARACTERISTICS: Low-growing circular mat, green in summer and fall, drying to straw or silvery in winter. Blue grama is sometimes referred to as "eyelash grass" because of the way its fringed, one-sided inflorescence sits on the top of its stalk, resembling an eyelash and curling when mature to look like a monocle.

NATIVE RANGE: Western and central North America, plains and forest openings, at elevations between 1,000 and 8,000 feet

SEASON OF BLOOM: Late summer

OUTSTANDING FEATURES: Characteristic "monocles" remain on plant throughout winter, providing winter and spring interest. Can be used successfully as a native turf that tolerates regular traffic and some shade; can be interplanted with native wildflowers and grasses to create a low-maintenance, informal meadow.

CULTURE

Soil: Will tolerate sandy or clay soils

Exposure: Sun to light shade

Water use: Low to moderate

Propagation: Seed, division

Care and maintenance: Very low; can be mowed periodically to remove seed heads, but mowing is not necessary.

LANDSCAPE USES: Low-water, low-maintenance turf; interplant with early-blooming bulbs and wildflowers, naturalizing, informal woodland garden, native pasture

WILDLIFE ATTRACTED: Wind-pollinated; butterfly habitat, provides shelter and forage for insects, birds, and mammals

HISTORICAL AND MODERN USES: Native American medicinal uses; an excellent range plant providing winter as well as summer forage.

A component of the shortgrass prairie, blue grama is one of the best native ground covers and takes moderately heavy traffic. Its tolerance of shade is unusual in a turfgrass, and though it will not be as dense as in sun, blue grama can be used as a turfgrass in light shade. The curled seed heads remain on the plant throughout the season for spring and winter interest. Often interplanted with buffalograss in a dry turfgrass blend, particularly in New Mexico, blue grama seeds readily and is more tolerant of colder zones (zones 3, 4, and 5) than buffalograss. To establish turf, a seeding rate of 3 to 4 pounds of blue grama per 1,000 square feet is recommended. It can also be established quickly from plugs planted 4 inches apart. It can be mowed or allowed to grow upright. To interplant blue grama with low-growing native wildflowers, seed the wildflowers in openings in the blue grama at the start of summer monsoons or in fall for growth in the next spring season. All the species listed as compatible with chocolate flower (see *Berlandiera lyrata*) will do well interplanted with blue grama; additional choices include prairie zinnia (*Zinnia grandiflora*) and Fendler's sundrops (*Calylophus hartwegii* subsp. *fendleri*). Blue grama is also an excellent companion to winter-hardy native cacti such as scarlet hedgehog (*Echinocereus coccineus* var. *coccineus*), claret cup (*Echinocereus triglochidiatus*), and pincushions (*Corphyantha* spp.). A related grass, side-oats grama (*Bouteloua curtipendula*), is an upright, 2-foot-tall, warm-season bunchgrass that is easily established on rocky slopes and hot, dry sites; in late summer, it bears seeds in two parallel rows on only one side of the flowering stalk. Black grama (*B. eriopoda*), another relative, is a rhizomatous grass native to desert grasslands.

Callirhoe involucrata

Callirhoe involucrata

WINE CUPS, PURPLE POPPY MALLOW
MALLOW FAMILY (*MALVACEAE*)
HERBACEOUS PERENNIAL
HEIGHT: 4 INCHES
WIDTH: 3 FEET
ZONE 4

CHARACTERISTICS: Medium-textured, sprawling, low-growing perennial ground cover with large, five-petaled, magenta-and-white cup-shaped flowers on upright stems above dark green, palmately lobed leathery leaves.

NATIVE RANGE: Rocky Mountain states and Great Plains (also, rarely, in Illinois and British Columbia)

SEASON OF BLOOM: All summer

OUTSTANDING FEATURES: Nonstop bloom all summer; flowers attractive to butterflies and bees; needs little, if any, supplemental water to thrive; best choice for hot, dry south-

or west-facing beds and in areas with reflected heat and sun.

CULTURE

Soil: Good drainage; thrives in excessively drained, coarse or cindery soils

Exposure: Full, hot sun

Water use: Low

Propagation: Seed; germinates best when sown or allowed to drop outdoors

Care and maintenance: Low. Allow seed to fall to naturalize.

LANDSCAPE USES: Ground cover, dry garden, butterfly garden, filler around taller plants, rock garden, hanging basket, borders

WILDLIFE ATTRACTED: Butterflies, bees

Because of its easy culture and its constant supply of large, beautiful flowers, wine cups is a favorite native plant of many gardeners. To attain best performance, be sure to provide adequate warmth, sun, and drainage. If soils are heavy, it will do best planted on a slope. As a ground cover, wine cups grows slowly, but will spread to form a dense, dark green cover. It also does well when planted at the top of retaining walls, where it will cascade downward to soften their edges. Wine cups combines well with other plants that thrive in the same conditions. Recommended companion plants include

Callirhoe involucrata

Maximilian's sunflower (*Helianthus maximilianii*), sundrops (*Calylophus* spp.), and many evening primrose species (*Oenothera pallida* subsp. *pallida, O. pallida* subsp. *runcinata, and O. caespitosa*), blue grama and side-oats grama (*Bouteloua gracilis* and *B. curtipendula*), and many sun-loving beardtongues such as Rocky Mountain penstemon (*Penstemon strictus*), Sunset Crater penstemon (*P. clutei*), phlox penstemon (*P. ambiguus*), scented penstemon (*P. palmeri*), and Eaton's firecracker (*P. eatonii*). It is also a delightful foreground companion to old-fashioned hollyhocks, butterfly bush (*Buddleia* spp.), and climbing roses.

Calylophus hartwegii

Calylophus hartwegii subsp. *fendleri*
(*Oenothera fendleri, O. hartwegii* subsp. *fendleri*)

FENDLER'S SUNDROPS
EVENING PRIMROSE FAMILY (*ONAGRACEAE*)
WOODY PERENNIAL
HEIGHT: 1 FOOT
WIDTH: 3 FEET
ZONE 4

CHARACTERISTICS: Upright, coarse-textured perennial with green leaves and pale stems; large yellow flowers, borne on the ends of upright narrow stems with neat green scalloped-edged leaves, have four square petals, which fade to orange or reddish pink and remain on the plant for a beautiful color contrast.

NATIVE RANGE: Southern Great Plains south to Texas and west to Arizona; on the Colorado Plateau, on dry mesas and limestone outcrops at elevations of 4,000 to 7,000 feet

SEASON OF BLOOM: All summer

OUTSTANDING FEATURES: This grasshopper-resistant, showy native perennial with 4-inch yellow flowers was the star performer and all-out winner in The Arboretum at Flagstaff's 1992 horticultural trial of evening primroses. Along with its beauty, it is extremely drought-tolerant and easy to grow. One by one, the constant supply of many flowers turn burnt orange to deep pink as they fade.

CULTURE

> *Soil:* Lean, well-drained
> *Exposure:* Full sun
> *Water use:* Low
> *Propagation:* Seed, cuttings
> *Care and maintenance:* Very low

LANDSCAPE USES: Rockery, dry garden, dry slopes, rock outcrops, small-area ground cover

WILDLIFE ATTRACTED: Butterflies and moths

Fendler's sundrops performs well with little irrigation and blooms best with limited water. Like few other drought-adapted natives, it comes into bloom in June, well before the monsoons start. Unlike many other evening primroses, it is a day bloomer, with its sunny blossoms open during most of the day. Day-old blossoms fade to orange and are quite attractive in combination with the yellow blooms of the next day. The combination of its green leaves, bright yellow flowers, and orange spent blossoms with gray-flowering shrubs such as sagebrushes (*Artemisia* spp.) can't be beat. Fendler's sundrops has many lovely compatible garden companions, including native cacti, succulents, bunchgrasses, and penstemons, as well as non-native garden species including lavenders (*Lavandula* spp.), Russian sage (*Perovskia atriplicifolia*), catmints (*Nepeta* spp.), and buckwheats (*Eriogonum* spp.) Three noteworthy companion plants are wine cups (*Callirhoe involucrata*), chocolate flower (*Berlandiera lyrata*), and purple three-awn (*Aristida purpurea* var. *purpurea*). Related species include lavenderleaf sundrops (*Calylophus lavandulifolius*), a southwestern native wildflower with clear bright yellow flowers and narrow gray-green foliage with the lacy look of French lavender, and dwarf sundrops (*C. serrulatus*), a compact heavy bloomer that bears cheery sun-yellow, four-petaled flowers above bright green serrated leaves from late spring through summer.

Calylophus hartwegii

Campanula rotundifolia

Campanula rotundifolia

HAREBELL, BLUEBELLS OF SCOTLAND, BLUEBELL BELLFLOWER
HAREBELL FAMILY (*CAMPANULACEAE*)
HERBACEOUS PERENNIAL
HEIGHT: 12–20 INCHES
WIDTH: SPREADING
ZONE 2

CHARACTERISTICS: Fine-textured, ground-hugging mat of bright green leaves; basal leaves rounded, stem leaves more elongate and very narrow. Many nodding, blue to purple, five-lobed, bell-shaped flowers with 1- to 2-inch corollas, borne on slender upright stems late spring through summer.

NATIVE RANGE: Northern Hemisphere

SEASON OF BLOOM: Spring through summer

OUTSTANDING FEATURES: This freely blooming and long-blooming perennial bears many nodding, bell-shaped, blue to purple flowers on narrow stems above a fine-textured mat of bright green leaves. With origins in the northern boreal regions of the world, it is extremely tolerant of cold and is hardy to zone 2. It will bloom bountifully in both sun and shade.

CULTURE

Soil: Any. A cool soil is best in hot areas.

Exposure: Sun to shade

Water use: Low to moderate

Propagation: Seed, division

Care and maintenance: Very low

LANDSCAPE USES: Small-area ground cover, wildflower meadow, shade garden, hanging basket, rockery or edging, butterfly garden. Good for edging or at the front of perennial border.

WILDLIFE ATTRACTED: Butterflies and bees

A good performer in very cold areas and cold microclimates, this dainty, heavily blooming perennial comes from the high mountains but does well at lower elevations, where it may benefit from planting in partial shade. It makes a particularly delightful specimen for hanging baskets, and its ability to drape and spill down makes it a great choice to soften stone walls and masonry or fill spaces between flagstones and pavers. Harebell is also a component of native meadows, where it grows in combination with grasses, sedges, and other wildflowers. To create your own high-elevation meadow, plant it with alpine bluegrass (*Poa alpina*), muttongrass (*Poa fendleriana*), alpine timothy (*Phleum alpinum*), spike trisetum (*Trisetum spicatum*), tufted hairgrass (*Deschampsia caespitosa*), ticklegrass (*Agrostis scabra*), Parry's primrose (*Primula parryi*), viscid Jacob's ladder (*Polemonium viscosum*), ebony sedge (*Carex ebenea*), and Parry's bellflower (*Campanula parryi*). Parry's bellflower has broad and usually solitary purple flowers on upright stems above the lowest mat of tiny bright green leaves. It blooms later in the season than *C. rotundifolia*. Both bellflowers are breathtaking with quaking aspen (*Populus tremuloides*), Canada violet and western dog violet (*Viola canadensis* and *V. adunca*), golden columbine (*Aquilegia chrysantha*), woolly cinquefoil (*Potentilla hippiana*), and old man's whiskers (*Geum triflorum*). They can be planted in the foreground in front of pearlseed (*Macromeria viridiflora*) and taperleaf (*Pericome caudata*), or with yellow monkeyflower (*Mimulus guttatus*) for a beautiful color contrast between yellow and blue.

Castilleja integra

Castilleja integra

WHOLELEAF INDIAN PAINTBRUSH
FIGWORT FAMILY (*SCROPHULARIACEAE*)
PERENNIAL WITH A WOODY ROOT
HEIGHT: 1 ½ FEET
WIDTH: 1 FOOT
ZONE 3

CHARACTERISTICS: Upright habit, medium-textured foliage; small, green tubular flowers above showy red bracts are borne in conspicuous, upright terminal spikes.

NATIVE RANGE: Western North America at elevations between 3,000 and 8,500 feet

SEASON OF BLOOM: Spring through fall

OUTSTANDING FEATURES: Showy vermilion flowers bloom in dense 3- to 6-inch spikes from spring to fall and are attractive to hummingbirds and butterflies.

CULTURE

Soil: Any

Exposure: Sun to light shade

Water use: Low to moderate

Propagation: Seed with grasses. Sow in fall or stratify seed for 1 to 2 months before planting.

Care and maintenance: Very low

LANDSCAPE USES: Wildflower meadow or grassland, hummingbird garden, naturalizing, container planting with native grasses

WILDLIFE ATTRACTED: Hummingbirds, butterflies

HISTORICAL AND MODERN USES: Dye plant

Wholeleaf Indian paintbrush is one of the most loved and most often recognized western wildflowers. The red, showy portion is actually a set of bracts that surrounds inconspicuous green flowers. This plant enjoys a hemiparasitic relationship with a host plant, usually a native grass. For successful seeding, the seeds should be sown in fall near the base of an already established native grass such as blue grama (*Bouteloua gracilis*). It will take several years after germination for paintbrush to bloom. If you are lucky to have paintbrush on your land, enjoy it. If you are tempted to dig plants in the wild, be forewarned that they are unlikely to survive transplant. With just a little patience, you will be able to grow your own paintbrush from seed. There are many different species of paintbrush with flower colors ranging from red to yellow and pink. For best results, try to plant species native to your area. Longleaved paintbrush (*Castilleja linariifolia*) is a branched plant with scarlet flowers and is native from the pinyon–juniper to aspen and mixed-conifer zones. Plains paintbrush (*C. sessiliflora*) has rose-pink flowers and is native from Canada to New Mexico and Texas.

Castilleja integra

Ceanothus fendleri

Ceanothus fendleri

FENDLER'S BUCKBRUSH
BUCKTHORN FAMILY (*RHAMNACEAE*)
MULTISTEMMED SHRUB
HEIGHT: 1–3 FEET
WIDTH: 3 FEET
ZONE 2

CHARACTERISTICS: Upright, dense shrub with gray-green leaves and small spines. Clusters of many small, white, fragrant, five-petaled flowers; petals are alternate with five stamens. Shiny seed capsules red at maturity.

NATIVE RANGE: Colorado Plateau, southwestern United States and Mexico, in pinyon–juniper woodlands and pine forests at elevations of 5,000 to 10,000 feet

SEASON OF BLOOM: Early summer

OUTSTANDING FEATURES: Durable shrub with shiny green leaves; covered in a haze of fragrant white flowers in summer; shiny apple-red seed capsules in late summer. Excellent wildlife value!

CULTURE

Soil: Any

Exposure: Sun to shade

Water use: Very low to moderate

Propagation: Root divisions and rhizomes, seed

Care and maintenance: Very low. Plants can be cut back to the ground periodically to rejuvenate growth.

LANDSCAPE USES: Shrub, butterfly plant, dry garden under pines with Gambel oaks, foundation planting, informal (unsheared) low hedge or garden border, wildlife habitat; excellent cover plant and honey plant.

WILDLIFE ATTRACTED: Butterflies and bees drink nectar; browsed by deer, porcupines, and rabbits; birds and small mammals eat seed.

HISTORICAL AND MODERN USES: Soap or hair tonic from blossoms, leaves used for medicinal tea, roots used as a lymphatic cleanser and vasoconstrictor.

This low-growing shrub can brighten a dark space with a haze of fragrant white flowers in summer. Buckbrush can be planted singly or in a mass planting to form a thicket as a barrier, garden edging, or wildlife habitat. It requires no fuss to make a substantial contribution to the garden. Two other common species of ceanothus found on the Colorado Plateau are readily adaptable to landscape use. Desert ceanothus (*Ceanothus greggii*) is a fine-textured, gray-leaved shrub found in chaparral and in pinyon–juniper woodlands with native oaks and Arizona cypress (*Cupressus arizonica* subsp. *arizonica*). It is very drought-tolerant, will thrive in bright hot sun and excessively drained soils and slopes, and bears crowded clusters of white flowers. It can occupy the same niche in landscapes that is filled by non-native cotoneasters. Deerbrush or white lilac (*Ceanothus integerrimus*) is an upright, spreading shrub to 8 feet tall with large, bright green leaves and large, 6-inch spikelike clusters of fragrant white (occasionally pink or bluish) flowers. It is native to open woodland and chaparral, where it is an important food plant for deer and other wildlife species and a honey plant for bees. All the wild lilacs (*Ceanothus* spp.) have lush early bloom, are easy to grow, and deserve a much wider use in high-elevation landscapes than they have received to date.

Clematis ligusticifolia

Clematis ligusticifolia

WHITE VIRGIN'S BOWER,
WESTERN WHITE CLEMATIS
BUTTERCUP FAMILY (*RANUNCULACEAE*)
DECIDUOUS VINE
HEIGHT: TO 20 FEET
WIDTH: SPREADING
ZONE 3

CHARACTERISTICS: Clambering vine; needs support; moderately coarse texture. Fragrant clusters of flowers to 1 inch across; flowers lack petals but have four white petaloid sepals. Male and female flowers are on separate plants; female flowers develop many persistent, plumed seeds.

NATIVE RANGE: Western North America along streams and in other moist places

SEASON OF BLOOM: All summer

OUTSTANDING FEATURES: Vigorous, bright green, deciduous climbing vine with an exceptionally fast growth rate; large clusters of fragrant white flowers; female plants have showy plumed seeds.

CULTURE

Soil: Any. Like most clematis species, it does best with organic matter in soil.

Exposure: Sun to light shade

Water use: Low to moderate

Propagation: Seed, cuttings

Care and maintenance: Tie onto trellis for support. Cut back periodically to control size or renew growth.

LANDSCAPE USES: Trellis, rock garden, ground cover, fragrance garden, yellow fall color accent

WILDLIFE ATTRACTED: Pollinated by bees; habitat for birds

HISTORICAL AND MODERN USES: Although the peppery-tasting leaves and stems of this plant were chewed by Native Americans and pioneers as a sore throat treatment, all parts of this plant are said to be poisonous. Flowers were traditionally used to treat migraine headaches.

Clematis ligusticifolia

White virgin's bower is a fast-growing vine that can be trained to quickly cover a trellis or support. It is also useful as a fast-growing ground cover. In its natural habitat it festoons willows (*Salix* spp.), cottonwoods (*Populus fremontii*), and other trees and shrubs. Many small white flowers and feathery seed heads give this otherwise coarsely textured plant a delicate air. Unlike cultivated clematis vines, it is a vigorous and aggressive grower in our region.

Cleome serrulata

Cleome serrulata

ROCKY MOUNTAIN BEEPLANT
CAPER FAMILY (*CAPPARACEAE*)
HERBACEOUS ANNUAL
HEIGHT: 3–4 FEET
WIDTH: 4 FEET
ZONE 3

CHARACTERISTICS: Upright, coarse-textured annual wildflower with large, bluish green, palmately compound leaves; lavender-pink, four-petaled, half-inch-long flowers with long stamens tipped with green anthers, borne in dense racemes often 3 to 5 inches long and occasionally up to 10 inches; long, succulent green seed pods.

NATIVE RANGE: Throughout most of North America except for easternmost United States, Alaska, and northern Canada

SEASON OF BLOOM: Late summer

OUTSTANDING FEATURES: A fast-growing annual that will germinate readily from seed sown outdoors in fall and left to overwinter; fragrant lavender-pink flowers with showy long stamens attract hummingbirds and bees.

CULTURE

Soil: Prefers disturbed soils

Exposure: Full sun

Water use: Low to moderate

Propagation: Direct-seed outdoors in autumn

Care and maintenance: Let seed fall; plants grow best in disturbed soils

LANDSCAPE USES: Wildflower meadow, roadsides and disturbed areas, hummingbird plant, honey plant, edible garden

WILDLIFE ATTRACTED: Hummingbirds, bees; doves eat seeds

HISTORICAL AND MODERN USES: A relative of the culinary caper, beeplant was historically cultivated by Native American farmers; seeds were eaten; leaves boiled and eaten as a potherb are high in calcium and vitamin A. Other uses include ceremonial, medicine, and dye plant.

This 3- to 4-foot upright annual wildflower frequently appears on roadsides and in construction cuts. Rocky Mountain beeplant's striking pink-purple flowers are attractive to hummingbirds and bees. Because it is an early colonizing species, it is an excellent choice for direct seeding in disturbed areas and waste places; as the landscape matures, beeplant will die out unless natural soil disturbances are present or created.

Cleome serrulata

Commelina dianthifolia

Commelina dianthifolia

DAYFLOWER
SPIDERWORT FAMILY (*COMMELINACEAE*)
HERBACEOUS PERENNIAL
HEIGHT: 1 FOOT
WIDTH: 1 FOOT
ZONE 2

CHARACTERISTICS: Fine- to medium-textured perennial with thickened, tuberous roots; green linear-lanceolate, somewhat succulent, alternate, grasslike, bright green leaves, with basal sheathing on upright to decumbent stems. Three-petaled, sky-blue flowers with six yellow stamens (three small sterile and three large fertile) above a boat-shaped spathe. Flower opens early in the morning and lasts most of the day.

NATIVE RANGE: Colorado, Arizona, New Mexico, and Mexico, in pine woods and mixed conifer forests at elevations between 3,500 and 9,500 feet

SEASON OF BLOOM: Mid- to late summer

OUTSTANDING FEATURES: The intense sky-blue flowers of this foot-tall native perennial wildflower emerge from a unique boatlike spathe every morning and last for a day.

CULTURE

Soil: Well-drained

Exposure: Shade to sun

Water use: Low to moderate

Propagation: Seed, cuttings

Care and maintenance: Very low. Avoid overwatering in fall when plant is dormant.

LANDSCAPE USES: Shade garden, naturalizing in pine-fescue woodland, container plant

WILDLIFE ATTRACTED: Pollinated by bees and other insects. (Because the flowers lack nectaries, pollinators gather only pollen.)

Like all members of the spiderwort family, dayflower is a monocot, with flower parts in threes and parallel leaf venation; its fruit is a three-sided capsule. The flowers are a delight to see in a woodland garden with other perennial wildflowers including fleabane (*Erigeron* spp.), pearlseed (*Macromeria viridiflora*), geranium-leaf and tall mountain larkspur (*Delphinium geraniifolium* and *D. scaposum*), purple geranium (*Geranium caespitosum*), creeping barberry (*Mahonia repens*), brickellbushes (*Brickellia* spp.), littleleaf alum root (*Heuchera parvifolia*), coral bells (*Heuchera sanguinea*), western spiderwort (*Tradescantia occidentalis*), bee balm (*Monarda fistulosa* var. *menthaefolia*), mountain phlox (*Linanthus nuttallii*), purple and Canada violets (*Viola adunca* and *V. canadensis*), and golden columbine (*Aquilegia chrysantha*). Compatible shrubs include wild currants and gooseberries (*Ribes* spp.), New Mexican raspberry (*Rubus neomexicanus*), New Mexican locust (*Robinia neomexicana*), mountain lover (*Paxistima myrsinites*), and coffeeberry (*Rhamnus californica*).

Commelina dianthifolia with *cleome serrulata* in background

Dalea purpurea

Dalea purpurea
(Petalostemon purpureum)

PURPLE PRAIRIE CLOVER, VIOLET PRAIRIE CLOVER
PEA FAMILY (*FABACEAE*)
HERBACEOUS PERENNIAL
HEIGHT: 2–3 FEET
WIDTH: 2–3 FEET
ZONE 3

CHARACTERISTICS: Medium-textured, upright perennial with stiff stems and an open growth habit; bright green, pinnately compound leaves are crowded along the stems almost to the inflorescence. Many violet-purple pea flowers, with five conspicuous yellow stamens, in dense spikes, followed by small pealike pods that contain one or two seeds.

NATIVE RANGE: Central North America, in dry open grasslands and plains

SEASON OF BLOOM: Summer

OUTSTANDING FEATURES: Dense spikes of sweet-scented, bright red-violet pea flowers at the ends of slender stems in summer. Very drought-tolerant and wind tolerant; deer resistant.

CULTURE

Soil: Any; will grow in poor, heavy soils and sterile soils

Exposure: Full sun

Water use: Low

Propagation: Seed

Care and maintenance: Very low

LANDSCAPE USES: Wildflower meadow, perennial garden, butterfly garden, flowers for cutting and drying

WILDLIFE ATTRACTED: Butterflies

HISTORICAL AND MODERN USES: Native American use as a poultice, a pulmonary aid, and as a beverage

Purple prairie clover will thrive in poor soils; a deep taproot allows it to tolerate a great deal of wind, sun, and drought, making it an ideal planting choice for barren, depleted soils and windswept gardens. Like many other legumes (members of the pea family), purple prairie clover fixes nitrogen from the air into the soil; it can actually provide nitrogen to improve soil fertility and help other plants grow. For a dense show of butterfly-attracting bloom from late spring into autumn, plant it with spotted gayfeather (*Liatris punctata*), a member of the

Dalea purpurea

aster family with similar growth form, flower color, and cultural needs; and blue flax (*Linum lewisii* var. *lewisii*), an early-blooming wildflower of similar form with sky-blue flowers. It is also a beautiful companion to Rocky Mountain penstemon (*Penstemon strictus*), butterfly milkweed (*Asclepias tuberosa*), yellow and red coneflowers (*Ratibida columnifera* and *R. columnifera* 'Mexican Hat'), and native groundsels (*Senecio* spp.). Mix purple prairie clover with other species from plains and open grasslands for a beautiful meadow that will provide habitat for butterflies, insects, and small mammals. White prairie clover (*Dalea candida*) is a white-flowering relative also attractive to butterflies and bees.

Datura wrightii

Datura wrightii
(Datura meteloides,
D. inoxia var. quinquecuspida)

SACRED DATURA
NIGHTSHADE FAMILY (*SOLANACEAE*)
ANNUAL OR HALF-HARDY PERENNIAL
HEIGHT: 3–4 FEET
WIDTH: 3–4 FEET
ZONE 5

CHARACTERISTICS: Coarse-textured, sprawling mound with large, hairy, ovate gray-green leaves. Fragrant, 8-inch, white-to-pale-lavender, trumpet-shaped blooms open in the evening. Seed pods, sometimes referred to as "Indian-apples," are round and spiny, contain many dark seeds.

NATIVE RANGE: Widely distributed in North America

SEASON OF BLOOM: Summer

OUTSTANDING FEATURES: Enormous, fragrant, white-to-pale-lavender trumpet flowers that open in the evening; thrives in hot, dry gardens.

CULTURE

Soil: Well-drained

Exposure: Full sun

Water use: Very low to low

Propagation: Seed

Care and maintenance: Very low

LANDSCAPE USES: Night garden, dry garden, naturalizing in sunny dry areas

WILDLIFE ATTRACTED: Hawk moths, which become intoxicated from the plant's nectar

HISTORICAL AND MODERN USES: Traditional use as "vision" plant, narcotic, and medicine. All parts of plant are poisonous if taken internally. Seed capsules were used as a food, probably after they were treated to dissipate the alkaloids.

Sacred datura is a plant to respect and admire. While it's not for every garden, few plants in the Temperate Zone produce flowers as large and seductive as its many white blossoms, and their hauntingly sweet fragrance is not toxic to enjoy. But because all parts of the plant are toxic if swallowed, sacred datura may require protection in the garden, especially if the garden is frequented by unattended children. Sacred datura is a plant of warm, sun-baked sites; in zones 4 and 5 it should be well protected in an enclosed courtyard or nestled against a wall or rocks that will radiate heat and protect it from low nighttime temperatures. In colder zones, or in gardens with poor drainage, treat it as an annual.

Delphinium geraniifolium

Delphinium geraniifolium

GERANIUM-LEAF LARKSPUR,
CLARK VALLEY LARKSPUR
BUTTERCUP FAMILY (*RANUNCULACEAE*)
HERBACEOUS PERENNIAL
HEIGHT: 2–3 FEET
WIDTH: 2 FEET
ZONE 2

CHARACTERISTICS: Coarse-textured, palmately lobed green leaves that look like geranium leaves form a neatly rounded mound; flowers densely crowded in upright, showy racemes to 3 feet tall; individual flowers consist of five petaloid sepals, the upper one prolonged into a spur.

NATIVE RANGE: Native only in northern Arizona, in canyons and forest edges and openings, at elevations of 7,000 to 9,500 feet

SEASON OF BLOOM: Early summer

OUTSTANDING FEATURES: Long-blooming perennial with tall spires of large, closely crowded purple flowers in summer and a rounded mound of green foliage from spring through autumn.

CULTURE:

Soil: Any; add organic matter to excessively drained and coarse soils.

Exposure: Sun to shade

Water use: Low to moderate

Propagation: Seed; will naturalize

Care and maintenance: Remove spent flower spikes to encourage repeat bloom.

LANDSCAPE USES: Back of border, wildflower meadow, hummingbird garden, butterfly garden, cutting garden

WILDLIFE ATTRACTED: Hummingbirds, butterflies

HISTORICAL AND MODERN USES: Dye plant. All parts are poisonous.

Geranium-leaf larkspur is one of the most spectacular drought-tolerant native perennials, drawing the eye across the landscape and luring both hummingbirds and butterflies with its graceful, upright flower spikes. Its palmately lobed leaves recall those of geranium or peony in their distinctive contour and lobing. It is remarkably easy to grow, accepting either full sun or light shade with equanimity. A prolific seeder, it will naturalize, germinating in spring if seed is allowed to fall to the ground. In the native garden, it combines equally well with plants from canyons, high meadows, and open forests.

Delphinium geraniifolium

Epilobium canum

Epilobium canum subsp. *latifolium*
(*Zauschneria californica* var. *latifolia; Z. latifolia, Z. arizonica*)

HARDY HUMMINGBIRD TRUMPET
EVENING PRIMROSE FAMILY (*ONAGRACEAE*)
WOODY PERENNIAL
HEIGHT: 2 FEET
WIDTH: 2 FEET
ZONE 5

CHARACTERISTICS: Medium-textured, clumping, upright perennial with oval bright green leaves that emerge from a woody caudex in spring. Multitudes of scarlet trumpet-shaped flowers to 3 inches long with four scarlet sepals, four apically notched scarlet petals, eight stamens, and a long style with a four-lobed stigma, in clusters at the ends of upright stems.

NATIVE RANGE: Southwestern United States, on rock outcrops and rocky slopes, in canyons, and along washes from 2,500 to 9,000 feet

SEASON OF BLOOM: Late summer and fall until killing frost

OUTSTANDING FEATURES: Late bloomer; fast-growing; large, brilliant, scarlet-red, trumpet-shaped flowers last until the first frost, attract hummingbirds

CULTURE

Soil: Well drained

Exposure: Full sun

Water use: Low

Propagation: Cuttings, seed

Care and maintenance: Very low; cut back tips early in season to encourage fullness and heavy bloom.

LANDSCAPE USES: Informal border, hummingbird garden, container plant, red color accent, late bloom, slope planting, rockery, mass planting

WILDLIFE ATTRACTED: Hummingbirds

Hardy hummingbird trumpet is a late bloomer; in cold zones, give it a southern or western exposure and a warm protected location to ensure plenty of time before the first frost to enjoy its large red flowers. It does best planted on slopes and among rocks and will benefit from a little extra late-summer water once the monsoons have ended. For a mass planting on a rocky slope, include with your choice of wild buckwheats—sulfur-flowered buckwheat (*Eriogonum umbellatum*), James's buckwheat (*E. jamesii*), Wright's buckwheat (*E. wrightii*), flat-topped buckwheat (*E. fasciculatum* var. *polifolium*), or any other wild buckwheat species local to your area. Hardy hummingbird trumpet is also attractive as a filler between shrubs; it is particularly beautiful alongside greenleaf manzanita (*Arctostaphylos patula*).

Epilobium canum

Ericameria nauseosa

Ericameria nauseosa
(Chrysothamnus nauseosus)

RUBBER RABBITBRUSH, CHAMISA
SUNFLOWER FAMILY (*ASTERACEAE*)
EVERGREEN SHRUB
SIZE: 5 FEET
HEIGHT: 5 FEET
ZONE 4

CHARACTERISTICS: Upright shrub with many slender, flexible branches; medium texture; narrowly linear leaves along felty stems; in late summer and autumn, covered entirely in cloudy clusters of yellow, rayless, quarter-inch-wide sunflowers.

NATIVE RANGE: Western North America, on dry slopes and mesas and in open grasslands and desert scrub

SEASON OF BLOOM: Late summer to autumn

OUTSTANDING FEATURES: This fast-growing, evergreen, drought-loving shrub has beautiful silver-blue foliage and late-season blooms of many rayless yellow sunflowers in large clusters.

CULTURE

Soil: Dry, well-drained

Exposure: Full sun

Water use: Very low to low

Propagation: Seed

Care and maintenance: Very low. Can be sheared to form a hedge or trained into various shapes.

LANDSCAPE USES: Dry garden, wildflower meadow, butterfly garden, accent plant, low-maintenance shrub, xeriscape, mass planting, screening, fast growth

WILDLIFE ATTRACTED: Butterflies and many other insect pollinators; eaten by rabbits and browsed by deer, elk, and pronghorn; provides shelter for birds and small mammals.

HISTORICAL AND MODERN USES: Navajo dye plant (flowers provide yellow dye, inner bark is a source of green dye). Used by Hopi for windbreaks and in arrows and wickerwork.

Known as chamisa in New Mexico, rubber rabbitbrush is widely planted in dry landscapes and is one of the most drought-tolerant shrubs for ornamental plantings. The silver-blue foliage contrasts beautifully with red soils or red-tinged masonry; it is equally striking when planted next to plants with yellow or red fall color. A related species, green rabbitbrush (*Chrysothamnus viscidiflorus*), has light green foliage and a more compact growth habit, 2 to 3 feet tall.

Erigeron compositus

Erigeron compositus
(Erigeron compositus var. discoideus)

DWARF MOUNTAIN FLEABANE, MAT DAISY
SUNFLOWER FAMILY (*ASTERACEAE*)
HERBACEOUS PERENNIAL
HEIGHT: 3 INCHES
WIDTH: 6 INCHES
ZONE 2

CHARACTERISTICS: Blue-gray divided leaves from a branching woody caudex form a fine-textured, ground-hugging cushion or small mound; many solitary heads of lavender-blue to pink ray flowers surround yellow disk flowers on upright naked stems.

NATIVE RANGE: Western United States, western Canada, and Greenland; on the Colorado Plateau, in a variety of habitats from openings in the ponderosa pine forest to alpine tundra, at elevations of 4,000 to above 11,500 feet

SEASON OF BLOOM: Early blooming, throughout summer

OUTSTANDING FEATURES: Called the finest of all rock garden daisies, this charming, diminutive herbaceous perennial bears lavender-blue to pink flowers with many narrow petals and yellow disks atop woolly, lacy, blue-gray foliage. Very drought-tolerant and wind tolerant.

CULTURE

Soil: Well drained

Exposure: Full sun to light shade

Water use: Low to moderate

Propagation: Seed

Care and maintenance: Very low

LANDSCAPE USES: Rock garden, alpine garden, small-area ground cover, native wildflower meadow, low edging, butterfly plant, container plant

WILDLIFE ATTRACTED: Butterflies

HISTORICAL AND MODERN USES: Native Americans used as a dermatological aid; common range plant.

This small mounding plant makes an attractive edging along paths or interplanted with rocks, mat-forming perennials like pussytoes, and low-growing native grasses such as sheep fescue (*Festuca ovina*) and Idaho fescue (*F. idahoensis*). Try it in the foreground to provide structure to other native fleabanes (*Erigeron divergens, E. speciosus*). To attract butterflies, plant in full sun among rocks. One sure-fire combination is dwarf mountain fleabane with pygmy bluets (*Houstonia wrightii*), Easter daisy (*Townsendia eximia*), pineleaf penstemon (*Penstemon pinifolius*), Lambert's locoweed (*Oxytropis lambertii*), blue starflower (*Ipomopsis multiflora*), perky Sue (*Tetraneuris argentea*), alpine sunflower (*Tetraneuris grandiflora*), and a choice of hairy false goldenaster (*Heterotheca villosa*), false goldenaster (*H. villosa* var. *foliolosa*), or Jones' false goldenaster (*H. jonesii*). Be sure to provide a source of shallow water nearby to give butterflies a drink and enhance the habitat value of your garden.

Erigeron flagellaris

Erigeron flagellaris

WHIPLASH DAISY, TRAILING FLEABANE
SUNFLOWER FAMILY (*ASTERACEAE*)
HERBACEOUS PERENNIAL
HEIGHT: 2—4 INCHES
WIDTH: SPREADING
ZONE 3

CHARACTERISTICS: Fine-textured perennial forms a low gray mat with many solitary upright flower heads, and produces new plants from buds on prostrate ground-level runners. Many very narrow white ray flowers surround a golden disk; each flowering head is borne singly at the top of a thin upright stem.

NATIVE RANGE: Western North America

SEASON OF BLOOM: Late spring through autumn; will rebloom frequently throughout season

OUTSTANDING FEATURES: This very low-growing native daisy spreads by above-ground runners and underground stems to create an easy-care, beautiful ground cover that will tolerate light foot traffic. Covered nonstop during the growing season with many narrow-petaled, solitary, white flowers with yellow centers that sway charmingly in the wind. Easy to grow!

CULTURE

Soil: Tolerates a broad range of soils

Exposure: Full sun to shade

Water use: Low to moderate (more to encourage dense growth and quick spreading); water during low rainfall periods.

Propagation: Divisions, seed

Care and maintenance: Very low. You may mow off dried seed heads.

LANDSCAPE USES: Ground cover (will take light foot traffic), gray color accent, filler or mass planting, butterfly garden, container plant

WILDLIFE ATTRACTED: Butterflies

HISTORICAL AND MODERN USES: Traditional uses include snakebite remedy and veterinary aid.

Whiplash daisy can be found in a variety of habitats and is a versatile landscaping plant. One of the finest native ground covers, it spreads rapidly when given regular water. It bears aboveground runners and roots along the stems in the same manner as strawberry plants and zebra plants. In one year in a Flagstaff garden, one 4-inch plant spread to cover a 3-foot-by-2-foot area. To initialize a dense mass planting, healthy plants can be divided easily and plugged into the ground at 1-foot intervals throughout the area to be established. The key to enjoying a dense ground cover of whiplash daisy is to water regularly during dry spells in spring, summer, and fall; failing to do so may cause it to die out entirely.

Erigeron speciosus

Erigeron speciosus
(*Erigeron speciosus var. macranthus*)

ASPEN FLEABANE
SUNFLOWER FAMILY (ASTERACEAE)
HERBACEOUS PERENNIAL
HEIGHT: 1 FOOT
WIDTH: 2 FEET
ZONE 4

CHARACTERISTICS: Low-growing, medium-textured, rhizomatous spreading perennial; leaves are variable, from smooth and shiny to dull and hairy. Many very narrow lavender ray flowers around a clear yellow disk; many flower heads, borne in clusters at ends of shoots.

NATIVE RANGE: Western North America, in many habitats at elevations of 6,000 to nearly 11,000 feet

SEASON OF BLOOM: All summer

OUTSTANDING FEATURES: Spreading, easy-to-grow perennial; lavender daisy-type flowers with golden disks; shiny to hairy green leaves.

CULTURE

Soil: Any

Exposure: Sun to shade

Water use: Low to moderate

Propagation: Seed

Care and maintenance: Very low

LANDSCAPE USES: Perennial garden, wildflower garden, container plant, filler or mass planting, shade garden, butterfly garden, rockery

WILDLIFE ATTRACTED: Butterflies

HISTORICAL AND MODERN USES: Used as an analgesic.

Aspen fleabane is easy to grow and a great choice to brighten up a dark space in a shady garden. It creates a free-flowering understory when planted beneath quaking aspen (*Populus tremuloides*) with red-twig dogwood (*Cornus sericea*), nodding groundsel (*Senecio bigelovii*), and scarlet bugler (*Penstemon barbatus*). Likewise, it will grow well under ponderosa pines provided needles are periodically taken away. The *Erigeron speciosus* complex consists of variable and intergrading species that are sold under various names in the native plant trade. For best results, and to avoid the confusion in naming, choose plants grown from local genotypes naturally occurring in conditions comparable to your planned garden use. By planting several species of native fleabanes, you can provide a variety of white, pink, and lavender narrow-petaled flowers that continuously bloom throughout the season. Two compatible species are three-nerve fleabane (*Erigeron subtrinervis*) and splendid daisy (*E. superbus*).

Erigeron speciosus

Eriogonum caespitosum

Eriogonum caespitosum

MATTED BUCKWHEAT
KNOTWEED FAMILY (POLYGONACEAE)
WOODY SUBSHRUB
HEIGHT: 3 INCHES
WIDTH: SPREADING
ZONE 4

CHARACTERISTICS: Fine-textured, very compact mat from a woody crown; felty, medium-gray-green leaves; clear yellow flowers in small heads on short stems in summer, aging to golden brown and remaining on plant throughout autumn.

NATIVE RANGE: Western United States, on dry hillsides

SEASON OF BLOOM: Early summer

OUTSTANDING FEATURES: Dense, low mat of gray-green leaves is entirely covered by many compact heads of small yellow flowers during its peak bloom; drought-tolerant, low maintenance.

CULTURE:

Soil: Well-drained

Exposure: Full sun or morning sun

Water use: Low

Propagation: Seed, division

Care and maintenance: Very low

LANDSCAPE USES: Small-area ground cover, rock garden, slope planting, butterfly garden

WILDLIFE ATTRACTED: Butterflies, bees

HISTORICAL AND MODERN USES: Culinary, medicinal, and ceremonial uses are likely but are not well documented.

This slow-growing buckwheat has the finest texture and forms the lowest mat of the yellow-flowering buckwheats. It is virtually maintenance free and is a very tidy, durable plant, remaining beautiful through seasons of drought and neglect. It is a suitable companion for cacti and woody plants native to sagebrush, pinyon–juniper, and dry ponderosa pine habitats. The yellow flowers of matted buckwheat contrast strikingly with blue to purple flowers of purple sage (*Salvia dorrii* var. *dorrii*), Salvia 'May Night', and coyote mint (*Monardella odoratissima*), and with the leaves of purple three-awn (*Aristida purpurea* var. *purpurea*).

Eriogonum caespitosum

Eriogonum jamesii var. *jamesii*

Eriogonum jamesii var. *jamesii*

JAMES'S BUCKWHEAT
KNOTWEED FAMILY (*POLYGONACEAE*)
WOODY PERENNIAL OR SUBSHRUB
HEIGHT: 18 INCHES
WIDTH: 2 FEET
ZONE 4

CHARACTERISTICS: Medium-textured subshrub bears an upright, open inflorescence atop low-growing basal leaves from a woody crown; leaves are gray-green above and felty white below. Many small, cream-colored flowers, on 18-inch stalks, in an open umbellate cyme, the inflorescences with 2- to 3-times-branched stalks, each branch subtended by conspicuous leaflike bracts. Dry flowers persist on plant.

NATIVE RANGE: Western plains, among rocks in pine and oak woodlands

SEASON OF BLOOM: Summer

OUTSTANDING FEATURES: Delicate cream-colored flowers, spreading and open atop a durable, dry-loving perennial with felty silver-green leaves. Cut flowers can be used in fresh or dried arrangements as a native "baby's breath."

CULTURE

Soil: Well-drained

Exposure: Sun to light shade

Water use: Low

Propagation: Seed

Care and maintenance: Very low

LANDSCAPE USES: Rock garden, butterfly garden, dry garden, dry border, cutting garden

WILDLIFE ATTRACTED: Butterflies and bees. Herbage provides browse for pronghorn.

HISTORICAL AND MODERN USES: Used by Native Americans as a heart medicine and an analgesic.

A tough plant! Beautiful and durable when planted in windswept, sunny areas in openings among Gambel, Arizona, or scrub oaks, ponderosa pines, pinyon pines, junipers, beargrass (*Nolina microcarpa*), and dry grasses. Plant with upright perennials including blue flax (*Linum lewisii* var. *lewisii*), scarlet gilia (*Ipomopsis aggregata*), and beardtongues. A good complement to early-blooming yellow-flowering plants and to other buckwheats.

Eriogonum jamesii var. flavescens

Eriogonum jamesii var. flavescens
(Eriogonum bakeri)

JAMES' GOLDEN BUCKWHEAT
KNOTWEED FAMILY (*POLYGONACEAE*)
WOODY SUBSHRUB
HEIGHT: 6 INCHES
WIDTH: 2 FEET
ZONE 3

CHARACTERISTICS: Leaves form a medium-textured, dense, upright mat above a branching woody caudex. Clear yellow flowers in dense clusters at the tips of naked stems borne 6 inches above the gray-green basal leaves.

NATIVE RANGE: Colorado Plateau states and Wyoming, in dry ponderosa and pinyon pine forests and open grasslands at elevations from 5,000 to 8,000 feet

SEASON OF BLOOM: Summer, persistent throughout autumn

OUTSTANDING FEATURES: Large, compact golden flower clusters top a low mound of gray-green leaves; flowers dry to a gold ochre and remain on plant until winter snows. Good for cutting or for dried arrangements.

CULTURE

Soil: Well-drained

Exposure: Full sun or morning sun

Water use: Very low to low

Propagation: Seed, division

Care and maintenance: Very low

LANDSCAPE USES: Small-area ground cover, dry garden, rockery, erosion control on slopes, butterfly plant, dry meadows

WILDLIFE ATTRACTED: Butterflies, bees, birds

HISTORICAL AND MODERN USES: Seeds edible

Forming a neat green mat, James' golden buckwheat is coarser in texture than matted buckwheat (*Eriogonum caespitosum*) and about twice its height. Plant with wildcandytuft (*Thlaspi montanum* var. *fendleri*), native grasses such as side-oats and blue grama (*Bouteloua curtipendula* and *B. gracilis*) and galleta grass (*Pleuraphis jamesii*), ponderosa pine (*Pinus ponderosa*), pinyon pine (*Pinus edulis*), three-leaf sumac (*Rhus trilobata*), mountain mahoganies (*Cercocarpus* spp.), junipers (*Juniperus deppeana, J. utahensis, J. monosperma,* and *J. scopulorum*), showy four-o'clock (*Mirabilis multiflora*), wax currant (*Ribes cereum*), native cacti, banana yucca (*Yucca baccata*), and other dry-loving natives. A very tough, resilient plant that contributes to garden and wildlife all year long.

Eriogonum racemosum

Eriogonum racemosum

REDROOT BUCKWHEAT
KNOTWEED FAMILY (*POLYGONACEAE*)
HERBACEOUS PERENNIAL
HEIGHT: 18 INCHES
WIDTH: 1 FOOT
ALL ZONES

CHARACTERISTICS: A medium-textured nearly flat basal clump of felty gray leaves forms early-season growth; this is augmented by an upright flower stalk in late summer. Fairy wands of small white to pink flowers with dark pink ribs on the back of petals, in dense racemes atop leafless, felty gray flowering stems; flowers dry until papery and remain on plant until heavy snows fall.

NATIVE RANGE: Texas to Colorado and California, in many habitats

SEASON OF BLOOM: Late summer

OUTSTANDING FEATURES: Large, velvety, pale-gray leaves form a neat basal rosette until summer, when dense, showy, pale pink blooms top this charming ground cover. Flowers age from creamy-pink to pink to russet and remain on the plant through autumn.

CULTURE

Soil: Any

Exposure: Sun to partial shade

Water use: Low to moderate

Propagation: Seed

Care and maintenance: Very low. Remove old flower stalks in fall or spring.

LANDSCAPE USES: Native garden, butterfly garden, small-area ground cover, silver foliage, edging plant, wild garden, woodland garden, dry or moist wildflower meadow

WILDLIFE ATTRACTED: Butterflies, bees

HISTORICAL AND MODERN USES: Edible seeds, medicinal uses of root

Plant redroot buckwheat in masses to create a drought-tolerant ground cover or low border. It can be planted in every zone on the Colorado Plateau and combines well with most low-growing, dry-loving plants. For best results, select plants of local sources and ecotypes. Some have nearly pink flowers, others creamy white, so buy plants in bloom to select for color.

Eriogonum racemosum

Eriogonum umbellatum

Eriogonum umbellatum

SULFUR-FLOWERED BUCKWHEAT
KNOTWEED FAMILY (POLYGONACEAE)
WOODY SUBSHRUB
HEIGHT: 4–12 INCHES
WIDTH: 2 FEET
ZONE 3

CHARACTERISTICS: Medium-textured, deep-green mound with late-season sulfur-yellow flowers in a variety of inflorescence forms, from open umbels to capitate heads, at the tips of upright stems, all showy and aging to rusty red when dry.

NATIVE RANGE: Western United States, in a variety of habitats

SEASON OF BLOOM: Summer through autumn

OUTSTANDING FEATURES: Many sulfur-yellow flowers, often tinged with red or purple, attract butterflies; flowers age to rusty red as they form seed.

CULTURE

Soil: Well-drained

Exposure: Sun to light shade

Water use: Low

Propagation: Seed

Care and maintenance: Very low

LANDSCAPE USES: Small-area ground cover, rockery, butterfly garden, wildflower meadow, slopes, openings between pines and in open meadows

WILDLIFE ATTRACTED: Butterflies, bees

HISTORICAL AND MODERN USES: Contains high amounts of vitamin K; has traditional uses in the treatment of excessive menstruation and bleeding.

This is the yellow-flowering buckwheat to choose for the ponderosa pine or mixed conifer zone. It also grows well at lower elevations. (As with all plants from a wide geographic range and varied habitats, try to choose local varieties and ecotypes.) It is beautiful when combined with greenleaf, pointleaf, or Pringle's manzanita (*Arctostaphylos patula, A. pungens,* or *A. pringlei*), pink- and purple-flowering penstemons (*Penstemon palmeri, P. linarioides, P. pseudospectabilis*), oblong-leaf false pennyroyal (*Hedeoma oblongifolia*), sweet scent (*Hedeoma hyssopifolium*), mountain mahogany (*Cercocarpus montanus*), white fir (*Abies concolor*), ponderosa pine (*Pinus ponderosa*), and Douglas fir (*Pseudotsuga menziesii* var. *interior*). Another compatible buckwheat, harder to find in the nursery trade but worth the search, is silver plant (*Eriogonum ovalifolium* var. *depressum*), a low mat of pure silver-gray leaves with dense clusters of pink to white flowers.

Eriogonum umbellatum

Erysimum capitatum var. *capitatum*

Erysimum capitatum var. *capitatum* (*Erysimum asperum*)

WESTERN WALLFLOWER
MUSTARD FAMILY (*BRASSICACEAE*)
HERBACEOUS PERENNIAL
HEIGHT: 2 FEET
WIDTH: 2 FEET
ZONE 2

CHARACTERISTICS: Medium-textured upright perennial with a basal rosette of toothed, gray-green, lance-shaped leaves. Flower stalk is upright to 2 ½ feet tall and bears narrow stem leaves. Many clear yellow flowers in a dense cluster on a terminal raceme, each three-quarters of an inch wide, with four clawed petals. Flowers open from the bottom up, and are followed by slender, erect, four-sided, 4-inch-long siliques or seed pods.

NATIVE RANGE: Throughout North America except easternmost and northernmost parts. On the Colorado Plateau, found in many habitats at elevations from 3,200 to

11,400 feet; common on slopes among oaks and in the ponderosa pine forest and into the spruce-fir and alpine tundra communities.

SEASON OF BLOOM: Early summer; plants often sprout secondary bloom well into the season.

OUTSTANDING FEATURES: Large, cheery racemes of yellow flowers. Early bloomer, long blooming season. Very easy to grow, and very popular with butterflies!

CULTURE

Soil: Well-drained

Exposure: Sun to light shade

Water use: Moderate

Propagation: Seed; sow in fall or summer

Care and maintenance: Very low. Let self-sow to naturalize.

LANDSCAPE USES: Butterfly garden, perennial border, slope planting, wildflower meadow, naturalizing

WILDLIFE ATTRACTED: Butterflies

HISTORICAL AND MODERN USES: Used as a poultice, analgesic, and gastrointestinal aid.

Erysimum capitatum var. *capitatum*

Our native wallflowers are perennials or sometimes short-lived biennials, but they reseed readily and often bloom the first year from seed. Like most members of the mustard family, western wallflower is often covered with butterflies throughout its entire bloom period. Plant it with blue flax (*Linum lewisii* var. *lewisii*), Rocky Mountain penstemon (*Penstemon strictus*), and Wheeler's wallflower (*Erysimum wheeleri*) to enjoy the beautiful color contrast of blue, orange, and purple wildflowers with the bright yellow wallflowers.

Erysimum wheeleri

Erysimum wheeleri
(*Erysimum asperum* var. *wheeleri*, *E. capitatum* var. *capitatum*)

WHEELER'S WALLFLOWER, MOUNTAIN WALLFLOWER
MUSTARD FAMILY (*BRASSICACEAE*)
HERBACEOUS PERENNIAL
HEIGHT: 2 ½ FEET
WIDTH: 1 FOOT
ZONE 2

CHARACTERISTICS: Medium-textured, upright perennial with a basal rosette of toothed, gray-green, lance-shaped leaves; flower stalk is upright to 2 ½ feet tall and bears narrow stem leaves. Many burnt-orange to maroon flowers in a dense cluster on a terminal raceme, each three-quarters of an inch wide, with four clawed petals. Flowers open from the bottom up, followed by slender, erect, four-sided, 4-inch-long siliques or seed pods.

NATIVE RANGE: Colorado, New Mexico, and Arizona, in open woodlands, canyons, and forests at elevations of 5,400 to 10,000 feet

SEASON OF BLOOM: Summer; long-blooming, with continued eruptions of flowers throughout the season

OUTSTANDING FEATURES: A butterfly magnet, most often seen covered with painted ladies and blues! Bears large, dense racemes of incredible burnt-orange to maroon flowers for the entire first half of the summer and lighter blooming through end of summer.

CULTURE

Soil: Well-drained

Exposure: Sun to light shade

Water use: Moderate

Propagation: Easy from seed in summer or fall

Care and maintenance: Let seed fall to naturalize; remove spent flowers to encourage repeat bloom.

LANDSCAPE USES: Naturalizing, wildflower meadow, butterfly garden, color accent, prolonged bloom

WILDLIFE ATTRACTED: Butterflies

Erysimum wheeleri

Although Wheeler's wallflower is actually no more than a distinct color form of western wallflower (*Erysimum capitatum* var. *capitatum*), we maintain its horticultural distinction because of the incredible and distinct flower coloration of Colorado Plateau endemic populations. In the gardens of The Arboretum at Flagstaff, it blooms for several months nonstop and is constantly covered with painted ladies and little blue butterflies. Plant it (like western wallflower) with blue flax (*Linum lewisii* var. *lewisii*) for color accent, and with western sneezeweed (*Hymenoxys hoopesii*), Richardson's goldflower (*Hymenoxys richardsonii*), and Arizona rubberweed (*Hymenoxys subintegra*) for continued butterfly action.

Fallugia paradoxa

Fallugia paradoxa

APACHE PLUME, FEATHER ROSE
ROSE FAMILY (*ROSACEAE*)
DECIDUOUS SHRUB
HEIGHT: 3–6 FEET
WIDTH: SPREADING
ZONE 4

CHARACTERISTICS: Fine- to medium-textured shrub with slender, white-barked branches and an upright, open habit. Will often form patches, spreading horizontally by underground stems. Dainty leaves are alternate, dull green, and pinnately dissected. Fragrant white flowers with yellow centers, resembling little roses, followed by many seeds with pink, feathery, 2-inch-long tails, held in large clusters that remain on the plant throughout the summer.

NATIVE RANGE: Southwest United States and Mexico, in a variety of habitats from high desert to ponderosa pine forest

SEASON OF BLOOM: Summer, ever-blooming

OUTSTANDING FEATURES: A wonderful, dry-loving, woody shrub. First the entire plant is covered with fragrant, pure white flowers that resemble roses, and then the flowers produce pink-plumed showy seed heads in pompom clusters that glow in the sunlight throughout summer. Exceedingly drought-tolerant.

CULTURE

Soil: Well-drained

Exposure: Full sun

Water use: Very low to low

Propagation: Seed, offsets, cuttings

Care and maintenance: Very low

LANDSCAPE USES: Extensive root system will hold slopes and prevent erosion; attractive as single accent plant

WILDLIFE ATTRACTED: Browse for deer

HISTORICAL AND MODERN USES: Branches were used as arrow shafts and outdoor brooms, leaves steeped for a hair wash, petals used medicinally, and roots used for cord to tie fencing and make ramadas.

Apache plume is a moderately rapid grower and will establish quickly. Plant it with other dry-loving trees and shrubs including junipers (*Juniperus* spp.), Gambel oak (*Quercus gambelii*), pines (*Pinus ponderosa* and *P. edulis*), New Mexican olive (*Forestiera neomexicana*), mountain mahogany (*Cercocarpus montanus*), Fremont wolfberry (*Lycium fremontii*), Fendler's buckbrush and wild lilac (*Ceanothus fendleri* and *C. greggii*), rabbitbrush (*Chrysothamnus* spp.), Mormon tea (*Ephedra* spp.), and common cliffrose (*Purshia stansburiana*). Compatible perennials include prickly poppy (*Argemone* spp.), little bluestem (*Schizachyrium scoparium*), needle-and-thread grass (*Hesperostipa comata*), native cacti, Parry's agave (*Agave parryi*), and banana yucca (*Yucca baccata*). Like other plants with plumose seeds, Apache plume is beautiful when planted in a location that will be backlit with afternoon sun and is a delightful companion to other plants with this characteristic, such as common cliffrose (*Purshia stansburiana*), a large upright shrub to 8 feet tall with leaves, flowers, and seeds similar to those of Apache plume; mountain mahogany, another upright shrub with single silvery plumose seeds; and old man's whiskers (*Geum triflorum*), a low, bright-green ground cover with deep pink plumose seeds. Plant together with the setting sun to their west.

Festuca arizonica

Festuca arizonica

ARIZONA FESCUE
GRASS FAMILY (*POACEAE*)
PERENNIAL BUNCHGRASS
HEIGHT: 10 INCHES TO 2 FEET;
SEED STALKS TO 3 FEET
WIDTH: 2 FEET
ALL ZONES

CHARACTERISTICS: Clumping bunchgrass with large, upright, wiry seed stalks to 3 feet tall; leaves pointed, with inrolled edges; spreading panicle of pointed florets in May and June, drying and persisting on plant throughout summer.

NATIVE RANGE: Southwest United States, in grasslands and pine forests, to 10,000 feet

SEASON OF BLOOM: Late spring and early summer

OUTSTANDING FEATURES: A tall-flowering, graceful, early-blooming grass with fine tufts of needlelike gray-green to blue-green leaves. The dominant grass of the ponderosa pine forest, this easy-to-grow native bunchgrass will thrive in a number of garden situations.

CULTURE

Soil: Any

Exposure: Sun to shade

Water use: Low to moderate

Propagation: Seed, division

Care and maintenance: Very low

LANDSCAPE USES: Wildflower meadow, ground cover (moderate traffic), erosion control, ornamental grass, early bloom, wildlife, bird, butterfly, and arthropod habitat

WILDLIFE ATTRACTED: Wind-pollinated; forage for elk, deer, antelope, small mammals; habitat for butterflies and birds.

HISTORICAL AND MODERN USES: Forage for cows. Most fescues can cause miscarriage in horses.

Plant Arizona fescue with other grasses including pine dropseed (*Blepharoneuron tricholepis*), mountain muhly (*Muhlenbergia montana*), spike muhly (*M. wrightii*), deergrass (*M. rigens*), mat muhly (*M. richardsonis*), muttongrass (*Poa fendleriana*), tufted hairgrass (*Deschampsia caespitosa*), little bluestem (*Schizachyrium scoparium*), and blue grama (*Bouteloua gracilis*) to form a durable meadow or natural ground cover. Makes a great matrix for interplanting any number of compatible native species, including silvery lupine (*Lupinus argenteus*), blue flax (*Linum lewisii* var. *lewisii*), native sagebrushes (*Artemisia* spp.), harebells (*Campanula rotundifolia*), Canada violet (*Viola canadensis*), mountain parsley (*Pseudocymopterus montanus*), goldenrod (*Solidago* spp.), wild asters (*Aster* spp.), and any number of cinquefoils—shrubby cinquefoil (*Potentilla fruticosa*), woolly cinquefoil (*P. hippiana*), partridge feather (*P. anserina*), bearded cinquefoil (*P. crinita*), and Thurber's cinquefoil (*P. thurberi*). Arizona fescue provides a shade-tolerant understory for ponderosa pine, aspen, white fir, and Douglas fir. In new plantings of aspen, it will soften the glare of reflected sunlight, reducing stress on the aspens. Arizona fescue is beautiful in autumn in combination with red-leaved shrubs such as big-tooth maple (*Acer grandidentatum*), three-leaf sumac (*Rhus trilobata*), smooth sumac (*R. glabra*), and vining western Virginia creeper (*Parthenocissus inserta*). Related species include Idaho fescue (*Festuca idahoensis*), which will thrive at elevations to 12,000 feet, and sheep fescue (*F. ovina*), which bears florets and seeds in tight, narrow panicles.

Fragaria ovalis

Fragaria ovalis
(*Fragaria virginiana* subsp. *glauca*)

WILD STRAWBERRY
ROSE FAMILY (*ROSACEAE*)
HERBACEOUS PERENNIAL
HEIGHT: 3–6 INCHES
WIDTH: SPREADING
ZONE 2

CHARACTERISTICS: Medium-textured, dense, low mat, spreading by runners to become a continuous ground cover; leaves have three leaflets, dark blue-green in summer turning to shades of red and purple in fall; white, five-petaled flowers, to 1 inch in diameter, yellow centers made up of many stamens and pistils; small, edible fruits.

NATIVE RANGE: Western North America; on the Colorado Plateau, at elevations between 7,000 and 11,000 feet

SEASON OF BLOOM: Spring

OUTSTANDING FEATURES: Attractive dark blue-green trailing ground cover that bears many white flowers followed by luscious berries; foliage turns red and purple in fall.

CULTURE

Soil: Add organic matter for vigorous growth

Exposure: Sun to shade

Water use: Moderate

Propagation: Offsets, stolons, divisions

Care and maintenance: Water regularly; add organic fertilizer to encourage blooms and berries; protect from slugs.

LANDSCAPE USES: Ground cover, shade garden, moist meadow, edible fruit, fall color

WILDLIFE ATTRACTED: Bees visit flowers; birds and small mammals relish fruits.

HISTORICAL AND MODERN USES: Edible fruit, leaves have herbal and medicinal uses

This high-elevation wild strawberry bears small but delicious fruit in summer. It makes a versatile, quick-spreading, very low ground cover and is attractive planted between native conifers and shrubs. Plants will tolerate light foot traffic, so it can also be grown between pavers or flagstones. To produce fruit, wild strawberry must be planted in full sun and will be at its best when given moderate, regular water and planted in a soil with organic amendments that also help the soil stay moist. Its deep red fall color is delightful! Wild strawberry mixes well in a meadow with native grasses and perennials of moderately moist habitats and is beautiful planted in a woodland garden in combination with agrimony (*Agrimonia striata*), Richardson's geranium (*Geranium richardsonii*), purple geranium (*G. caespitosum*), geranium-leaf larkspur (*Delphinium geraniifolium*), alkali pink (*Sidalcea neomexicana*), wild rose (*Rosa woodsii*), white virgin's bower (*Clematis ligusticifolia*), western Virginia creeper (*Parthenocissus inserta*), Thurber's cinquefoil (*Potentilla thurberi*), and Utah serviceberry (*Amelanchier utahensis*).

Frasera speciosa

Frasera speciosa (Swertia radiata)

DEERS' EARS, ELKWEED, MONUMENT PLANT
GENTIAN FAMILY (*GENTIANACEAE*)
HERBACEOUS PERENNIAL
HEIGHT: LEAVES 1 FOOT; FLOWER STALKS TO 6 FEET
WIDTH: 2 FEET
ZONE 2

CHARACTERISTICS: Coarse-textured perennial bears an upright flower stalk to 6 feet tall with purple-tinged light green leaves in whorls of four to six, held high above large basal rosettes of shiny, upright leaves shaped like giant deers' ears. Silvery-green, four-petaled flowers with purple spots, alternate pointed green sepals and two fringed purple nectar glands at the base of each lobe; arranged on short stalks in leaf axils of huge flowering stalks.

NATIVE RANGE: Western North America; on the Colorado Plateau, in a variety of rich soil in open pine forests and mixed aspen-conifer forests at elevations of 5,000 to 10,500 feet

SEASON OF BLOOM: Summer

OUTSTANDING FEATURES: Unforgettable! The flowers of deers' ears are like nothing else you've ever seen. Tall stalks of four-pointed, silvery-green flowers with purple spots and double purple nectar glands attract insects and butterflies, then age gracefully to showy, pale green seed pods.

CULTURE

Soil: Moist; best with organic matter

Exposure: Full sun to shade

Water use: Low to moderate

Propagation: Seed; plants require several years to reach full blooming size.

Care and maintenance: Best with summer water. Let seed fall to naturalize.

LANDSCAPE USES: Accent or specimen plant, naturalizing in shade or full sun, plant at the edges of forests or meadows

WILDLIFE ATTRACTED: Butterflies and other insects; grazed by elk

HISTORICAL AND MODERN USES: Cold remedy, analgesic, antidiarrheal

Usually associated with moist meadows, deers' ears is also found in clearings in the ponderosa pine forest. Place this showy plant beneath aspens along with columbines, wax

Frasera radiata

currant (*Ribes cereum*), orange mountain gooseberry (*Ribes pinetorum*), harebells (*Campanula rotundifolia*), and silvery lupine (*Lupinus argenteus*); use it as a mass planting in open meadows; or use it as a single specimen plant or accent in a large container.

Gaillardia pinnatifida

Gaillardia pinnatifida

CUTLEAF BLANKETFLOWER, HOPI BLANKETFLOWER,
RED DOME BLANKETFLOWER
SUNFLOWER FAMILY (*ASTERACEAE*)
HERBACEOUS PERENNIAL
HEIGHT: 1 $^{1}/_{2}$ FEET
WIDTH: 2 FEET
ZONE 3

CHARACTERISTICS: Medium-textured upright perennial from a branched caudex; leaves are green, hairy, and pinnately lobed, to 3 inches long. Rusty red disk flowers form a rounded 1 $^{3}/_{4}$-inch dome, surrounded by a wispy fringe of sparse yellow ray flowers.

NATIVE RANGE: Southwest United States and Mexico in fields, plains, mesas, and clearings in ponderosa pine forests

SEASON OF BLOOM: Early summer, long blooming

OUTSTANDING FEATURES: This unique, easy-care perennial blooms long and freely. Its many heads of rusty red disk flowers form rounded domes with wispy skirts of sparse, narrow yellow rays.

CULTURE

Soil: Any

Exposure: Full sun

Water use: Low

Propagation: Seed, division; will naturalize

Care and maintenance: Very low

LANDSCAPE USES: Sunny border, wildflower meadow, accent plant, butterfly garden, companion for grasses, naturalizing, dry garden

WILDLIFE ATTRACTED: Butterflies, honeybees

HISTORICAL AND MODERN USES: Native American medicinal use, including analgesic and diuretic

Like all blanketflowers, cutleaf blanketflower is easy to grow and blooms heavily throughout the summer. It will do well in warm, dry locations and provide satisfaction to those who want a truly "no-maintenance" garden. A related species, great blanketflower or Indian blanket (*Gaillardia aristata*), is native throughout North America and is a common component of many commercial wildflower mixtures; it has large flowers with bright red centers (disks and inner part of ray flowers) and yellow-tipped ray flowers for months on end. Blanketflowers do well in combination with other dry-loving wildflowers, grasses, shrubs, and native cacti. The assemblage of gold, adobe, and burgundy is most pleasing with plants whose flowers or leaves have hues of blue, gray, straw, or olive green, and against reddish soils and rocks.

Gaillardia pinnatifida

Gaillardia pulchella

Gaillardia pulchella

FIREWHEEL
SUNFLOWER FAMILY (*ASTERACEAE*)
HERBACEOUS ANNUAL
HEIGHT: 2 FEET
WIDTH: 2 FEET
ZONE 3

CHARACTERISTICS: Medium-textured, upright, bushy, leafy-stemmed annual; yellow-tipped, red-petaled "daisy" flowers to 3 inches wide with purple and gold disk flowers; tips of rays divided into three sharp lobes.

NATIVE RANGE: California east to Missouri and Louisiana, as well as Mexico, in open areas and on roadsides

SEASON OF BLOOM: Early summer to autumn

OUTSTANDING FEATURES: Many large, yellow-tipped, red ray flowers with purple and golden disks; easy to establish from seed; long blooming and attractive to butterflies; good cut flower.

CULTURE

Soil: Any

Exposure: Full sun

Water use: Low

Propagation: Seed

Care and maintenance: Reseeds prolifically! Let seed drop to establish next year's plants.

LANDSCAPE USES: Butterfly garden, dry garden, wildflower meadow, naturalizing, container garden

WILDLIFE ATTRACTED: Butterflies, honeybees

Gaillardia pulchella

Firewheel is an easy-to-grow annual that brightens any sunny, dry garden. Plant it in a warm location with other dry-loving wildflowers and native grasses.

Geranium caespitosum

Geranium caespitosum

PURPLE GERANIUM, JAMES' GERANIUM,
PINEYWOODS GERANIUM
GERANIUM FAMILY (*GERANIACEAE*)
HERBACEOUS PERENNIAL
HEIGHT: 1–2 FEET
WIDTH: 2 FEET
ZONE 2

CHARACTERISTICS: Medium-textured, mounding perennial with few to many stems from a definitely woody caudex becomes open and upright at time of bloom; leaves are deeply lobed, palmate, and dark green, turning to purple and red with autumn chill. Magenta-purple, five-petaled flowers three-quarters of an inch across with whitish streaks, in pairs or not, on slender pedicels; flowers are followed by cranesbill-shaped seed pods.

NATIVE RANGE: Southwest United States and Mexico, in a wide variety of habitats

SEASON OF BLOOM: Early summer to late summer

OUTSTANDING FEATURES: Rich magenta-purple flowers rise on short stems above deeply lobed leaves. A versatile plant that does well in sun or shade, beautifying many locations in the garden with its special flower color.

CULTURE

Soil: Any

Exposure: Sun to shade

Water use: Low to moderate

Propagation: Seed

Care and maintenance: Very low

LANDSCAPE USES: Perennial border, butterfly garden, shade or woodland garden, naturalizing, dry garden.

WILDLIFE ATTRACTED: Butterflies

HISTORICAL AND MODERN USES: Root used for female healing and as an astringent. Good forage for sheep. Children can make "scissors" and other playthings from needle-like seed capsules.

Purple geranium will grow well in a wide variety of garden situations, from moist shade to dry sun. It will grow taller in moist soils and remain compact in dryer conditions. It is captivating in high-elevation landscapes, planted under aspen or ponderosa pines. The rich magenta flowers are beautiful when planted in combination with goldenrod (*Solidago* spp.), redroot buckwheat (*Eriogonum racemosum*), wild larkspurs (*Delphinium* spp.), columbines (*Aquilegia caerulea* and *A. chrysantha*), other native geraniums, and taperleaf (*Pericome caudata*). It also combines well with non-native hardy geraniums. Two quite similar related native geranium species are Fremont's geranium (*Geranium fremontii*), which differs from purple geranium in its pale purple flowers and lack of glands on stem leaves, and sticky purple geranium (*G. viscosissimum*), a stout, mounding, many-flowered plant with bright rose-purple flowers, common in middle to subalpine elevations; as its name implies, all parts are sticky.

Geranium caespitosum

Geranium richardsonii

Geranium richardsonii

RICHARDSON'S GERANIUM, WHITE GERANIUM
GERANIUM FAMILY (*GERANIACEAE*)
HERBACEOUS PERENNIAL
HEIGHT: 2 FEET
WIDTH: 3 FEET
ZONE 3

CHARACTERISTICS: Medium-textured, often sprawling perennial with palmately lobed leaves; white, five-petaled flowers to 1 inch wide, sometimes tinged with pink and usually with purple veins, followed by cranesbill-shaped seed pods.

NATIVE RANGE: Alaska south to California, Arizona, and New Mexico; on the Colorado Plateau at elevations of 4,500 to 11,500 feet, in a variety of habitats, usually in moist soils

SEASON OF BLOOM: Early to late summer, long-blooming

OUTSTANDING FEATURES: Its sprawling habit makes this geranium a good filler or softener. Bearing many five-petaled white flowers throughout summer and into autumn, it will grow in a variety of conditions and is very cold tolerant.

CULTURE

Soil: Any; moist

Exposure: Sun to shade

Water use: Moderate to high

Propagation: Seed

Care and maintenance: Very low

LANDSCAPE USES: Butterfly garden, mixed conifer or aspen garden, riparian garden, white-flower garden, high-elevation wildflower meadow with native grasses and sedges, background or filler plant, fall color.

WILDLIFE ATTRACTED: Butterflies

HISTORICAL AND MODERN USES: Used to stop nosebleeds because it contains a high amount of tannin, an astringent.

Richardson's geranium has a more open, sprawling habit than the other native geraniums and can be planted next to masonry to soften the edges. The rich, dark green, palmately lobed leaves contrast nicely with the white bark of aspen (*Populus tremuloides*), the red bark of red-twig dogwood (*Cornus sericea*), and the yellow flowers of golden columbine (*Aquilegia chrysantha*). Its fall foliage provides a wide spectrum of colors with the first frosty night. A good plant to select for filler or cover between specimen plants, it does best with regular moisture and combines well in the garden with other moisture-loving perennials including Canada violet (*Viola canadensis*), purple violet (*V. adunca*), and alkali pink checkerbloom (*Sidalcea neomexicana*).

Geranium richardsonii

Geum triflorum

Geum triflorum

OLD MAN'S WHISKERS,
PRAIRIE SMOKE
ROSE FAMILY (*ROSACEAE*)
HERBACEOUS PERENNIAL
HEIGHT: 4 INCHES
WIDTH: SPREADING
ALL ZONES

CHARACTERISTICS: Medium-textured mat of bright green, upright, pinnately divided leaves, supported by large, thickened brown rhizomes; unusual nodding, rosebudlike, maroon to pink flowers held above reflexed pink bracts in early spring, followed by persistent pink feathery seeds.

NATIVE RANGE: Western North America

SEASON OF BLOOM: One of the earliest spring bloomers, repeat-blooms with summer rains.

OUTSTANDING FEATURES: Large drifts of feathery, fernlike leaves stay green all winter; spreads by vigorous rhizomes. Heads of long, iridescent, pink feathery seeds that persist throughout the summer give the plant both its common names.

CULTURE

Soil: Any

Exposure: Sun to partial shade

Water use: Low to moderate; requires more water during drought.

Propagation: Seed, division

Care and maintenance: Very low

LANDSCAPE USES: Ground cover (will take moderate traffic), native prairie or meadow, filler

WILDLIFE ATTRACTED: Butterflies

HISTORICAL AND MODERN USES: Good forage for sheep

Interplant old man's whiskers with bulbs for a showy early bloom. One of the few truly evergreen perennials in the high elevations, this plant remains green throughout the winter and can photosynthesize and grow through several feet of snow. This plant will grow in a variety of conditions: In dry pine forests it tolerates a fair amount of heat and drought,

Geum triflorum

while in mountain meadows it can thrive in heavy, seasonally saturated soils. Although its thick rhizomes enable it to survive long periods of drought, it can get very crisp during dry spells. To be at its best in dry gardens it should receive regular water throughout periods of prolonged drought during spring, summer, and fall. Beautiful when planted with pussytoes (*Antennaria parvifolia*), twinberry (*Lonicera involucrata*), Parry's bellflower (*Campanula parryi*), and harebells (*Campanula rotundifolia*).

Glandularia bipinnatifida

Glandularia bipinnatifida
(Verbena bipinnatifida)

DAKOTA VERVAIN
VERBENA FAMILY (*VERBENACEAE*)
HERBACEOUS PERENNIAL
HEIGHT: TO 18 INCHES
WIDTH: 1–2 FEET
ZONE 4

CHARACTERISTICS: Sprawling perennial with dark green, long-haired leaves with edges curled under, sunken veins, much divided into long, narrow lobes; covered with flowers. Many bright-pink to red-violet, fragrant, tubular flowers with five notched, flaring lobes to half-inch wide, in large, somewhat flat terminal clusters.

NATIVE RANGE: South Dakota to Alabama, Texas, and Arizona; on the Colorado Plateau, along roadsides, on rocky dry slopes, mesas, and in open coniferous forests, at elevations of 5,000 to 10,000 feet

SEASON OF BLOOM: Summer to fall, long-blooming

OUTSTANDING FEATURES: Rounded clusters of bright-pink, fragrant, tubular flowers bloom all season, making this drought-tolerant prairie perennial a bold addition to any sunny garden.

CULTURE

Soil: Dry

Exposure: Full sun

Water use: Low

Propagation: Seed

Care and maintenance: A few extra waterings will extend blooming season.

LANDSCAPE USES: Wildflower meadow, dry garden, butterfly garden, container plant

WILDLIFE ATTRACTED: Butterflies, bees

This prairie native is at home in parched, windblown terrain. Plant Dakota vervain with bluestems (*Schizachyrium scoparium, Andropogon gerardii, Andropogon saccharoides* var. *torreyana,* and *Bothriochloa bardinodis*), side-oats grama (*Bouteloua curtipendula*), sunflowers, showy goldeneye (*Heliomeris multiflora* var. *multiflora*), wine cups (*Callirhoe involucrata*), phlox penstemon (*Penstemon ambiguus*), and dropseeds (*Sporobolus* spp.), or as a simple flowering accent dispersed among dry-loving, gray-leaved shrubs, yuccas, and boulders.

Helianthella quinquenervis

Helianthella quinquenervis

LITTLE SUNFLOWER,
ASPEN SUNFLOWER
SUNFLOWER FAMILY (*ASTERACEAE*)
HERBACEOUS PERENNIAL
HEIGHT: 2–4 FEET
WIDTH: 2 FEET
ALL ZONES

CHARACTERISTICS: Coarse-textured, upright perennial with bright-green hairy leaves to 10 inches long with five prominent veins. Yellow rays and slightly darker yellow disks on 3- to 4-inch flowers, solitary or in few-flowered clusters; dark brown seeds.

NATIVE RANGE: South Dakota to Montana, south to Mexico, rare in Oregon; on the Colorado Plateau, in mountain meadows, slopes and clearings in coniferous forests at elevations of 5,000 to 10,000 feet

SEASON OF BLOOM: Summer to fall

OUTSTANDING FEATURES: Nodding, solitary, yellow heads with yellow centers above large, upright leaves make a bold accent in the garden. A great magnet for birds.

CULTURE

Soil: Seasonally moist

Exposure: Sun

Water use: Low to moderate

Propagation: Seed

Care and maintenance: Very low

LANDSCAPE USES: Perennial garden, tall border, montane and subalpine open meadows, butterfly garden

WILDLIFE ATTRACTED: Butterflies, birds, small animals

Little sunflower is a good plant for open sunny spots in regularly irrigated gardens or at high elevations. It will do well between aspens and conifers including ponderosa pine, limber pine, Douglas fir, Colorado blue spruce, Engelmann spruce, bristlecone pine, white fir, and subalpine fir. Plant little sunflower with Arizona mule's ears (*Wyethia arizonica*) and showy goldeneye (*Heliomeris multiflora* var. *multiflora*) for a continuous sunflower display and a continuous buffet for birds and animals.

Helianthella quinquenervis

Helianthus maximilianii

Helianthus maximilianii

MAXIMILIAN'S SUNFLOWER, MICHAELMAS DAISY
SUNFLOWER FAMILY (*ASTERACEAE*)
ZONE 4
HERBACEOUS PERENNIAL
SIZE: 3–10 FEET
WIDTH: SPREADING

CHARACTERISTICS: Upright, multistemmed, coarse-textured perennial with bright green, narrow, folded leaves; arises in dense clumps from heavy roots. Many yellow, 3-inch sunflowers on tall flowering stalks continue to bloom down the stems until the first killing frost. Fruits are achenes about an eighth of an inch long.

NATIVE RANGE: Western North America, in grasslands and foothills

SEASON OF BLOOM: Late summer into fall

OUTSTANDING FEATURES: Three-inch yellow sunflowers range along tall stalks on this fast-growing perennial. Loves warmth and reflected light; makes an excellent flowering hedge. Beloved of children and birds alike.

CULTURE

Soil: Warm; can thrive in both dry and damp soils.

Exposure: Full sun

Water use: Low to high

Propagation: Seed, divisions, cuttings

Care and maintenance: Cut back to ground in winter or spring in colder zones; may need support where watered frequently.

LANDSCAPE USES: Flowering hedge, screen, back of border, along fences or walls, scattered in meadows; yellow fall color accent

WILDLIFE ATTRACTED: Butterflies, honeybees, birds, other wildlife

HISTORICAL AND MODERN USES: Flowers, seeds, leaves, and thick sections of roots are all edible and eaten by humans; good forage for livestock

This cheery, coarse-textured perennial can be used to create long-blooming hedges as well as sunflower houses or mazes for children. It will attract butterflies, birds, and other wildlife. A fast grower, it can be planted from a 4-inch pot and used as a screen by its second season. It gives incredible bloom while asking only for blazing sun, little water, and a warm place to grow. Great planted along streets, walks, and walls. Plant with purple coneflowers (*Echinacea purpurea*), other sunflowers, and tall garden plants such hollyhocks, larkspur, foxgloves, and cosmos. While at its best with full sun and warmth, it will make an attractive, although less spectacular, garden specimen when planted in morning sun or partial shade. Maximilian's sunflower will also hold its own in getting established when interplanted with weeds and non-native grasses. Though extremely tolerant of drought, it will also take wet conditions. Maximilian's sunflower is an aggressive plant and should be kept out of flower beds with rich soil.

Heliomeris multiflora

Heliomeris multiflora var. *multiflora* (*Viguiera multiflora*)

SHOWY GOLDENEYE
SUNFLOWER FAMILY (*ASTERACEAE*)
HERBACEOUS PERENNIAL
HEIGHT: 3 FEET
WIDTH: 3 FEET
ZONE 2

CHARACTERISTICS: Open, fine-textured, branched perennial herb with opposite leaves. Many heads of 1 ½-inch yellow sunflowers with yellow rays and darker disks throughout late summer until fall; dark-hulled seeds remain on dried flower heads.

NATIVE RANGE: Southwestern Montana to New Mexico, southern Arizona, Nevada, and eastern California; on the Colorado Plateau, at elevations between 4,500 and 9,500 feet on dry slopes and in mountain meadows, often in ponderosa pine forests

SEASON OF BLOOM: Late summer to autumn

OUTSTANDING FEATURES: This charming, fine-textured native is literally covered with abundant golden yellow sunflowers in summer and on into fall. Butterflies visit the blooms; birds and small mammals banquet on the seeds.

CULTURE

Soil: Any

Exposure: Full sun

Water use: Very low to low

Propagation: Seed

Care and maintenance: Very low. Leave seed-filled heads on plant to provide food for birds and wildlife; enough seed will drop to the ground to self-sow.

LANDSCAPE USES: Wildflower meadow, butterfly garden, dry garden, naturalizing, mass planting; bird and wildlife plant

WILDLIFE ATTRACTED: Butterflies, birds, small mammals

HISTORICAL AND MODERN USES: Seeds edible; plants good for forage.

Showy goldeneye is a charming, sunny plant that extends summer cheer into the autumn. It behaves well in a small or cultivated garden where it can be planted to form a low hedge or border. Great for mass plantings and naturalizing to create a sea of golden sunflowers. Butterflies, birds, and small mammals will abound and eat sunflower seeds. A perfect late-season complement to blanketflowers (*Gaillardia* spp.), blue flax (*Linum lewisii* var. *lewisii*), and lanceleaf tickseed (*Coreopsis lanceolata*) in dry wildflower meadows, or planted as filler between yuccas, Apache plume (*Fallugia paradoxa*), and common cliffrose (*Purshia stansburiana*) on slopes. An annual relative, annual goldeneye (*Heliomeris longifolia* var. *annua*), is coarser textured, with a more upright growth habit and an even showier display of flowers; it establishes easily from seed.

Hesperostipa comata

Hesperostipa comata (Stipa comata)

NEEDLE-AND-THREAD GRASS
GRASS FAMILY (*POACEAE*)
TUFTED PERENNIAL BUNCHGRASS
HEIGHT: 2 FEET; FLOWER STALK TO 4 FEET
WIDTH: 2 FEET
ZONE 4

CHARACTERISTICS: Coarse-textured, tufted, perennial bunchgrass with basal leaves, tall upright flower stalk to 4 feet. Large, open panicles of sparsely arranged green florets age to a spectacular straw-colored inflorescence with showy, long-tailed seeds.

NATIVE RANGE: Western and central North America

SEASON OF BLOOM: Summer

OUTSTANDING FEATURES: A dramatic, tall, coarse-textured, drought-tolerant bunchgrass whose pointed seeds and conspicuous trailing, slender, 6-inch awns give it its common name. Entire dried seed stalks are beautiful in dried arrangements

CULTURE

Soil: Well-drained; can tolerate sandy, gravelly, and rocky soils.

Exposure: Full sun

Water use: Low to moderate

Propagation: Seed

Care and maintenance: Very low

LANDSCAPE USES: Wildflower meadow, perennial bunchgrass, ornamental accent grass, roadsides and disturbed areas, with other tall grasses and wildflowers, wildlife habitat

WILDLIFE ATTRACTED: Butterflies, birds, arthropods, small mammals

HISTORICAL AND MODERN USES: Sharp-pointed seeds used as needles.

This graceful, imposing native grass serves as a dramatic accent plant because of its tall stature and showy seed heads. These attractive seeds can, however, be very hazardous to domestic animals, quickly drilling into their ears and throats, so plant needle-and-thread grass only if you have no pets. Combine it with other tall grasses including sand dropseed (*Sporobolus cryptandrus*), big bluestem (*Andropogon gerardii*), and alkali sacaton (*Sporobolus airoides*). Plant it en masse where it will be backlit to enjoy the full impact of long-awned seeds glistening in the sun and moving in the wind.

Hesperostipa comata

Heterotheca jonesii

Heterotheca jonesii
(Chrysopsis caespitosa, C. jonesii)

JONES' FALSE GOLDENASTER
SUNFLOWER FAMILY (*ASTERACEAE*)
HERBACEOUS PERENNIAL
HEIGHT: 1–2 INCHES
WIDTH: SPREADING
ZONE 4

CHARACTERISTICS: Fine-textured, silver-leaved mat to 2 inches tall grows from a creeping belowground caudex. Many small yellow daisies with yellow centers, held just above the leaves, solitary or in twos or threes.

NATIVE RANGE: Found only in Utah, where it grows in ponderosa pine, manzanita, and Douglas fir communities on sandstone and sand at elevations between 5,000 to 8,500 feet

SEASON OF BLOOM: Early to late summer

OUTSTANDING FEATURES: Very low-growing, gray-leaved perennial wildflower forms a tight mat, covered with many small yellow asterlike flowers all summer; thrives in hot, dry conditions.

CULTURE

Soil: Well-drained

Exposure: Full sun

Water use: Low

Propagation: Seed, division

Care and maintenance: Very low

LANDSCAPE USES: Small-area ground cover for small no-traffic areas, rock garden, butterfly garden, dry garden

WILDLIFE ATTRACTED: Butterflies

This very fine textured ground cover thrives with warmth and dry conditions, blooming regularly throughout the summer growing season. At The Arboretum at Flagstaff Jones' false goldenaster has done well in sunny, moderately dry, sloping beds, where it is grown in the foreground of greenleaf manzanita (*Arctostaphylos patula*), Arizona fescue (*Festuca arizonica*), and dry-loving native penstemons. It resembles whiplash daisy (*Erigeron flagellaris*) in form and texture and forms a similar-looking mat when not in bloom.

Heterotheca villosa

Heterotheca villosa
(Chrysopsis villosa)

HAIRY FALSE GOLDENASTER
SUNFLOWER FAMILY (*ASTERACEAE*)
HERBACEOUS PERENNIAL
HEIGHT: 4–20 INCHES
WIDTH: 2 FEET
ZONE 4

CHARACTERISTICS: Medium-textured, compact, mounding perennial with upright stems from a woody crown and taproot; light gray to gray-green, woolly leaves to 1¼ inches long along the stems; many terminal clusters of golden yellow daisies 4 inches across with yellow rays and darker yellow disks.

NATIVE RANGE: Central and Western North America; common on the Colorado Plateau on dry slopes, mesas, and plains at elevations to 8,500 feet

SEASON OF BLOOM: Summer to fall

OUTSTANDING FEATURES: Goldenasters shine in the wild garden because of their long period of bloom, profuse bright yellow flowers that attract butterflies, and ability to thrive with nearly complete neglect.

CULTURE

Soil: Any

Exposure: Sun to light shade

Water use: Low to moderate

Propagation: Seed, cuttings

Care and maintenance: Very low

LANDSCAPE USES: Dry wildflower meadow, naturalizing, butterfly garden, small-area ground cover, dry garden

WILDLIFE ATTRACTED: Butterflies

HISTORICAL AND MODERN USES: Traditional medicinal applications, including toothache; modern use as insecticide/insect repellent

Plant hairy false goldenaster in harsh locations with other plants requiring very low maintenance, or in a garden setting, either dry or irrigated, where its low growth habit makes it a suitable candidate for use as a border or edging plant. A related, less common variety known as false goldenaster, *Heterotheca villosa* var. *foliosa*, is a more upright plant, with spreading, ascending stems covered with small, gray, sessile leaves and many small, light yellow asters in tall spikes. It blooms later than hairy false goldenaster and has a much finer texture. When used in combination in the landscape, these two varieties provide a virtually nonstop show of yellow, butterfly-attracting bloom from May until October.

Heterotheca villosa

Heuchera parvifolia

Heuchera parvifolia

LITTLELEAF ALUM ROOT
SAXIFRAGE FAMILY (*SAXIFRAGACEAE*)
HERBACEOUS PERENNIAL
HEIGHT: 2 FEET
WIDTH: 1 FOOT
ZONE 2

CHARACTERISTICS: Medium-textured, loose rosette of dark green scalloped leaves that grow from a woody caudex. Small, cream-colored, nodding bells in interrupted panicles on upright stalks 10 inches to 2 feet tall; the conspicuous portion of the flower is the calyx of five sepals and five tiny petals.

NATIVE RANGE: Alberta to New Mexico and west to Idaho and Nevada; found among many plant communities on the Colorado Plateau, often in rocky places, at elevations of 4,000 to 10,500 feet

SEASON OF BLOOM: Summer, long-blooming

OUTSTANDING FEATURES: One of the easiest woodland plants to grow; takes shade or sun; bears airy clusters of many tiny bell-shaped flowers on upright stalks above a rosette of dark green leaves.

CULTURE

Soil: Any

Exposure: Shade to sun

Water use: Low to moderate

Propagation: Seed, division, leaf cuttings

Care and maintenance: Very low

LANDSCAPE USES: Perennial border, edging, rock garden, hummingbird and butterfly garden

WILDLIFE ATTRACTED: Hummingbirds, butterflies

HISTORICAL AND MODERN USES: Astringent

Littleleaf alum root is an easy-to-grow woodland plant that does equally well in a rockery, a sunny cultivated bed, or a shade garden. It will spread horizontally with time. In dry locations it will look its best with occasional supplemental water.

Heuchera rubescens

Heuchera rubescens

PINK ALUM ROOT
SAXIFRAGE FAMILY (*SAXIFRAGACEAE*)
HERBACEOUS PERENNIAL
HEIGHT: 4–12 INCHES
WIDTH: 1 FOOT
ZONE 2

CHARACTERISTICS: Compact low mound of deep green leaves from a branched, woody caudex. Flowers are pink-tinged white to lavender-pink, in narrow panicles on a short stalk; stamens visibly extend beyond the sepals.

NATIVE RANGE: Oregon to Utah, Arizona, and California; on the Colorado Plateau, often found in rock outcrops at elevations between 5,000 and 10,000 feet

SEASON OF BLOOM: Late summer

OUTSTANDING FEATURES: A delightfully compact rock garden plant with delicate pink flowers on short stalks above scalloped leaves.

CULTURE

Soil: Any

Exposure: Shade to sun

Water use: Low to moderate

Propagation: Seed, division

Care and maintenance: Very low

LANDSCAPE USES: Shade garden, rockery, hummingbird garden, container planting, low border or edging

WILDLIFE ATTRACTED: Hummingbirds

Pink alum root can be distinguished from littleleaf alum root (*Heuchera parvifolia*) by its conspicuous stamens and pinkish to red-tinged sepals; the stamens of littleleaf alum root are hidden within its cream-colored sepals, and its flowers are borne on slender spires to 2 feet tall. Pink alum root can be planted in the foreground of taller littleleaf alum root and coral bells (*Heuchera sanguinea*) for a hummingbird-enticing border or bed. With its compact habit, it grows well beside other low plants, including bluebells (*Campanula rotundifolia* and *C. parryi*) and whiplash daisy (*Erigeron flagellaris*). Like the other heuchera species, pink alum root is quite drought-tolerant but will benefit from occasional supplemental water.

Heuchera rubescens

Heuchera sanguinea

Heuchera sanguinea

CORAL BELLS, BLOOD ALUM ROOT
SAXIFRAGE FAMILY (*SAXIFRAGACEAE*)
HERBACEOUS PERENNIAL
HEIGHT: 2 FEET
WIDTH: 2 FEET
ZONE 3

CHARACTERISTICS: Fine-textured flowers on leafless 2-foot stalks above a basal clump of dark green rounded leaves; deep pink to carmine red flowers in dense, cymose panicles.

NATIVE RANGE: Arizona, New Mexico, and northern Mexico, on shaded hillsides and moist, rocky areas in the shade at 4,000 to 8,500 feet

SEASON OF BLOOM: Early to late summer, long-blooming

OUTSTANDING FEATURES: Dainty, bell-shaped, bright rosy-red flowers dangling from tall stalks attract hummingbirds and provide great late-season bloom. Drought-tolerant, blooms well in sun or shade. Flowers are long lasting in cut bouquets and hold up well in dried arrangements.

CULTURE

Soil: Well drained; best with organic matter, but tolerant of mineral soils

Exposure: Sun to shade

Water use: Low to moderate

Propagation: Seed, division

Care and maintenance: Very low. Remove old flower stalks for repeat bloom.

LANDSCAPE USES: Small-area ground cover, perennial border, shade garden, rockery, container, hummingbird garden, woodland garden, dry garden, cutting garden

WILDLIFE ATTRACTED: Hummingbirds, butterflies

HISTORICAL AND MODERN USES: Used to treat diarrhea caused by drinking alkali water; rootstock has astringent properties.

Coral bells is a versatile, showy wildflower of proven value and long-standing use as a garden perennial. Though it naturally occurs in moist, shaded, and protected locations, it will tolerate a wide variety of conditions in the garden; in temperate climates it is tolerant of full sun and low water, although it blooms best with some occasional additional water. The red blooms attract hummingbirds and butterflies. Often the plant blooms late enough in the season to show off its bright flowers when most other garden perennials have been knocked down by frost. Try coral bells with other alum root species (*Heuchera* spp.) and upright beardtongues (*Penstemon* spp.) for a variety of colors and bloom times. For a late-season display, plant it in the foreground with autumn joy sedum (*Sedum spectabile* 'Autumn Joy') and small-flowered white prairie aster (*Symphyotrichum falcatum*), and alongside golden columbine (*Aquilegia chrysantha*).

Heuchera sanguinea

Humulus americanus "hops"

Humulus americanus
(Humulus lupulus var. lupuloides)

AMERICAN HOP
HEMP FAMILY (*CANNABACEAE*)
HERBACEOUS PERENNIAL VINE
HEIGHT: TO 20 FEET
WIDTH: CLAMBERING, SPREADING
ZONE 4

CHARACTERISTICS: Coarse-textured, rough-stemmed, bright-green twining vine with large, sandpapery, opposed leaves. Flowers lack petals but have five creamy white sepals; male flowers are arranged in loose panicles in leaf axils; female flowers are in short spikes in pairs, each pair subtended by a leaflike bract.

NATIVE RANGE: Throughout North America; found on the Colorado Plateau at elevations of 4,200 to 9,500 feet in riparian areas or moist canyons, in coniferous forests, and on rocky slopes

SEASON OF BLOOM: Summer, followed by drooping 3- to 4-inch catkins of oat-colored bracts that persist into winter

OUTSTANDING FEATURES: Fast-growing twining vine has large, hairy, three-lobed leaves. Female flowers produce "hops," large, fragrant, drooping clusters of overlapping oat-colored bracts that rustle in the wind and can be used in home brewing or a number of herbal concoctions.

CULTURE

Soil: Any

Exposure: Sun to partial shade

Water use: Low to high

Propagation: Seed

Care and maintenance: Dies back to the ground; remove old dead growth in early spring.

LANDSCAPE USES: Fast-growing vine for trellis, fence, or ground cover on slopes; edible garden, fragrance garden

WILDLIFE ATTRACTED: Pollinated by butterflies; dense habit creates a safe haven for insects and small wildlife

HISTORICAL AND MODERN USES: Hops are used to make beer, a relaxing potpourri or a sedative tea, or in dried arrangements. Pollen and hops are restful; combine dried hops with rose petals, mugwort, and lavender to make "dream pillows."

Both male and female plants are necessary to produce fruits (hops) on the female plants. American hop is a great plant for screening and masking landscape problems, or for quick cover on disturbed slopes. This fast-growing vine can cover a 6-foot fence within the first month of one growing season. Hops does well grown on a trellis with a warm southern exposure. It combines well in the landscape with other plants from streamside habitats such as yerba mansa (*Anemopsis californica*) and cardinal flower (*Lobelia cardinalis*). With its propensity to vine around other plants, it should be kept off newly planted trees, shrubs, and perennials.

Humulus americanus female flowers

Hymenoxys hoopesii

Hymenoxys hoopesii
(Helenium hoopesii, Dugaldia hoopesii)

WESTERN SNEEZEWEED, ORANGE MOUNTAIN DAISY, OWL'S CLAWS
SUNFLOWER FAMILY (*ASTERACEAE*)
HERBACEOUS PERENNIAL
HEIGHT: 3 FEET
WIDTH: 3 FEET
ALL ZONES

CHARACTERISTICS: Coarse texture; early-season basal rosette of bright green shiny leaves, becoming upright and multistemmed later in season. Many bright yellow daisies at tips of shoots with darker yellow disks, surrounded by ray flowers that curve backward with age.

NATIVE RANGE: Wyoming to Oregon, south to New Mexico, Arizona, and California; rare in Montana. Often abundant in rich soil of coniferous forests and mountain meadows of the Colorado Plateau at elevations between 7,000 and 11,000 feet.

SEASON OF BLOOM: Late spring through early summer

OUTSTANDING FEATURES: Tall, shiny-leaved perennial is distinguished by long-lasting candelabras of yellow daisies with recurved petals and dark yellow centers. Beautiful, durable, and one of the few plants that elk avoid eating. Extremely cold hardy in all zones.

CULTURE

Soil: Best with some organic matter

Exposure: Full sun

Water use: Low to moderate

Propagation: Seed

Care and maintenance: Very low

LANDSCAPE USES: Butterfly plant, wildflower meadow, naturalizing, back of border or pond

WILDLIFE ATTRACTED: Butterflies, bees, many other insects, birds. Elk and deer resistant.

HISTORICAL AND MODERN USES: Entire plant used as analgesic for sore muscles (external use only; entire plant is toxic). Yellow dye obtained from flower heads.

A signature plant of high-elevation meadows, western sneezeweed is one of the best choices for very cold areas in the garden. In addition to its tolerance of extreme cold and its long, showy flowering period, lack of palatability makes it a sure bloomer in gardens frequented by elk. Its recurved petals give the plant one of its common names, owl's claws. Although a massive display of western sneezeweed produces some pollen, don't let the name deter you from enjoying this beauty in your garden. It combines well with other plants of high mountain meadows; compatible species include western blue flag (*Iris missouriensis*), silvery lupine (*Lupinus argenteus*), geranium-leaf larkspur (*Delphinium geraniifolium*), Rocky Mountain penstemon (*Penstemon strictus*), scarlet bugler (*Penstemon barbatus*), asters and fleabanes, orange mountain gooseberry (*Ribes pinetorum*), shrubby cinquefoil (*Potentilla fruticosa*), alpine timothy (*Phleum alpinum*), tufted hairgrass (*Deschampsia caespitosa*), and ebony sedge (*Carex ebenea*).

Hymenoxys hoopesii

Hymenoxys richardsonii

Hymenoxys richardsonii

RICHARDSON'S GOLDFLOWER,
COLORADO RUBBERWEED
SUNFLOWER FAMILY (*ASTERACEAE*)
PERENNIAL SUBSHRUB
HEIGHT: 2 FEET
WIDTH: 2 FEET
ZONE 2

CHARACTERISTICS: Small but upright subshrub with fine-textured branches and leaves; many small yellow flower heads with 9 to 14 widely spaced, squared, notched, and slightly reflexed yellow rays and deep golden yellow disks

NATIVE RANGE: Saskatchewan to Alberta, south to New Mexico and Arizona. Found on the Colorado Plateau at elevations between 5,000 and 9,000 feet, often in openings in pine forests.

SEASON OF BLOOM: Late summer until autumn

OUTSTANDING FEATURES: A tough, drought-tolerant plant with bright green leaves and copious small golden yellow flowers in late summer; highly attractive to butterflies.

CULTURE

Soil: Any; very tolerant of poor soils

Exposure: Sun

Water use: Low

Propagation: Seed

Care and maintenance: Cut off flowering stalks after seed drop.

LANDSCAPE USES: Butterfly garden, dry garden, dry wildflower meadow, naturalizing with grasses

WILDLIFE ATTRACTED: Butterflies

HISTORICAL AND MODERN USES: Native American medicine; bark used as chewing gum by Native Americans in New Mexico; dye plant. Toxic to livestock, especially to sheep, but eaten only when other forage is scarce.

Out on the range, the presence of Richardson's goldflower, a humble plant when out of bloom, has long been recognized as an indication of overgrazing. However, as a butterfly plant, tolerant of a wide variety of landscape situations and natural conditions, Richardson's goldflower shines. Its many blooms are often entirely covered with swarms of small blue butterflies. It grows well in poorly drained spots and windswept locations and can be used as a low-growing natural wind fence to protect other plants and hold blowing soils. Because of their toughness and abundant yellow flowers, goldflowers (in both genera *Hymenoxys* and *Tetraneuris*) make wonderful drought-tolerant ornamentals. Those compatible with Richardson's include old man (*Hymenoxys bigelovii*), the first yellow aster seen in late spring in many pine forests, where it does best in full sun to filtered light. It bears large, solitary golden heads of 3-inch flowers atop a felty silver stem to 2 feet tall, held above soft, gray basal leaves. Perky Sue (*Tetraneuris argentea*) is another early-blooming perennial from pinyon–juniper woods of eastern Arizona and New Mexico, with a bonus of a light repeat bloom in the fall. It has fuzzy, narrow, silver-gray leaves, bears solitary yellow daisies on many upright stems 6 to 8 inches tall, thrives on rocky, poor soils, and is hardy to zone 3.

Hymenoxys subintegra

Hymenoxys subintegra

ARIZONA RUBBERWEED
SUNFLOWER FAMILY (*ASTERACEAE*)
HERBACEOUS BIENNIAL AND/OR PERENNIAL
HEIGHT: 2 FEET
WIDTH: 2 FEET
ZONE 4

CHARACTERISTICS: Basal rosette of silver leaves in first year; upright flowering stalks to 2 ½ feet tall in second year; many 1-inch golden yellow daisies with reflexed ray flowers and deep golden disks on tall stalks.

NATIVE RANGE: Utah and Arizona, in dry forests and openings in ponderosa pine, aspen and spruce-fir communities at elevations of 5,500 to 8,500 feet

SEASON OF BLOOM: Summer through fall

OUTSTANDING FEATURES: A good plant for dry, sunny spots; many golden yellow daisy flowers and silver leaves; self-seeds.

CULTURE

Soil: Well-drained; does well in rocky soil

Exposure: Full sun

Water use: Low

Propagation: Seed

Care and maintenance: Very low; for continued presence in the garden, plant every other year and let seed fall.

LANDSCAPE USES: Dry garden, wildflower garden, rockery, dry border, butterfly garden, silver accent. Plant with conifers and native grasses; good on slopes.

WILDLIFE ATTRACTED: Butterflies

Arizona rubberweed, a wildflower of coniferous forests and dry soils, is a short-lived perennial or biennial that performs best in dry, sunny areas at elevations of 5,500 to 8,500 feet. The first year it appears as a silver-leaved basal rosette; in its second season it shoots straight up to display a tower of coarse silvery leaves topped with a branched inflorescence holding many goldflowers and creating an enticing perch for butterflies and bees in midsummer. A related biennial species, alpine sunflower (*Tetraneuris grandiflora*), bears solitary 3- to 4-inch yellow sunflowers at the end of each stem and requires light shade and moderate water. Native to high alpine meadows in the Rocky Mountains, alpine sunflower is cold tolerant in all zones; it can be planted successfully in colder, moister locations than Arizona rubberweed. Old man (*Hymenoxys bigelovii*) is a perennial early-bloomer with solitary, golden yellow, 2-inch daisies atop an upright, woolly stem. Native to ponderosa pine forests from 5,500 to 7,500 feet in New Mexico and Arizona, old man is hardy to zone 4 and will brighten locations in light shade to full sun in the early part of the blooming season.

Ipomopsis aggregata

Ipomopsis aggregata
(Gilia aggregata)

SCARLET GILIA, SKYROCKET
PHLOX FAMILY (*POLEMONIACEAE*)
HERBACEOUS BIENNIAL
HEIGHT: 3 FEET
WIDTH: 1 FOOT
ZONE 3

CHARACTERISTICS: Upright, medium-textured perennial, forming a 4- to 6-inch-wide basal rosette of finely divided leaves the first year, in the second year shooting up to form an upright plant with many trumpetlike, five-lobed, scarlet flowers on tall stalks throughout the summer. Pink and, rarely, white flowers have also been reported.

NATIVE RANGE: Western North America; on the Colorado Plateau, in open areas and forest openings at elevations from 5,000 to 8,500 feet

SEASON OF BLOOM: Mid- to late summer

OUTSTANDING FEATURES: One of the brightest hummingbird attractors; forms a beautiful basal rosette of gray-green leaves the first year and produces tall, congested spikes of trumpetlike scarlet flowers throughout the summer in the second year. Very easy to grow from seed and very rewarding.

CULTURE

Soil: Well-drained

Exposure: Sun to light shade

Water use: Low

Propagation: Seed

Care and maintenance: Very low. Let seed disperse to naturalize.

LANDSCAPE USES: Best in mass planting, wildflower meadow, dry garden; excellent for naturalizing along roadsides and in disturbed places

WILDLIFE ATTRACTED: Hummingbirds, hawk moths; browsed by deer, pronghorn, and livestock

HISTORICAL AND MODERN USES: Native American medicinal and ceremonial use

Although the flowers of scarlet gilia are red at lower elevations, at higher elevations they often fade from red to pink to white late in the season. Plants at lower elevations bloom earlier, when hummingbirds are present; at high elevations hummingbirds have left for warmer haunts by the time scarlet gilia blooms, and the pink to white flowers instead attract hawk moths as night pollinators. All species of *Ipomopsis* establish easily from seed. Related species (sometimes classified as varieties of scarlet gilia) include pink gilia (*Ipomopsis aggregata* x *tenuitiba*), a naturally occurring hybrid hardy to zone 2, with fuzzy gray foliage that bears tall spikes of longer-tubed pink flowers than scarlet gilia, and Arizona skyrocket (*I. aggregata* var. *arizonica*), a local endemic from the cinder hills northeast of Flagstaff, hardy to zone 5, with brilliant red star-shaped blooms on 2-foot stalks. Two blue-flowered species are blue starflower (*I. longiflora*), an annual with pale blue trumpet flowers borne above airy green threadlike foliage that does well in limestone soils and on dry soils; and many-flowered skyrocket (*I. multiflora*), a low-growing, blue-flowered perennial with dense clusters of blue tubular flowers in late summer. Plant scarlet gilia beside the earlier-blooming scarlet bugler (*Penstemon barbatus*) and Eaton's firecracker (*P. eatonii*) for continued red hummingbird flowers in the landscape. Other plants with a similar flower include Bridges' penstemon (*P. rostriflorus*), the very late-blooming cardinal penstemon (*P. cardinalis*), and pineleaf penstemon (*P. pinifolius*).

Iris missouriensis

Iris missouriensis

WESTERN BLUE FLAG
IRIS FAMILY (*IRIDACEAE*)
RHIZOMATOUS PERENNIAL
HEIGHT: 2–3 FEET
WIDTH: CLUMPING
ALL ZONES

CHARACTERISTICS: Upright clumping perennial with bright green straplike leaves. Lilac-blue flowers 4 to 5 inches across, with pale throats, three narrow petals, and a fall of three wider sepals; after flowering, plants develop three-celled seed capsules.

NATIVE RANGE: British Columbia to North Dakota, south to New Mexico and Arizona; on the Colorado Plateau, along streams, in wet meadows, and in moist forest clearings at elevations between 4,500 and 9,500 feet.

SEASON OF BLOOM: Late spring, early summer

OUTSTANDING FEATURES: Pale lilac-blue irises with pale throats atop clumps of bright green straplike leaves; attractive to butterflies in late spring to early summer. Will tolerate cold, poorly drained soils. Excellent cut flowers; seed pods and stems are useful in dried arrangements.

CULTURE

Soil: Seasonally moist

Exposure: Full sun to light shade

Water use: Moderate to high

Propagation: Division, seed

Care and maintenance: Divide older clumps periodically to invigorate.

LANDSCAPE USES: Naturalizing, plant with other bulbs and spring ephemerals, butterfly garden

WILDLIFE ATTRACTED: Butterflies

HISTORICAL AND MODERN USES: Rootstocks and leaves are poisonous if eaten.

Western blue flag is very cold-tolerant and will grow with wet feet and frigid soils; plant with other high-elevation, moisture-loving species including quaking aspen (*Populus tremuloides*), golden columbine (*Aquilegia chrysantha*), wild valerians (*Valeriana occidentalis* and *V. arizonica*), pussytoes (*Antennaria* spp.), leafy-bract aster (*Symphyotrichum foliaceum* var. *canbyi*), geranium-leaf larkspur (*Delphinium geraniifolium*), skyrockets (*Ipomopsis aggregata* and *I. aggregata* x *teunituba*), sego lily (*Calochortus nuttallii*), bluebells (*Campanula parryi* and *C. rotundifolia*), silvery lupine (*Lupinus argenteus*), alpine timothy (*Phleum alpinum*), tufted hairgrass (*Deschampsia caespitosa*), weeping brome (*Bromus frondosus*), rabbitbrush (*Chrysothamnus viscidiflorus*), Richardson's goldflower (*Hymenoxys richardsonii*), and Lambert's locoweed (*Oxytropis lambertii*). Beautiful early-season accompaniment to the bark of twinberry (*Lonicera involucrata*) and the flowers of Arizona honeysuckle (*Lonicera arizonica*). An excellent color contrast to mountain sorrel (*Oxyria digyna*), with its heart-shaped succulent green leaves, red stems, red seed heads, and beautiful beet-hued fall color. To create or utilize an existing "stream" feature in the landscape, plant western blue flag, alkali pink (*Sidalcea neomexicana*), yellow monkeyflower (*Mimulus guttatus*), and upright bunchgrasses like deergrass (*Muhlenbergia rigens*) and muttongrass (*Poa fendleriana*) along the edges of a course of river rock placed along a depression or natural drainage.

Koeleria macrantha

Koeleria macrantha
(Koeleria nitida, K. cristata)

PRAIRIE JUNE GRASS
GRASS FAMILY (*POACEAE*)
PERENNIAL BUNCHGRASS
HEIGHT: LEAVES 4—8 INCHES; FLOWER SPIKE TO 2$\frac{1}{2}$ FEET
WIDTH: 1 FOOT
ZONE 3

CHARACTERISTICS: Clumping bunchgrass with a tuft of bright green basal leaves and an upright flower spike to 2 $\frac{1}{2}$ feet tall. The pale spikelets are arranged in a narrow, spikelike panicle 1 to 7 inches long, three-eighths of an inch wide, and tapering at both ends. As spikelets mature, the glistening, translucent scales surrounding each seed are exposed to light; they remain conspicuously shiny all summer long.

NATIVE RANGE: Circumboreal; North America except eastern seaboard states; in western United States, in a wide range of habitats at elevations of 4,000 to 10,000 feet

SEASON OF BLOOM: Summer, particularly June. Spikelets remain on the plant through the season.

OUTSTANDING FEATURES: Glistening upright flowering spikes shine like bright candles in the filtered light of the forest. Greens up early in spring; pointed bright leaves form a neat, compact tuft.

CULTURE

Soil: Any. Amend coarse soils with organic matter.

Exposure: Sun to light shade

Water use: Low to moderate

Propagation: Seed

Care and maintenance: Very low. Prevent overgrazing early in season.

LANDSCAPE USES: Ornamental bunchgrass, accent plant, wildflower meadow, wildlife, pasture and forage plant

WILDLIFE ATTRACTED: Wind-pollinated; food and habitat for birds, large and small mammals

HISTORICAL AND MODERN USES: Native Americans use plant for flour to make breads and cake. Seeds are edible. June grass also provides excellent forage, particularly after the monsoons.

Prairie June grass is an outstanding bunchgrass that deserves more use in the landscape. When the narrow flower spikes open briefly at anthesis—the time when the plant extends its anthers to disperse pollen—they shine in open pyramids. After anthesis, they resume their tight, narrow form. The shiny flower spikes draw the eye across the landscape and serve as a seasonal focal point. In nature, Prairie June grass often is found growing with muttongrass (*Poa fendleriana*), another native bunchgrass with flowers in tall, more open panicles, often tinged with purple. This lovely pair transfers well to the garden. Bring in silvery lupine (*Lupinus argenteus*), canyon lupine (*Lupinus latifolius* subsp. *parishii*), woolly cinquefoil (*Potentilla hippiana*), and pussytoes (*Antennaria parvifolia*) for a beautiful, low-maintenance understory for pines and aspens.

Koeleria macrantha

Krascheninnikovia lanata

Krascheninnikovia lanata
(Ceratoides lanata, Eurotia lanata)

WINTERFAT
GOOSEFOOT FAMILY (*CHENOPODIACEAE*)
EVERGREEN SHRUB OR SUBSHRUB
HEIGHT: 1—3 FEET
WIDTH: 3 FEET
ZONE 3

CHARACTERISTICS: Upright, densely hairy shrub of fine to medium texture. Many small flowers age to persistent seed heads; monoecious (male and female parts are borne in separate flowers on the same plant); produces abundant seeds.

NATIVE RANGE: Western North America; on the Colorado Plateau, among grasses on dry plains and mesas below 7,000 feet

SEASON OF BLOOM: Late summer to fall

OUTSTANDING FEATURES: Silver-leaved evergreen shrub blanketed with a dense coat of woolly white seed heads in fall. Excellent in dried arrangements.

CULTURE

Soil: Tolerates alkaline soil but does poorly in very saline soil

Exposure: Full sun

Water use: Low

Propagation: Seed

Care and maintenance: Very low

LANDSCAPE USES: Dry garden, silver foliage, fall and winter interest, excellent forage and wildlife plant, excellent for erosion control

WILDLIFE ATTRACTED: Birds and mammals

HISTORICAL AND MODERN USES: Reported to have Native American medicinal uses as a treatment for burns and fever. One of the most valuable fall and winter forage plants, especially for sheep.

With felty bundles of soft gray to white leaves and inflated, nutritious, woolly-white seed heads, this drought-tolerant shrub is unsurpassed in winter beauty. Its persistent seed heads and densely white-hairy stems shimmer when backlit by the autumn sun. Birds and mammals value winterfat for seed and forage during the cold season. As an ornamental plant, it combines nicely with common cliffrose (*Purshia stansburiana*), antelope bitterbrush (*Purshia tridentata*), Apache plume (*Fallugia paradoxa*), and dry-loving native grasses for a durable, low-maintenance landscape.

Krascheninnikovia lanata

Linanthus nuttallii

Linanthus nuttallii
(Linanthastrum nuttallianum)

MOUNTAIN PHLOX
PHLOX FAMILY (*POLEMONIACEAE*)
HERBACEOUS PERENNIAL
HEIGHT: 8 INCHES
WIDTH: 1 INCH
ZONE 4

CHARACTERISTICS: Fine-textured trailing perennial has narrow, spreading stems with upright tips: three shiny, needlelike leaflets arranged like the fingers of a hand appear whorled on the stems. Long-tubed flowers with five white petals and yellow centers cover the plant in summer.

NATIVE RANGE: Western United States and Mexico; on the Colorado Plateau, in openings in ponderosa pine forest and in canyons, at elevations of 5,500 to 8,000 feet.

SEASON OF BLOOM: Early summer to autumn; long-blooming

OUTSTANDING FEATURES: Star-shaped, long-tubed, white flowers with yellow centers cover the tips of this trailing perennial; three-fingered leaves are deep green and shiny. A neat-looking, low-maintenance plant that will attract butterflies throughout the season.

CULTURE

Soil: Well-drained

Exposure: Sun to partial shade

Water use: Low to moderate

Propagation: Tip cuttings, seed

Care and maintenance: Very low; let seed fall to naturalize.

LANDSCAPE USES: Naturalizing, edging for other summer flowers, rock garden or front of mixed border, trailing over rocks and walls, hanging basket or container, butterfly garden, slope planting or canyon garden

WILDLIFE ATTRACTED: Butterflies

HISTORICAL AND MODERN USES: Navajo medicinal use

This trailing, fine-textured native perennial has been shown to perform well and flowers continuously throughout the summer in The Arboretum at Flagstaff's rock garden and in other local landscapes. With proven ability to remain healthy looking and vigorous under dry conditions with very little maintenance, this plant deserves more frequent use. Its beautiful needlelike foliage is prickly to the touch and shiny to behold. Once established, mountain phlox will bloom heavily and look good even with drought and neglect. It is covered with white blooms throughout the summer and can be planted in full sun or used to brighten slopes in canyons and semi-shady gardens. Great in the foreground of mountain lover (*Paxistima myrsinites*), silvery lupine, native asters and fleabanes, and red-flowering wildflowers such as Bridges' penstemon (*Penstemon rostriflorus*) and scarlet bugler (*P. barbatus*); plant on slopes with hardy hummingbird trumpet (*Epilobium canum*) and brickellbushes (*Brickellia* spp.), bracken fern (*Pteridium aquilinum*), and buckwheats (*Eriogonum* spp.).

Linum lewisii

Linum lewisii var. *lewisii*
(*Linum perenne* subsp. *lewisii*, *L. perenne* var. *lewisii*)

BLUE FLAX
FLAX FAMILY (*LINACEAE*)
HERBACEOUS PERENNIAL
HEIGHT: 2 FEET
WIDTH: 2 FEET
ZONE 3

CHARACTERISTICS: Arching, upright, open, fine-textured, gray-leaved perennial with short, narrow leaves. Cornflower-blue, five-petaled flowers to 1 inch wide, on the tips of every stem in loose clusters; flowers close in the afternoon.

NATIVE RANGE: Western North America; found along roadsides and in forest clearings and other open places

SEASON OF BLOOM: Early spring into summer; occasional repeat bloom with monsoonal rain

OUTSTANDING FEATURES: Blue flax blooms with an airy haze of cornflower-blue, five-petaled flowers with yellow centers from spring through early summer. Extremely cold-hardy, fast-growing, low-maintenance, and easy to grow from seed.

CULTURE

Soil: Well-drained

Exposure: Full sun

Water use: Very low to moderate

Propagation: Seed

Care and maintenance: Very low; let seed fall to naturalize.

LANDSCAPE USES: Wildflower meadow, butterfly plant, naturalizing, early bloom, low-maintenance garden, roadsides and disturbed areas

WILDLIFE ATTRACTED: Butterflies

HISTORICAL AND MODERN USES: Like those of its domesticated relatives, the fibers of blue flax are used for many purposes including cordage, nets, mats, and basketry.

Blue flax is one of the easiest native wildflowers to grow; if sown in fall, plants will bloom in their first spring season. It thrives in harsh climates and will flower throughout windy, dry spring days. Flax does well with other low-maintenance wildflowers such as blanket-flowers (*Gaillardia* spp.), plains tickseed (*Coreopsis lanceolata*), prickly poppy (*Argemone* spp.), California poppy (*Eschscholtzia californica*), scented penstemon (*Penstemon palmeri*), galleta grass (*Pleuraphis jamesii*), blue grama (*Bouteloua gracilis*), side-oats grama (*B. curtipendula*), dropseeds (*Sporobolus* spp.), switchgrass (*Panicum virgatum*), and other dry-loving wildflowers and grasses of the western plains. For a spectacular color combination, plant blue flax with Wheeler's wallflower (*Erysimum wheeleri*), Rocky Mountain penstemon (*Penstemon strictus*), stemless Townsend daisy (*Townsendia exscapa*), and early-blooming yellow-flowered species including New Mexican and threadleaf woollywhite (*Hymenopappus mexicanus* and *H. filifolius*), many-flowered groundsel (*Senecio spartioides* var. *multicapitatus*), mat groundsel (*S. actinella*) and Richardson's goldflower (*Hymenoxys richardsonii*). Blue flax is a variable species of wide distribution, long available in commercial wildflower mixes; for best results, try to obtain seed produced from local sources and genotypes.

Linum lewisii

Lithospermum multiflorum

Lithospermum multiflorum

PUCCOON, PRETTY STONESEED, MANY-FLOWERED GROMWELL
BORAGE FAMILY (*BORAGINACEAE*)
HERBACEOUS PERENNIAL
HEIGHT: 1–2 FEET
WIDTH: 2 FEET
ZONE 4

CHARACTERISTICS: Moderately fine-textured upright perennial with several to many hairy stems and narrow, alternately arranged, light green leaves. Deep yellow, symmetrical, tubular flowers with five rounded corolla lobes; tubes about 1 inch long, flowers up to 1 inch across; in nodding, terminal racemes, followed by the shiny nutlets that give this plant one of its common names "pretty stoneseed."

NATIVE RANGE: Wyoming south to New Mexico, Arizona, and Mexico; on the Colorado Plateau, throughout the pinyon–juniper woodlands and ponderosa pine forest on slopes, in openings, and in clearings at 5,400 to 9,500 feet.

SEASON OF BLOOM: Late spring to early summer, long-blooming

OUTSTANDING FEATURES: Clusters of pretty yellow tubular flowers that attract butterflies; drought tolerance; ease of care; attractive, neat growth habit

CULTURE

Soil: Any

Exposure: Sun to shade

Water use: Low to moderate

Propagation: Seed; sow outdoors in fall.

Care and maintenance: Very low; let seeds drop to naturalize.

LANDSCAPE USES: Plant beneath ponderosa pines in full sun to light shade; shade garden, naturalizing, revegetating forest understory

WILDLIFE ATTRACTED: Butterflies

HISTORICAL AND MODERN USES: Native Americans obtained purple dye from the thick, woody roots.

Like many other members of the borage family, puccoon is an early bloomer and has hairy, entire leaves. It can be reestablished in forested areas by removing excess needles from beneath trees. After planting, water in well and reapply a shallow layer of pine needles as a water-retaining mulch. A reliable bloomer with a neat appearance, puccoon also grows well in casual, sunny gardens and is especially eye-catching when planted beside blue flax (*Linum lewisii* var. *lewisii*), redroot buckwheat (*Eriogonum racemosum*), and other dry-loving wildflowers.

Lithospermum multiflorum

Lobelia cardinalis

Lobelia cardinalis
(*Lobelia cardinalis* subsp. *graminea*)

CARDINAL FLOWER, SCARLET LOBELIA
HAREBELL FAMILY (*CAMPANULACEAE*)
HERBACEOUS PERENNIAL
HEIGHT: 2–3 FEET
WIDTH: 2 FEET
ZONE 3

CHARACTERISTICS: Medium-textured, upright perennial with dark green leaves and tall flower spikes in late summer. Two-lipped, tubular, cardinal-red flowers have two smaller upper lobes and three larger lower lobes, stamens united in a column, flowers to 1 ½ inches long on spikelike racemes to 3 feet tall.

NATIVE RANGE: North and Central America, in drainages, seeps, springs, and hanging gardens at elevations of 2,700 to 7,500 feet

SEASON OF BLOOM: Late summer into fall

OUTSTANDING FEATURES: A beautiful native wildflower for wet places. Upright stalks of showy, bright red, hummingbird-attracting flowers on tall stalks; late-season bloom.

CULTURE

Soil: Constantly moist during blooming season

Exposure: Sun to light shade

Water use: Moderate to high

Propagation: Seed, cuttings, division

Care and maintenance: Low; keep moist.

LANDSCAPE USES: Water garden or stream, moist shade garden or meadow, hummingbird garden, butterfly garden, container plant

WILDLIFE ATTRACTED: Butterflies, hummingbirds, bees

HISTORICAL AND MODERN USES: Cardinal flower is potentially poisonous to humans if ingested, due to the presence of the alkaloid lobeline. Several Native American groups smoke the leaves for medicinal purposes.

Worth the water! Cardinal flowers are highly variable across western North America; some varieties bear deep pink flowers, some have nearly purple leaves. Cardinal flower is wonderful at the back of wet borders; it can be planted in moist places along with shooting stars (*Dodecatheon* spp.), buttercups (*Ranunculus* spp.), and other moisture-loving plants including cutleaf coneflower (*Rudbeckia laciniata*), yellow monkeyflower (*Mimulus guttatus*), cardinal monkeyflower (*M. cardinalis*), Lewis' monkeyflower (*M. lewisii*), alpine timothy (*Phleum alpinum*), native sedges (*Carex* spp.), Parry's primrose (*Primula parryi*), wild candytuft (*Thlaspi montanum* var. *fendleri*), and mountain lobelia (*Lobelia anatina*). The related mountain lobelia is a delicate and heavily blooming rhizomatous perennial native of moist mountain meadows, marshy places, and streams in New Mexico, Arizona, and Mexico. It bears many spikes of up to eight deep-lavender, five-petaled, tubular flowers with white throats on erect, bright green slender stems from summer into fall. Mountain lobelia can be planted in front of cardinal flower for a beautiful color combination or used in hanging baskets or borders in place of cultivated lobelias. Both native lobelias are hardy to zone 3.

Lobelia cardinalis

Lupinus argenteus

Lupinus argenteus

SILVERY LUPINE
PEA FAMILY (*FABACEAE*)
HERBACEOUS PERENNIAL
HEIGHT: 3 FEET
WIDTH: 2 ½ FEET
ZONE 3

CHARACTERISTICS: Upright, many-branched, coarse-textured perennial with leafy stems, silver-gray palmate leaves. Many lavender pea flowers in dense racemes at the ends of stems, long-lasting and fragrant; followed by dehiscent, pealike hairy seed pods that split and twist, self-sowing their three to six seeds. White and pink color forms are sometimes found.

NATIVE RANGE: Western North America; on the Colorado Plateau, at elevations of 3,200 to 10,000 feet

SEASON OF BLOOM: Early summer to late summer

OUTSTANDING FEATURES: Profuse, fragrant lavender pea flowers in showy spikes on this sturdy, nearly shrublike, coarse-textured perennial; hairy, silver leaves glow beautifully when backlit in sunshine. A tough, tap-rooted plant that thrives and looks great when other plants are wilting from drought stress; uncommonly drought-tolerant once established.

CULTURE

Soil: Any

Exposure: Sun to light shade

Water use: Low (once established) to moderate

Propagation: Seed

Care and maintenance: Very low

LANDSCAPE USES: Wildflower meadow, butterfly plant, fragrance garden, naturalizing, perennial bed, dry garden

WILDLIFE ATTRACTED: Butterflies, bees; seeds are eaten by birds

HISTORICAL AND MODERN USES: Possibly poisonous to livestock due to the presence of alkaloids. Like other members of the pea family, lupines enhance soil fertility by fixing atmospheric nitrogen. Native Americans have used the crushed leaves as a poultice to relieve poison ivy blisters.

As with any species with different varieties from many habitats and locations, try to obtain seed of local varieties and genotypes. Silvery lupine is compatible with other species of open meadows, ponderosa pine forests, oak woodlands, and open grasslands. For a high-elevation aspen grove, plant with aspens, Arizona fescue (*Festuca arizonica*), taperleaf (*Pericome caudata*), Canada violet (*Viola canadensis*), Richardson's geranium (*Geranium richardsonii*), and golden or Rocky Mountain columbine (*Aquilegia chrysantha* or *A. caerulea*). For a simple, low-maintenance shade garden, try combining silvery lupine with Fendler's meadow rue (*Thalictrum fendleri*), whiplash daisy (*Erigeron flagellaris*), and scarlet bugler (*Penstemon barbatus*). Two related varieties, canyon lupine (*Lupinus latifolius* subsp. *parishii*) and giant lupine (*L. latifolius* subsp. *leucanthus*), do well in high-elevation gardens; both are hardy to zone 4 and look great when planted with ferns and coneflowers. Canyon lupine is an early-blooming variety that bears large, showy spikes of pink pea flowers and thrives with partial shade and moderate moisture. Giant lupine has white to ivory pea flowers in a 3- to 5-foot-tall raceme above a stout basal mound of coarse, dark green, palmate leaves. In areas above 6,500 feet it should be given a warm, protected site to prevent frosting of its late-season blooms. King's lupine (*L. kingii*) is a silver-leaved, low-growing annual lupine with many small purple flowers. It naturalizes in sunny areas and blooms in midsummer. All lupines are visited regularly by butterflies.

Machaeranthera canescens

Machaeranthera canescens (Aster canescens)

HOARY TANSYASTER
SUNFLOWER FAMILY (*ASTERACEAE*)
HERBACEOUS TO SOMETIMES WOODY-BASED PERENNIAL
SIZE: 2 FEET
WIDTH: SPREADING
ZONE 2

CHARACTERISTICS: Upright, fine-textured, many-branched perennial with small gray leaves; variable in form. Numerous small purple asters in heads with violet to purple ray flowers and yellow disk flowers.

NATIVE RANGE: Throughout western North America

SEASON OF BLOOM: Late summer to fall, long-blooming

OUTSTANDING FEATURES: A multitude of small purple asters with yellow centers cover this late-blooming wildflower. It is drought-tolerant, a heavy bloomer, and quite attractive to butterflies.

CULTURE

Soil: Any

Exposure: Full sun to light shade

Water use: Low

Propagation: Seed

Care and maintenance: Very low

LANDSCAPE USES: Butterfly garden, wild garden, naturalizing or wildflower meadow, mass planting

WILDLIFE ATTRACTED: Butterflies

HISTORICAL AND MODERN USES: Native American medicinal use; gynecological aid; respiratory and throat aid

Late in the season this hoary, gray-leaved plant, covered with yellow-centered purple asters, is usually very conspicuous, adding to the sun-drenched glory of late summer days. To create a spectacular and lingering grand finale to the season, plant hoary tansyaster along with other late-blooming beauties including small-flowered white aster (*Virgulus falcatus*), showy goldeneye (*Heliomeris multiflora* var. *multiflora*), rubber rabbitbrush (*Ericameria nauseosa*), broom groundsel (*Senecio spartioides*), apricot mallow and cowboy's delight (*Sphaeralcea coccinea* and other species of *Sphaeralcea*), showy four-o'clock (*Mirabilis multiflora*), and a host of warm-season native grasses including mountain muhly (*Muhlenbergia montana*), deergrass (*M. rigens*), Richardson's muhly (*M. richardsonii*), needle-and-thread grass (*Hesperostipa comata*), dropseeds (*Sporobolus* spp.), switchgrass (*Panicum virgatum*), Scribner's rosette grass (*Dicanthelium oligosanthes* var. *scribnerianum*), and big and little bluestems (*Schizachyrium scoparium* and *Andropogon gerardii*).

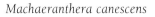

Machaeranthera canescens

Macromeria viridiflora

Macromeria viridiflora

PEARLSEED, GIANT TRUMPETS
BORAGE FAMILY (*BORAGINACEAE*)
HERBACEOUS PERENNIAL
HEIGHT: 3 FEET
WIDTH: 3 FEET
ZONE 3

CHARACTERISTICS: Arching, upright, medium-textured, shrublike perennial dies back to the ground each winter and quickly grows to 3 feet tall in spring. Grayish green, prominently veined, lance-shaped hairy leaves to 7 inches long; pale green tubular flowers to 3 inches long, borne in clusters in leaf axils, followed by pearly white seeds.

NATIVE RANGE: Arizona, New Mexico, and Mexico, on rocky slopes, roadsides, canyons, and valleys in coniferous forests at mid to higher elevations

SEASON OF BLOOM: Early summer

OUTSTANDING FEATURES: This graceful, unusual perennial quickly shoots to 3 feet tall in spring and will thrive in a wide variety of conditions. After its intriguing ghostly pale green flowers are past, it sets pearly white seed that remains in the leaf axils until heavy snows knock it down.

CULTURE

Soil: Well-drained

Exposure: Sun to shade

Water use: Low to moderate

Propagation: Seed

Care and maintenance: Very low; rake away previous season's old growth in spring.

LANDSCAPE USES: Accent plant, woodland garden, foundation garden, slope planting

WILDLIFE ATTRACTED: Butterflies

HISTORICAL AND MODERN USES: Ceremonial use of dried flowers and leaves by Hopi

Pearlseed is an excellent choice to combine with other perennials and woody medium-sized shrubs including wild rose (*Rosa woodsii*), taperleaf (*Pericome caudata*), bracken (*Pteridium aquilinum*), orange mountain gooseberry (*Ribes pinetorum*), shrubby cinquefoil (*Potentilla fruticosa*), pussytoes (*Antennaria* spp.), Fendler's meadow rue (*Thalictrum fendleri*), silvery lupine (*Lupinus argenteus*), bee balm (*Monarda fistulosa* var. *menthaefolia*), and milkweeds (*Asclepias tuberosa, A. speciosa,* and *A. asperula*).

Macromeria viridiflora

Mahonia repens

Mahonia repens
(Berberis repens)

CREEPING BARBERRY
BARBERRY FAMILY (*BERBERIDACEAE*)
EVERGREEN SHRUB
HEIGHT: 6 INCHES TO 1 FOOT
WIDTH: SPREADING
ZONE 2

CHARACTERISTICS: Coarse-textured, creeping, woody-stemmed ground cover to 1 foot tall; shiny, dark green, pinnately divided leaves, leaflets spiny or smooth-edged; roots along stems. Yellow, six-petaled, six-sepaled flowers in elongated, dense, many-branched clusters, followed by large clusters of dark blue-black to reddish berries.

NATIVE RANGE: Western North America; on the Colorado Plateau, in coniferous forests at elevations between 5,000 and 9,000 feet

SEASON OF BLOOM: Spring to early summer, long-blooming

OUTSTANDING FEATURES: Low-growing, woody-stemmed ground cover with shiny dark green leaves, large clusters of many clear yellow flowers in late spring; colorful new leaves and fall growth, ranging from bronze to deep red and purple. Edible blue berries attract wildlife and can be made into jellies and jams.

CULTURE

Soil: Any

Exposure: Shade to sun

Water use: Low to moderate

Propagation: Cuttings, seed, division

Care and maintenance: Shear, mow, or prune out old stems to maintain compact growth form; water occasionally to encourage faster growth.

LANDSCAPE USES: Ground cover (will take some traffic), shade garden, wildlife habitat, naturalizing in shade; erosion control on slopes

WILDLIFE ATTRACTED: Birds, small animals. Deer- and elk-resistant

HISTORICAL AND MODERN USES: Roots are used for a bitter tonic and to make medicine for gall bladder and liver congestion—excellent for hangovers. Roots and bark used an antiseptic. Yellow dye from roots. Edible fruit used to make jams, jellies, and medicines.

Because creeping barberry spreads by underground stolons and roots where its stems touch the ground, it is an excellent plant for control of surface soil erosion. Creeping barberry is an attractive ground cover for shady areas, where it can be planted among Gambel oaks, pines, and junipers; in sunny places it will form a dense ground cover. For a very low maintenance, bird-attracting, and beautiful landscape, combine it with Oregon grape (*Mahonia aquifolium*), a western North American native proven to be reliable, durable, and lovely in landscapes from California to Maine. Interplant creeping barberry with bulbs for an early spring display. All related species of barberry (*Mahonia* spp.) produce edible berries and are attractive to birds for food and shelter. Fendler's barberry (*M. fendleri*) is a deciduous shrub with small, shiny, dark green leaves, yellow flowers, red berries, and striking fall color. In hot, dry areas, plant Fremont barberry (*M. fremontii*), an 8-foot-tall evergreen shrub with prickly, hollylike leaves, yellow flowers, and red berries, with other dry shrubs including common cliffrose (*Purshia stansburiana*), pinyon and ponderosa pines, junipers, sagebrush (*Artemisia* spp.), fernbush (*Chamaebatiaria millefolium*), yuccas (*Yucca* spp.), and green ephedra (*Ephedra viridis*); or use it as a barrier plant, bird plant, and blue-gray color accent; it is hardy to zone 4. Red barberry (*M. haematocarpa*) is another similar dry-loving native shrub from hot, dry habitats; it has hollylike evergreen gray foliage, fragrant yellow flowers, and red berries and is hardy to zone 5.

Melampodium leucanthum

Melampodium leucanthum

BLACKFOOT DAISY, PLAINS BLACKFOOT DAISY
SUNFLOWER FAMILY (*ASTERACEAE*)
WOODY-BASED PERENNIAL
HEIGHT: 1 FOOT
WIDTH: 2 FEET
ALL ZONES

CHARACTERISTICS: Medium-textured, dense, mounding perennial with opposite leaves. Many showy, half-inch daisies have white ray flowers with purple veins surrounding yellow disk flowers.

NATIVE RANGE: Colorado and Kansas south to Texas and west to New Mexico and Arizona. Found on the Colorado Plateau on dry rocky slopes, in desert grasslands, and in oak woodlands at elevations to 5,000 feet, often on limestone outcrops.

SEASON OF BLOOM: Starts in early summer, blooms all summer

OUTSTANDING FEATURES: Deep-rooted, low-growing perennial wildflower forms neat mounds and is covered with many white-petaled, yellow-centered daisy flowers all summer long. Good cut flower. Extremely drought-tolerant!

CULTURE

Soil: Well-drained

Exposure: Full sun

Water use: Very low

Propagation: Seed

Care and maintenance: Very low

LANDSCAPE USES: Dry garden, rock garden, border, slope planting, naturalizing

WILDLIFE ATTRACTED: Butterflies

Blackfoot daisy thrives in hot, dry locations, where it is always a heavy bloomer. In zones 4 and 5, be sure to give it the warmest location possible. Plant with other dry-loving species of grassy plains, rocky places, and oak woodlands for a low-maintenance garden. It is a suitable companion to scrub oak (*Quercus turbinella*), junipers (*Juniperus* spp.), manzanitas (*Arctostaphylos pungens* and *A. pringlei*), wild lilacs and buckbrushes (*Ceanothus fendleri, C. greggii, C. integerrimus*), common cliffrose (*Purshia stansburiana*), three-leaf sumac (*Rhus trilobata*), sugar bush (*Rhus ovata*), desert olive (*Forestiera neomexicana*), Indian ricegrass (*Achnatherum hymenoides*), New Mexico needlegrass (*Hesperostipa neomexicana*), Parry's agave (*Agave parryi*), beargrass (*Nolina macrocarpa*), scented penstemon (*Penstemon palmeri*), showy four-o'clock (*Mirabilis multiflora*), Eaton's firecracker (*Penstemon eatonii*), and desert marigold (*Baileya multiradiata*). It is particularly effective planted on rocky slopes.

Melampodium leucanthum

Mertensia ciliata

Mertensia ciliata

MOUNTAIN BLUEBELLS, CHIMING BELLS,
TALL FRINGED BLUEBELLS
BORAGE FAMILY (*BORAGINACEAE*)
HERBACEOUS PERENNIAL
HEIGHT: 3–4 FEET
WIDTH: 3 FEET
ZONE 2

CHARACTERISTICS: Erect or ascending, coarse-textured, many-stemmed perennial with broad, ovate, pale green leaves; large colonies of upright stems form from spreading rootstock. Pink buds in scorpioid cymes open to nodding, clear blue flowers to five-eighths of an inch long.

NATIVE RANGE: Western North America; on the Colorado Plateau, at elevations between 6,000 and 12,500 feet, where it is a component of mountain brush, aspen, Douglas fir, limber pine, ponderosa pine, lodgepole pine, spruce-fir, and alpine tundra communities.

SEASON OF BLOOM: Early to late summer

OUTSTANDING FEATURES: Delicate pink buds in coiled clusters unfurl to become nodding, bell-shaped, sky-blue flowers. Will do well in the coldest microclimates, even with frigid and seasonally saturated soils.

CULTURE

Soil: Moist

Exposure: Sun to filtered light

Water use: Moderate

Propagation: Seed, division

Care and maintenance: Very low

LANDSCAPE USES: Shade garden, perennial garden, woodland garden, mountain meadow, naturalizing

WILDLIFE ATTRACTED: Bees; Rocky Mountain pika makes "hay" of stems and leaves and stores for winter food; porcupines graze leaves.

Mountain bluebells is an upright, coarse-textured perennial with blue flowers native throughout western North America. It grows well in cool, moist, sunny and shady garden situations and combines successfully with other native perennials from moist meadow habitats including deers' ears (*Frasera speciosa*), harebells (*Campanula rotundifolia*), Parry's bluebells (*C. parryi*), geranium-leaf larkspur (*Delphinium geraniifolium*), pink ipomopsis (*Ipomopsis aggregata* x *tenuituba*), western blue flag (*Iris missouriensis*), Parry's primrose (*Primula parryi*), alkali pink (*Sidalcea neomexicana*), leafy Jacob's ladder (*Polemonium foliosissimum*), and golden mountain banners (*Thermopsis divaricarpa* or *T. montana*). Other related species are Flagstaff bluebells (*Mertensia franciscana*), from wet canyons and moist meadows of northern Arizona and Utah at elevations of 6,000 to 11,000 feet, and MacDougal's bluebells (*M. macdougalii*), a northern Arizona endemic found mostly in open ponderosa pine forests, at elevations of 6,000 to 9,000 feet. MacDougal's bluebells, one of the earliest spring bloomers around Flagstaff, grows from 5 to 16 inches tall. A spring ephemeral, it bears lavender-tinged blue flowers above upright, smooth leaves from March to June, sets seed, and promptly disappears until the next spring. Flagstaff bluebells is similar in appearance to mountain bluebells, but sports clear blue flowers and has hairs on the upper edges of the leaves and on the edges of the sepals. Like mountain bluebells, Flagstaff bluebells does best with regular water and will bloom well in partial sun or shade. Growing all three species in the same garden can create a nearly summerlong succession of bluebells; be sure to give MacDougal's bluebells a warmer, somewhat drier place in the garden than its higher-elevation relatives, and provide a moist location for Flagstaff and mountain bluebells.

Mimulus cardinalis

Mimulus cardinalis

CARDINAL MONKEYFLOWER
FIGWORT FAMILY (*SCROPHULARIACEAE*)
HERBACEOUS PERENNIAL
HEIGHT: 1—2 FEET
WIDTH: 2 FEET
ZONE 4

CHARACTERISTICS: Sprawling, coarse-textured native perennial with bright green, opposite leaves with serrate edges and succulent stems. Spectacular 2-inch-long, vermilion to scarlet, snapdragon-like, two-lipped flowers at stem tips, three lobes of lower lip notched, upper lip arched upward, yellow stamens project beyond corolla; flowers followed by many tiny seeds in a two-sided capsule.

NATIVE RANGE: Utah to Oregon, south to northwestern Mexico; on the Colorado Plateau in moist areas at elevations of 2,000 to 8,500 feet, usually in the shade

SEASON OF BLOOM: All summer, long-blooming

OUTSTANDING FEATURES: Many large, vermilion to scarlet flowers and cheery light green foliage grace this hummingbird-attracting, water-loving, fast-growing perennial.

CULTURE

Soil: Moist

Exposure: Sun to light shade

Water use: Moderate to high

Propagation: Seed, cuttings, root division. Reseeds freely.

Care and maintenance: Trim older shoots back periodically to encourage compact growth; keep moist during season of active growth.

LANDSCAPE USES: Water feature, irrigated garden, container plant, salad garden

WILDLIFE ATTRACTED: Hummingbirds

HISTORICAL AND MODERN USES: Traditional medicinal uses; young stems and leaves can be eaten in salads.

Cardinal monkeyflower is striking planted with yellow monkeyflower (*Mimulus guttatus*), cardinal flower (*Lobelia cardinalis*), alkali pink (*Sidalcea neomexicana*), American bistort (*Polygonum bistortoides*), blue-eyed grass (*Sisyrinchium demissum*), sedges (*Carex* spp.), and other plants that thrive along streams and moist places. Plant in the foreground of cutleaf coneflower (*Rudbeckia laciniata*), leafy Jacob's ladder (*Polemonium foliosissimum*), and silvery lupine (*Lupinus argenteus*). The vermilion to scarlet flowers are beautiful in combination with light blue, yellow, or white flowers.

Mimulus cardinalis

Mimulus guttatus

Mimulus guttatus

YELLOW MONKEYFLOWER, YELLOW-STREAM MONKEYFLOWER,
SEEP MONKEYFLOWER
FIGWORT FAMILY (*SCROPHULARIACEAE*)
HERBACEOUS PERENNIAL
HEIGHT: 2 FEET
WIDTH: 2 FEET
ZONE 3

CHARACTERISTICS: Upright, coarse-textured, herbaceous perennial with bright green leaves with toothed margins arranged oppositely along hollow stems; upper leaves are sessile. Two-lipped, broad, yellow, snapdragon-like flowers with hairy throats, sometimes with red dots; two lobes of upper lip point upward, three lobes of lower lip point downward; flowers to 1 ½ inches long and 1 ¼ inches wide, in upper leaf axils, are followed by papery seed capsules filled with many minute seeds.

NATIVE RANGE: Western North America, in moist places below 9,500 feet

SEASON OF BLOOM: Early summer to late summer

OUTSTANDING FEATURES: Broad, yellow, snapdragon-like flowers, with hairy throats, on tall spikes borne above plants; attractive to hummingbirds; great for wet places.

CULTURE

Soil: Moist

Exposure: Full sun to partial shade

Water use: Moderate to high

Propagation: Seed, cuttings, division. Stem cuttings will root in water.

Care and maintenance: Keep moist to wet; will self-sow.

LANDSCAPE USES: Hummingbird garden, container garden, seasonally moist areas, water features, perennial garden

WILDLIFE ATTRACTED: Hummingbirds

HISTORICAL AND MODERN USES: Leaves and flowers can be eaten in salads.

If you have a wet spot or a water feature in the garden (or can remember to keep a container watered), yellow monkeyflower will reward you with nonstop bloom and visiting hummingbirds. Compatible species include Mexican rush (*Juncus mexicanus*), western blue flag (*Iris missouriensis*), alkali pink (*Sidalcea neomexicana*), scarlet monkeyflower (*Mimulus cardinalis*), fowl mannagrass (*Glyceria striata*), bee balm (*Monarda fistulosa* var. *menthaefolia*), and cutleaf coneflower (*Rudbeckia laciniata*). Yellow monkeyflower is also a lovely plant to establish in roadside ditches and wet drainages. Once established, it may die out without water, but seeds will germinate with the spring thaw, and plants are very fast-growing, blooming the first season from seed.

Mimulus lewisii

Mimulus lewisii

Lewis' monkeyflower, pink monkeyflower,
purple monkeyflower
Figwort family (*Scrophulariaceae*)
Herbaceous perennial
Height: 1—3 feet
Width: 2 feet
Zone 3

CHARACTERISTICS: Several erect, stout, herbaceous stems from a perennial rootstock; leaves are lance-shaped, toothed, and light green; upper leaves lack petioles. Two-lipped flowers are penstemon-like, pink or magenta to rose red, borne singly or severally on long pedicels, throats of flowers pinkish to golden yellow and often lined with red dots.
NATIVE RANGE: Western North America, in moist places
SEASON OF BLOOM: Summer

OUTSTANDING FEATURES: Rosy-pink tubular flowers with rounded corolla lobes and golden, open throats that reveal red dots within. A choice plant for moist gardens, containers, and water features; provides nectar to hummingbirds.

CULTURE

Soil: Moist

Exposure: Sun to light shade

Water use: Moderate to high

Propagation: Cuttings, seed

Care and maintenance: Trim older shoots back periodically to encourage compact growth; keep moist during season of active growth.

LANDSCAPE USES: Moist perennial garden, shade garden, hummingbird garden, complement to water features

WILDLIFE ATTRACTED: Hummingbirds

In the wild, Lewis' monkeyflower grows along streams and in mountain meadows and seeps. In the garden, it needs water, and its culture and uses are much the same as those of cardinal monkeyflower (*Mimulus cardinalis*). It often can be grown successfully at elevations lower than its natural range.

Mirabilis multiflora

Mirabilis multiflora

SHOWY FOUR-O'CLOCK, COLORADO FOUR-O'CLOCK, MARAVILLA
FOUR-O'CLOCK FAMILY (*NYCTAGINACEAE*)
HERBACEOUS PERENNIAL
HEIGHT: 2 FEET
WIDTH: 3 FEET
ZONE 4

CHARACTERISTICS: Coarse-textured mound of many blue-gray to green opposite leaves in spring, from a large, tuberous root. New growth is magenta; old growth bleaches to white and dries in winter. A long succession of many flat-faced, tubular, magenta flowers in groups of three to six, with yellow stamens, open in the afternoon and close by late morning. Borne in an involucre, they lack true petals; their showy part is their petaloid calyx of fused sepals. Flowers are followed by rounded, dark brown, ribbed seeds.

NATIVE RANGE: Southwestern United States and Texas; on the Colorado Plateau, in dry plant communities from 2,100 to 7,500 feet; may grow under protection of pinyon pine or junipers in harsh, dry locations.

SEASON OF BLOOM: All summer

OUTSTANDING FEATURES: Dense blue-gray mound of broad, pointed leaves is covered with magenta tubular flowers that open in the late afternoon. Aboveground parts bleach to an interesting, many-branched skeleton in winter. A most attractive plant that requires no care and will thrive in many harsh conditions; very drought-tolerant.

CULTURE

Soil: Any; tolerant of clay soils

Exposure: Full sun to light shade

Water use: Very low to low

Propagation: Seed; will naturalize

Care and maintenance: Pull away dead top growth in spring.

LANDSCAPE USES: Dry garden with plants from dry ponderosa pine and pinyon–juniper plant communities, hummingbird garden, butterfly garden, naturalizing, disturbed sites, erosion control

WILDLIFE ATTRACTED: Hummingbirds, butterflies

HISTORICAL AND MODERN USES: Large root used medicinally for various ailments such as reducing swelling; also used as a tea.

Showy four-o'clock is a durable, beautiful perennial that maintains its neat, mounding form without pruning. Despite its lush appearance, this plant is incredibly tolerant of cold and drought and thrives in difficult situations, due largely to its enormous underground root. Several closely related native species grow on the Colorado Plateau. Spreading four-o'clock (*Mirabilis oxybaphoides*) is a sprawling, many-branched perennial with vivid red-violet flowers throughout the summer, which does best with partial shade; broad-leaf four-o'clock (*M. decipiens*) and scarlet four-o'clock (*M. coccinea*) are two long-blooming, upright wildflowers. All the wild four-o'clocks are great in combination with native cacti, woolly locoweeds (*Oxytropis sericeus* and *Astragalus mollissimus*), Lambert's locoweed (*Oxytropis lambertii*), hardy hummingbird trumpets (*Epilobium canum* subsp. *latifolium*), apricot and globe mallows (*Sphaeralcea ambigua, S. fendleri,* and *S. coccinea*), white-flowering evening primroses including *Oenothera caespitosa, O. pallida* subsp. *pallida,* and *O. pallida* subsp. *runcinata,* groundsels (*Senecio* spp.), Richardson's goldflower (*Hymenoxys richardsonii*), wild buckwheats (*Eriogonum* spp.), and warm-season grasses including Indian ricegrass (*Acnatherum hymenoides*), buffalograss (*Buchloe dactyloides*), and black grama (*Bouteloua eriopoda*). Upright drought-tolerant perennials including prairie clover (*Dalea purpurea*), scented penstemon (*Penstemon palmeri*), desert penstemon (*P. pseudospectabilis*), purple- and rose-flowered sages (*Salvia dorrii* and *S. pachyphylla*), prince's plume (*Stanleya pinnata*), largeflower flame flower (*Talinum calycinum*), azure blue sage (*Salvia azurea*), banana yucca (*Yucca baccata*), Parry's agave (*Agave parryi*), double bubble mint (*Agastache cana*), and false yucca (*Hesperaloe parviflora*) have complementary form and texture and will keep hummingbirds coming back for nectar throughout the summer. Purplemat (*Nama hispidum*) is a low-growing plant with flowers of similar form and complementary color; when planted with showy four-o'clock it mirrors the appearance of its flowers on a diminutive scale.

Monarda fistulosa

Monarda fistulosa var. menthaefolia
(Monarda menthifolia,
M. fistulosa subsp. fistulosa var. menthaefolia)

BEE BALM, WILD BERGAMOT
MINT FAMILY (*LAMIACEAE*)
HERBACEOUS PERENNIAL
HEIGHT: 2 FEET
WIDTH: 3 FEET
ZONE 3

CHARACTERISTICS: Upright to arching, medium-textured, herbaceous perennial, spreading to form a dense basal cluster of fragrant leaves that elongate to tall, leafy, square stems. Tubular, lavender-pink flowers in whorls at branch ends give rise to white-bracted seed heads.

NATIVE RANGE: Western North America, in small canyons and washes, often in limestone soil

SEASON OF BLOOM: All summer, long-blooming

OUTSTANDING FEATURES: There is nothing quite like the sight of bee balm when painted ladies and other butterflies cover the blooms; it is also attractive to various bees and an occasional hummingbird. Profuse, showy, lavender-pink flowers in summer; yellow fall color; edible leaves used as a seasoning.

CULTURE

Soil: Best with summer moisture

Exposure: Sun or light shade

Water use: Low to moderate

Propagation: Cuttings, seed, division

Care and maintenance: Responds generously to regular water and organic soil. Keep water off leaves, and plant in an area with good air circulation to prevent powdery mildew.

LANDSCAPE USES: Herb garden, riparian habitat or streamside, butterfly garden. Bee balm spreads where moisture is present and may need to be contained in the ground or grown in a pot.

WILDLIFE ATTRACTED: Butterflies, bees, hummingbirds

HISTORICAL AND MODERN USES: Used as a seasoning and an edible green by the Hopi. Culinary herb, seasoning, and tea. All monardas contain thymol, a compound that is effective against fungi and bacteria.

Bee balm can be used to flavor foods and make teas; the fragrance of the plant is reminiscent of oregano, and it can be used as a mild substitute for Greek or Mexican oregano. Relatives include scarlet bee balm (*Monarda didyma*), native to the eastern United States, which has bright scarlet flowers and grows to 3 feet tall, and lemon bee balm (*M. citriodora* subsp. *austromontana*), which has white to rosy-pink flowers surrounded by similar colored bracts and produces a distinctive smell of lemon when the leaves are crushed. Spotted horsemint (*M. pectinata*) has pink flowers in summer; spotted bee balm (*M. punctata*) is a short-lived perennial native to the Great Plains, with pinkish-purple bracts subtending yellow flowers with purple spots in tall spikes. Plant bee balm with other natives from the same habitat zone. These include butterfly milkweed (*Asclepias tuberosa*), showy milkweed (*A. speciosa*), wild rose (*Rosa woodsii*), cutleaf coneflower (*Rudbeckia laciniata*), dayflower (*Commelina dianthifolia*) lady fern (*Athyrium filix-femina*), mountain lover (*Paxistima myrsinites*), golden columbine (*Aquilegia chrysantha*), Rocky Mountain columbine (*A. caerulea*), silvery lupine (*Lupinus argenteus*), Parish's snowberry (*Symphoricarpos rotundifolius* var. *parishii*), creeping barberry (*Mahonia repens*), geranium-leaf larkspur (*Delphinium geraniifolium*), western valerian (*Valeriana occidentalis*), and tasselbush (*Brickellia grandiflora*).

Monardella odoratissima

Monardella odoratissima

COYOTE MINT, MOUNTAIN PENNYROYAL
MINT FAMILY (*LAMIACEAE*)
HERBACEOUS PERENNIAL
HEIGHT: 1 FOOT
WIDTH: 1 FOOT
ZONE 4

CHARACTERISTICS: Mounding, fine-textured, gray-green perennial; dense clusters of tubular lavender flowers in summer; all parts of plant are fragrant.

NATIVE RANGE: California and Nevada north to British Columbia; on the Colorado Plateau, in forest openings from 3,500 to 11,000 feet

SEASON OF BLOOM: Summer into autumn, long-blooming

OUTSTANDING FEATURES: Neat, mounding perennial with a powerful minty scent and lavender flowers in clusters at tips of gray, leafy stems. Very tolerant of sun and drought.

CULTURE

Soil: Any

Exposure: Full sun to light shade

Water use: Low to moderate

Propagation: Seed, cuttings

Care and maintenance: Very low

LANDSCAPE USES: Perennial border, fragrance garden, bee plant, ethnobotanic, tea and herb garden, slope planting, rockery, mixed conifer planting

WILDLIFE ATTRACTED: Bees

HISTORICAL AND MODERN USES: Tea, emmenagogue (promoting menstruation), insect repellent

Plant this minty gray-leaved beauty where you can brush up against it and enjoy its sharp, clean fragrance. It makes a delightful tea. Lovely when planted in the foreground with golden columbine (*Aquilegia chrysantha*) and Whipple's penstemon (*Penstemon whippleanus*). Plant in filtered light as understory specimen with limber pine (*Pinus flexilis*), aspen (*Populus tremuloides*), common juniper (*Juniperus communis* var. *depressa*), Rocky Mountain juniper (*J. scopulorum*), alligator juniper (*J. deppeana*), ponderosa pine (*Pinus ponderosa*), and Gambel oak (*Quercus gambelii*). Despite its delicate appearance, coyote mint is tolerant of dry, hot growing conditions once established. Beautiful in combination with low-growing native stonecrops (*Rhodiola* spp.) and alum roots (*Heuchera* spp.). Glenn Keator, author of Complete Garden Guide to the Native Perennials of California, recommends the purple flowers of coyote mint and the rich red-orange flowers of hardy hummingbird trumpet (*Epilobium canum* subsp. *latifolium*) as a lovely late-season contrast.

Monardella odoratissima

Muhlenbergia montana

Muhlenbergia montana

MOUNTAIN MUHLY
GRASS FAMILY (*POACEAE*)
PERENNIAL BUNCHGRASS
HEIGHT: 2 ¹/₂ FEET
WIDTH: 2 FEET
ZONE 3

CHARACTERISTICS: Upright, medium-sized, medium-textured bunchgrass; large open panicles of awned, green florets aging to straw and persisting until heavy snows.

NATIVE RANGE: Colorado Plateau, Rocky Mountains, and Great Basin; on the Colorado Plateau, abundant on dry mesas, rocky hills, and in woodlands and forest openings at elevations between 4,500 and 9,000 feet.

SEASON OF BLOOM: Late summer through fall

OUTSTANDING FEATURES: A dense-growing, moderately large bunchgrass that flowers after the summer rains. After blooming, mountain muhly bears loose panicles of awned seed heads that shimmer in sun and wind from late summer throughout fall. Easy to establish from plants or seed.

CULTURE

Soil: Any, well-drained or seasonally dry

Exposure: Sun to moderate shade

Water use: Low to moderate

Propagation: Seed, division

Care and maintenance: Very low

LANDSCAPE USES: Wildflower meadow; naturalizing; butterfly, bird, and wildlife habitat; understory; reclamation of disturbed and degraded areas

WILDLIFE ATTRACTED: Wind-pollinated; provides food and shelter for butterflies, insects, mammals, and birds.

HISTORICAL AND MODERN USES: A good source of forage early in the year, but becomes unpalatable at maturity.

Mountain muhly is abundant throughout its range. It combines well with other high-elevation muhlys (*Muhlenbergia wrightii, M. rigens, M. richardsonii*), Arizona fescue (*Festuca arizonica*), pine dropseed (*Blepharoneuron tricholepis*), and blue grama (*Bouteloua gracilis*) for low-maintenance native grass plantings, and it can also be interplanted with a variety of compatible shrubs and wildflowers. With its beauty and ease of growth, mountain muhly deserves consideration as a ground cover or an understory planting in high-elevation landscapes.

Muhlenbergia rigens

Muhlenbergia rigens

DEERGRASS
GRASS FAMILY (*POACEAE*)
PERENNIAL BUNCHGRASS
HEIGHT: 3–5 FEET
WIDTH: 3 FEET
ZONE 4

CHARACTERISTICS: Arching, upright, coarse-textured, clumping bunchgrass; green florets in dense spikelets to 5 feet tall, aging to straw color.

NATIVE RANGE: Southwest United States and Mexico; on the Colorado Plateau below 7,500 feet on open slopes and in forests and in moist meadows, arroyos, and streambeds.

SEASON OF BLOOM: Summer to fall

OUTSTANDING FEATURES: Dramatic, arching form; tall, narrow, green spikelike inflorescences that age to straw color and remain on plant until heavy snows fall.

CULTURE

Soil: Will grow in most soils with seasonal moisture

Exposure: Sun to light shade

Water use: Low to moderate

Propagation: Seed, division

Care and maintenance: Very low; in gardens with a high level of maintenance or where fire is a concern, tease away dried leaves in spring.

LANDSCAPE USES: Ornamental, accent plant, wildlife and bird habitat, container plant, wildflower meadow, stream planting

WILDLIFE ATTRACTED: Wind-pollinated; habitat for birds and small animals

HISTORICAL AND MODERN USES: Basketry

Its coarse texture and dramatic stature make deergrass a good native substitute for the invasive non-natives pampas grass and hardy pampas grass in gardens throughout the Southwest. It will achieve its maximum stature with warmth and adequate moisture, growing to 3 feet at higher elevations but taller in warmer parts of its range. Deergrass is a valuable plant in basket-making. Another basketry plant, beargrass (*Nolina microcarpa*), is similar in form, and these two species are complementary in dry gardens. Plant deergrass with cardinal monkeyflower (*Mimulus cardinalis*) and tall sedge (*Carex senta*) at the edges of water features, or with three-leaf sumac (*Rhus trilobata*), wax currant (*Ribes cereum*), and pale wolfberry (*Lycium pallida*) for wildlife plantings in drier locations. In warmer, lower areas, plant deergrass with bush muhly (*Muhlenbergia porteri*), ring muhly (*M. torreyi*), and bullgrass (*M. emersleyi*), along with native shrubs, for excellent cover and wildlife habitat.

Muhlenbergia wrightii

Muhlenbergia wrightii

Spike muhly
Grass family (*Poaceae*)
Perennial bunchgrass
Height: 1–2 feet
Width: 2 feet
Zone 4

CHARACTERISTICS: Upright, spreading grass often grows wider than it is high, occasionally rooting along trailing stolons and appearing rhizomatous. Sharp-pointed, tapering leaves; green florets, in upright compact spikes to 4 inches long, age to gray-black and remain on plant until inundated by snows.

NATIVE RANGE: Southwest United States and Mexico; on the Colorado Plateau, on open slopes at elevations to 8,500 feet

SEASON OF BLOOM: Summer

OUTSTANDING FEATURES: Fine-textured, upright green leaf blades and narrow, upright flowering spikes

CULTURE

Soil: Any

Exposure: Full sun

Water use: Low to moderate

Propagation: Seed, division

Care and maintenance: Very low

LANDSCAPE USES: Naturalizing, informal ground cover, wildflower meadow

WILDLIFE ATTRACTED: Wind-pollinated; wildlife habitat and forage

HISTORICAL AND MODERN USES: Grazing, forage

Spike muhly is a durable, wiry native grass. Plant it in open, sunny locations with other grasses, wildflowers, and forbs. Its low growth habit and black seed heads give spike muhly a distinctive appearance in the landscape. Bare soils are almost always an invitation to weeds, so planting native grasses between other plants and on neglected patches of bare ground is a good way to prevent erosion, provide cover for birds and small animals, and keep weeds from gaining a foothold in the garden.

Oenothera caespitosa

Oenothera caespitosa

WHITE-TUFTED EVENING PRIMROSE, TUFTED EVENING PRIMROSE
EVENING PRIMROSE FAMILY (*ONAGRACEAE*)
HERBACEOUS PERENNIAL
HEIGHT: 6 INCHES TO 1 FOOT
WIDTH: 1 FOOT
ZONE 4

CHARACTERISTICS: Moderately coarse-textured herbaceous perennial; the petals are borne on top of the long, thin, seed-bearing ovary, which resembles a stem, directly above a basal rosette of narrow 1- by 7-inch leaves, soft gray to green, hairy or smooth; leaf margins entire, toothed or nearly pinnately divided. Fragrant, four-petaled, 3- to 4-inch white flowers with four reflexed sepals, eight conspicuous yellow stamens, and a four-lobed stigma, petals fading to pink or purple with age. Each flower opens in the afternoon and remains open until it fades with the heat of the next day. Flowers are followed by persistent woody seed capsules.

NATIVE RANGE: Western North America; on the Colorado Plateau, at elevations between 4,000 and 8,700 feet on dry stony slopes and well-drained soils in openings in ponderosa pine forests and throughout many habitats and plant communities.

SEASON OF BLOOM: Early summer to late summer, with a six-week blooming period

OUTSTANDING FEATURES: Large, fragrant, white flowers open in the afternoon and fade to persistent pink the next day. Long blooming season. Great magnet for hawk moths.

CULTURE

Soil: Well-drained

Exposure: Full sun

Water use: Very low to low

Propagation: Seed, cuttings

Care and maintenance: Very low. Let seed fall to naturalize.

LANDSCAPE USES: Slope planting, roadsides and disturbed areas, rockery, fragrance garden, night garden, container, dry garden, dry wildflower meadow, front of dry border

WILDLIFE ATTRACTED: Hawk moths

HISTORICAL AND MODERN USES: Many Native American medicinal uses

The blooms of white-tufted evening primrose are striking and fragrant. It is said that if you listen carefully you can actually hear them pop open and unfurl. It's also known as "kleenex plant" and "handkerchief plant" because the thin white blossoms look like dainty handkerchiefs or tissues littering roadsides. The flowers bloom in late afternoon and fade by midmorning of the next day, so they are better in afternoon light, and best of all in the evening, when pollinating hawk moths hover like nocturnal hummingbirds and extend their long proboscises to sip the nectar. Consider planting them near an observation blind for evening viewing. Plant white-tufted evening primrose in a dry, well-drained location. If you have heavy or moist soil, the plant will survive but may be short-lived; let seeds fall to the ground, and replacement plants will self-sow with time. For a dramatic color contrast, plant white-tufted evening primrose with other dry-loving species that have large purple, pink, orange, or white flowers, such as southwestern prickly poppy (*Argemone pleiacantha*) and sacred datura (*Datura wrightii*).

Oenothera caespitosa

Oenothera elata

Oenothera elata
(Oenothera hookeri)

HOOKER'S EVENING PRIMROSE
EVENING PRIMROSE FAMILY (*ONAGRACEAE*)
HERBACEOUS BIENNIAL
HEIGHT: 2–4 FEET
WIDTH: 2 FEET
ALL ZONES

CHARACTERISTICS: Medium-textured, upright, many-stemmed perennial with a compact bright green basal rosette. Four-petaled, 2 ½ -inch, yellow flowers with reflexed green sepals, borne in large terminal clusters, petals fading to orange with age.

NATIVE RANGE: Western United States; roadsides, pinyon–juniper woodlands, clearings in the ponderosa pine forest, and moist drainages at elevations between 3,500 and 9,500 feet

SEASON OF BLOOM: All summer long until autumn; a heavy bloomer

OUTSTANDING FEATURES: A summerlong progression of large, pale yellow flowers, fading to orange, on upright stems above bright green leaves. This plant will succeed in rough, tough places. Very easy to grow!

CULTURE

Soil: Any. Moisture is a plus.

Exposure: Sun to light shade

Water use: Low to moderate

Propagation: Seed. Let seed drop to renew planting.

Care and maintenance: Very low. Will accept drought but grows larger and lusher with regular water.

LANDSCAPE USES: Naturalizing, tall wildflower meadow or pasture, butterfly plant, tall plant for back of border, container plant

WILDLIFE ATTRACTED: Butterflies, hawk moths

HISTORICAL AND MODERN USES: Seeds eaten by Native Americans and Europeans.

To combine plants of like flower but different form, try planting Hooker's evening primrose behind Missouri evening primrose (*Oenothera macrocarpa*), which is a foot tall with 4-inch yellow flowers, dark green leaves, and cascading habit, and dandelion-leaf evening primrose (*Oenothera flava*), a ground-hugger with bright green, scalloped leaves like dandelion greens and a very fragrant, 3-inch, lemon-custard-colored flower that draws in hawk moths like airplanes to a landing strip. All three of these species will reseed freely and bloom throughout summer.

Oenothera elata

Oenothera pallida subsp. *pallida*

Oenothera pallida subsp. *pallida*

PALE EVENING PRIMROSE
EVENING PRIMROSE FAMILY (*ONAGRACEAE*)
HERBACEOUS PERENNIAL
HEIGHT: 1 1/2 FEET
WIDTH: 2 FEET
ZONE 4

CHARACTERISTICS: Medium-textured, spreading, rhizomatous perennial, with narrow gray leaves and upright stems; wider than it is tall. Many four-petaled, 3-inch, white flowers open in the afternoon and remain open until midmorning, fading to rose-pink.

NATIVE RANGE: Western United States; on the Colorado Plateau, at elevations of 3,000 to 7,500 feet in dry plant communities including shadscale-greasewood, mixed warm-desert shrub, blackbrush, sagebrush-rabbitbrush, pinyon–juniper, mountain brush, and ponderosa pine.

SEASON OF BLOOM: Summer; repeat-blooms

OUTSTANDING FEATURES: Deliciously fragrant lemon-scented, ghostly white flowers atop silver-gray leaves; wonderful in the night garden; drought-tolerant; self-sows easily.

CULTURE

Soil: Well-drained, warm

Exposure: Full sun

Water use: Low to moderate

Propagation: Seed, cuttings

Care and maintenance: Very low; self-sows easily

LANDSCAPE USES: Fragrance garden, dry native wildflower meadow, rockery, moonlight or night-pollinator garden, white-flower garden, naturalizing

WILDLIFE ATTRACTED: Hawk moths

HISTORICAL AND MODERN USES: Native American medicinal uses

Although it provides a reliable source of nice large white flowers, pale evening primrose is not necessarily the most beautiful of the native evening primroses. Its intoxicating lemon fragrance is what makes this one so outstanding—it is simply the best among night-bloomers of the Colorado Plateau. Hardy to zone 4, it needs strong, reflected warmth and blazing sun to do its best and bloom heavily. It makes an excellent mass planting with prickly poppies (*Argemone* spp.) and California poppies (*Eschscholtzia* spp.), verbena (*Verbena* spp.), native cacti, paper-flowers (*Psilostrophe* spp.), prairie zinnia (*Zinnia grandiflora*), and showy four-o'clocks (*Mirabilis multiflora*). Plant pale evening primrose where you can enjoy its delightful fragrance, its night bloom (beautiful when bathed in moonlight), and its fascinating relationship with visiting pollinators.

Oenothera pallida subsp. *pallida*

Oenothera pallida subsp. *runcinata*

Oenothera pallida subsp. *runcinata* (*Oenothera runcinata*)

CREEPING EVENING PRIMROSE
EVENING PRIMROSE FAMILY (*ONAGRACEAE*)
HERBACEOUS PERENNIAL
HEIGHT: 2 ½ FEET
WIDTH: 3 FEET
ZONE 4

CHARACTERISTICS: Upright, multibranched, spreading, medium-textured wildflower has deeply incised, wavy-edged, sawtoothed leaves, narrow and gray; nearly woody, red-tinged stems, covered with flowers. Many 2-inch, four-petaled, white flowers, fading to pink with age, with eight yellow stamens and yellow, four-lobed stigmas; new flowers emerge each day.

NATIVE RANGE: Southwestern United States; on dry hills and plains, 3,500 to 7,000 feet

SEASON OF BLOOM: Nonstop from May to September

OUTSTANDING FEATURES: Parade of white flowers all summer long that attract hawk moths; incredibly tough, thrives on stress; one of the most dry-loving native perennials grown; self-sows and spreads quickly by underground runners.

CULTURE

Soil: Well-drained

Exposure: Sun to light shade

Water use: Very low to low

Propagation: Seed, cuttings, division; offsets can be transplanted throughout growing season.

Care and maintenance: Very low

LANDSCAPE USES: Low-maintenance garden, wildflower meadow, dry garden, plant with dry-loving grasses, in openings in ponderosa pine and pinyon–juniper and in sunny, excessively drained and windswept areas. Naturalizes; will compete with many grasses and weedy species. Rhizomes and heavy top growth can help stabilize bare soils.

WILDLIFE ATTRACTED: Hawk moths

If you have a barren, overgrazed, windswept piece of land, you could begin to establish your garden with starts of creeping evening primrose. This beautiful, ever-blooming perennial will thrive in the most demanding and stressful situations including strong winds and poor, rocky, and excessively dry soils. Creeping evening primrose looks most pleasing when planted with Lambert's locoweed (*Oxytropis lambertii*), woolly locoweed (*Astragalus mollissimus*), cowboy's delight (*Sphaeralcea coccinea*), galleta grass (*Pleuraphis jamesii*), Indian ricegrass (*Achnatherum hymenoides*), blue flax (*Linum lewisii* var. *lewisii*), showy four o'clock (*Mirabilis multiflora*), phlox penstemon (*Penstemon ambiguus*), wild rosemary (*Poliomintha incana*), threadleaf groundsel (*Senecio flaccidus* var. *flaccidus*), badlands mules' ears (*Wyethia scabra*), sand sage (*Artemisia filifolia*), and saltbush (*Atriplex* spp.). It also makes a wonderful, easy-care dry garden planted in the foreground with wild rose (*Rosa woodsii*), three-leaf sumac (*Rhus trilobata*), and wax currant (*Ribes cereum*).

Oxytropis lambertii

Oxytropis lambertii

LAMBERT'S LOCOWEED, PURPLE LOCOWEED
PEA FAMILY (*FABACEAE*)
HERBACEOUS PERENNIAL
HEIGHT: 1 FOOT
WIDTH: 1 FOOT
ZONE 3

CHARACTERISTICS: Medium-textured basal rosette of felt-covered, silvery, upright, pinnately divided leaves from a deep taproot, with densely crowded, upright flower spikes. Many vibrant magenta-red to lavender-purple pea flowers, lightly fragrant, in crowded racemes to 6 inches tall, followed by leathery, beaked, pealike pods.

NATIVE RANGE: Western North America, in forest openings at elevations of 5,000 to 8,000 feet

SEASON OF BLOOM: Early to late summer; long-lasting

OUTSTANDING FEATURES: Silvery, featherlike leaves and upright spikes of strikingly bright, iridescent pea flowers. Cold- and drought-tolerant.

CULTURE

Soil: Well-drained

Exposure: Sun to filtered light

Water use: Low

Propagation: Seed

Care and maintenance: Very low

LANDSCAPE USES: Accent plant, dry border, rock garden, butterfly garden, wildflower meadow with grasses, planting under aspens, ponderosa, limber, and bristlecone pines

WILDLIFE ATTRACTED: Many butterflies, including sulphurs; hummingbirds

HISTORICAL AND MODERN USES: Poisonous. Eaten readily by livestock, often with fatal effect. Lambert's locoweed is also reported to have been used by Native Americans in various ways.

This versatile locoweed occurs naturally in many different habitats, from hot, dry grasslands to aspen woodland, moist upland meadows, and clearings in the ponderosa pine forest. Flower color is unparalleled. Plant Lambert's locoweed with bristlecone pines (*Pinus aristata*), columbines (*Aquilegia* spp.), nodding brome (*Bromus frondosus*), alpine prickly currant (*Ribes montigenum*), mountain ash (*Sorbus dumosa*), red elderberry (*Sambucus microbotrys*), common juniper (*Juniperus communis* var. *depressa*), Wright's goldenrod (*Solidago wrightii*), and high-elevation penstemons (*Penstemon barbatus* and *P. whippleanus*) for a beautiful subalpine garden that will tolerate strong winds and a short growing season. Or combine it with any number of likely companions from one of its many other native habitats. A related species, silky or white locoweed (*Oxytropis sericea*), is similar in appearance, with silky leaves and white flowers in tall racemes. It combines beautifully with Lambert's in a low border or rockery. Because its consumption induces the frequently fatal locoism in cattle, horses, and sheep, care should be taken to keep all livestock away from locoweed.

Oxytropis lambertii

Panicum virgatum

Panicum virgatum

SWITCHGRASS, WAND PANIC GRASS
GRASS FAMILY (*POACEAE*)
PERENNIAL BUNCHGRASS
HEIGHT: BLADES 2 FEET; FLOWER STALKS TO 5 FEET
WIDTH: 2 FEET
ZONE 3

CHARACTERISTICS: Coarse-textured, rhizomatous bunchgrass with upright inflorescences to 5 feet tall. Leaf blades are wide, flat, and bright green, becoming a colorful russet or red-orange in fall. Single-seeded florets arranged in airy, open panicles bear plump, round, edible seeds from summer to fall.

NATIVE RANGE: Western Hemisphere

SEASON OF BLOOM: Summer to fall

OUTSTANDING FEATURES: Large, open inflorescences atop 5-foot stalks. Plump, rounded seeds are edible by people, birds, and animals. The entire plant turns a beautiful red-orange color in autumn.

CULTURE

Soil: Any

Exposure: Sun

Water use: Low to moderate

Propagation: Seed, division

Care and maintenance: Very low. Like many prairie species, switchgrass can be rejuvenated by burning.

LANDSCAPE USES: Accent plant, wildflower meadow or tallgrass prairie, mass planting, erosion control, wildlife habitat, container plant

WILDLIFE ATTRACTED: Wind-pollinated; food for birds, butterflies, and mammals

HISTORICAL AND MODERN USES: An important grass of the plains, valued for forage, pasture, and erosion control. Seeds are edible.

For beautiful color contrast, plant switchgrass beside gray-leaved perennials and shrubs with yellow and red fall color such as three-leaf sumac (*Rhus trilobata*) and smooth sumac (*R. glabra*), along with prairie sage (*Artemisia ludoviciana*), Great Basin sagebrush (*A. tridentata*), and fringed sagebrush (*A. frigida*). All switchgrasses bear hard, edible seeds, and most display dramatic yellow fall color. Related species include Scribner's rosette grass (*Dichanthelium oligosanthes* var. *scribnerianum*), a trailing, low-growing, rhizomatous species with airy open seed panicles and culms and leaf blades resembling bamboo, which turn a golden yellow in autumn. Nurseries are producing many horticultural selections and named varieties of switchgrass, and these are quickly coming into use in ornamental plantings. *Panicum virgatum* 'Trailblazer' is a sod-forming native turfgrass with yellow-orange fall and winter color. *P. virgatum* 'Heavy Metal' is an ornamental silver-leaved variety that forms a beautiful mass planting at Red Butte Botanic Garden in Salt Lake City.

Parthenocissus inserta

Parthenocissus inserta
(Parthenocissus quinquefolia)

WESTERN VIRGINIA CREEPER, WESTERN FIVE-LEAVED IVY
GRAPE FAMILY (*VITACEAE*)
DECIDUOUS VINE
HEIGHT: 3–15 FEET
WIDTH: SPREADING, CLAMBERING
ZONE 4

CHARACTERISTICS: Coarse-textured, climbing, sprawling woody vine with thickened nodes; alternate, palmately compound leaves turn a deep crimson with the first autumn cold snap. Small inconspicuous flowers with yellow-green petals in clusters opposite the leaves, followed by bunches of bluish-black berries to a quarter-inch wide.

NATIVE RANGE: Ohio to Wyoming, south to New Mexico and Arizona; often found in riparian areas at elevations of 3,000 to 7,000 feet

SEASON OF BLOOM: Early summer

OUTSTANDING FEATURES: Large, shiny, bright green leaves, clusters of small yellow-green flowers followed by berries that attract birds and other wildlife. Wonderful brilliant red in fall. Will climb masonry and wood without support.

CULTURE

Soil: Moderate moisture; some organic matter

Exposure: Sun to shade

Water use: Moderate

Propagation: Seed, cuttings, division

Care and maintenance: Does best with regular water; not as aggressive as Virginia creeper, its eastern counterpart.

LANDSCAPE USES: Screening, ground cover, softening rocky edges, training on fences or masonry, slope planting for drainages and damp canyons; wildlife habitat and food

WILDLIFE ATTRACTED: Food and cover for birds and small mammals

HISTORICAL AND MODERN USES: Navajo medicinal use; Southern Tewa food and beverage; Jemez pueblo arts and crafts. Pliable vines can be used as natural cordage and as garden ties.

Like most other riparian species, western Virginia creeper is a fast grower and can be used to obtain quick cover and screening wherever ample water is available. Its red fall color is breathtaking. Plant it near gray-leaved perennial sagebrushes (*Artemisia* spp.), red-twig dogwood (*Cornus sericea*), and late-blooming white-flowered perennials like small-flowered white prairie aster (*Symphyotrichum falcatum*) for a lovely late-season color contrast. Canyon grape (*Vitis arizonica*), in the same family, is a sprawling, scrambling woody vine with tendrils, often found in nature festooning entire trees and shrubs and forming huge thickets. Canyon grape offers excellent cover for wildlife, edible fruit for animals, especially birds, and flowers attractive to bees. Its fruit can also be used for jelly, wine, and juice. Male and female flowers of canyon grape are found on separate plants; to ensure fruit production, make sure both are present. Canyon grape has the same cultural needs as western creeper and is often found growing alongside it in moist canyons, drainages, roadsides, and streams; its large, heart-shaped, sandpapery green leaves turn bright yellow in fall. Plant western Virginia creeper in natural drainages with canyon grape and other riparian species like Arizona sycamore (*Platanus wrightii*) or Fremont cottonwood (*Populus fremontii*), wild rose (*Rosa woodsii*), American hop (*Humulus americanus*), willows (*Salix* spp.), golden columbine (*Aquilegia chrysantha*), and cutleaf coneflower (*Rudbeckia laciniata*) for a dreamy, cool, moist haven for people, animals, and butterflies.

Paxistima myrsinites

Paxistima myrsinites
(Paxystima myrsinites, Pachystima myrsinites)

MOUNTAIN LOVER
BITTERSWEET FAMILY (*CELASTRACEAE*)
WOODY PERENNIAL
HEIGHT: 2 FEET
WIDTH: 2 FEET
ZONE 3

CHARACTERISTICS: Fine-textured, bright green, upright evergreen shrub has tiny, bright green, leathery leaflets with toothed margins, to 1 inch long, on thin woody stems. Tiny maroon to reddish-brown flowers, in clusters of two to three in leaf axils in spring, have four petals and four pointed sepals; flowers are followed by tiny green fruits.

NATIVE RANGE: British Columbia south to California, Arizona, and New Mexico; on the Colorado Plateau, in coniferous forests from pinyon–juniper to spruce-fir communities, often in moist shady locations, at elevations of 6,000 to 10,000 feet

SEASON OF BLOOM: Spring

OUTSTANDING FEATURES: One of the few broad-leafed evergreen shrubs native to the Colorado Plateau. Tiny but charming maroon flowers in spring; shiny, pointed, leathery leaves. Tolerates extreme cold and heavy snow load. Stems and leaves can be used as cut greens in floral arrangements.

CULTURE

Soil: Best with some soil organic matter and moisture

Exposure: Sun to shade

Water use: Low to moderate

Propagation: Cuttings

Care and maintenance: Remove injured tips of branches in spring. In sunny, exposed areas, protect from dieback with a winter cover of juniper branches or landscape cloth.

LANDSCAPE USES: Hedge, border or foundation planting, shade garden; can be sheared to create a low formal hedging.

WILDLIFE ATTRACTED: Browsed by deer

This delicate-looking but surprisingly hardy native shrub can be used as a sheared or informal hedge, to create a low wall or barrier, or even trained as a small topiary. It is drought-tolerant within its natural range, but care must be given to provide supplemental water during times of extended winter drought or lack of snow cover. Compatible woody plant species include wild rose (*Rosa woodsii*), littleleaf mockorange (*Philadelphus microphyllus*), and cliff fendlerbush (*Fendlera rupicola*). Mountain lover provides a handsome garden framework or a deep green backdrop that sets off many flower colors. For a rich color contrast, plant it with desert and Bridges' penstemons (*Penstemon pseudospectabilis* and *P. rostriflorus*), sparse-flowered goldenrod (*Solidago sparsiflora*), Richardson's geranium (*Geranium richardsonii*), and Indian pink (*Silene laciniata*). For a neat garden edging, plant a dense row of native violets (*Viola adunca* or *V. canadensis*) in front of a low hedge of mountain lover.

Penstemon barbatus

Penstemon barbatus

SCARLET BUGLER
FIGWORT FAMILY (*SCROPHULARIACEAE*)
HERBACEOUS PERENNIAL
HEIGHT: 1 1/2 –4 FEET
WIDTH: 2 FEET
ZONE 4

CHARACTERISTICS: Low basal mat of dark green, shiny leaves, often tinged with red-violet; upright, open panicles of flowers on tall, often solitary stalks. Many tubular, two-lipped, scarlet flowers to 1 1/2 inches long with a yellow bearded chin and enclosed stamens; flowers nod downwards from slender pedicels in an elongate, loosely flowered panicle atop a tall, upright stalk.

NATIVE RANGE: Utah, Colorado, Arizona, and south into Mexico, at elevations of 4,000 to 10,000 feet

SEASON OF BLOOM: Early summer; repeat bloom late in season

OUTSTANDING FEATURES: Clusters of nodding scarlet flowers with gold beards attract hummingbirds. Striking as a single accent or in a mass planting. Unusual for a penstemon, scarlet bugler tolerates light shade and heavy soils; it is equally at home in sunny, moderately dry gardens. Leaves turn purple with winter chill, contrasting beautifully with snow and ice.

CULTURE

Soil: Any

Exposure: Sun to shade

Water use: Low to moderate

Propagation: Seed, division

Care and maintenance: Cut off spent flowers for repeat bloom later in season. Let seeds of late blooms fall to the ground to naturalize.

LANDSCAPE USES: Hummingbird plant, shade garden, roadside, butterfly garden, rockery

WILDLIFE ATTRACTED: Hummingbirds, butterflies

HISTORICAL AND MODERN USES: Native American medicinal and ceremonial use; Navajo dye plant

Penstemon barbatus

Scarlet bugler is one of the few shade-tolerant penstemons. Its tall stalks of narrow-throated, tubular soft red flowers make it an imposing plant along roadsides or lining paths and driveways. Combine it in the garden with lupines (*Lupinus* spp.), Fendler's meadow rue (*Thalictrum fendleri*), purple geranium (*Geranium caespitosum*), and wild currants and gooseberries (*Ribes* spp.). Scarlet bugler blooms midseason; to extend your garden's season of usefulness to hummingbirds, plant it with the later-blooming scarlet gilia (*Ipomopsis aggregata*), the low-growing many-flowered Bridges' penstemon (*Penstemon rostriflorus*), and the tall, upright, sun-loving Eaton's firecracker (*P. eatonii*) for a continuous show of nectar-laden red flowers.

Penstemon clutei

Penstemon clutei

SUNSET CRATER PENSTEMON
FIGWORT FAMILY (*SCROPHULARIACEAE*)
HERBACEOUS PERENNIAL
HEIGHT: 2 FEET
WIDTH: 2 FEET
ZONE 4

CHARACTERISTICS: Coarse-textured, spreading, open perennial has many upright stems, each topped by an arching panicle of many flowers; leaves are blue-gray, opposite, and toothed. Hot rose-pink tubular flowers to 2 inches long with the throat swollen on one side, a wide mouth displaying white markings and a smooth staminode; the flowers are on 1- to 2-foot, usually leafy, panicles that are often interrupted toward the base.

NATIVE RANGE: A northern Arizona endemic found only in the volcanic, cindery soils of dry pine forests near Sunset Crater National Monument, at about 7,000 feet elevation

SEASON OF BLOOM: Summer, long-blooming; repeat bloom with smaller spikes later in the season

OUTSTANDING FEATURES: Bright rose-pink flowers in tall spikes contrast with blue-gray, many-toothed leaves. A rare plant in nature, but readily available from nursery sources that have cultivated it for years before the passage of rare plant laws. Be sure to obtain plants only from cultivated sources. Very drought-tolerant and sun loving. Naturalizes!

CULTURE

Soil: Any. Will tolerate cindery and heavy clay soils.

Exposure: Full sun

Water use: Very low to low

Propagation: Seed, cuttings; will naturalize freely

Care and maintenance: Low. Cut off spent flower stalks to encourage repeat bloom; remove old, dead stalks in spring.

LANDSCAPE USES: Dry garden, hummingbird garden, naturalizing, wildflower meadow, butterfly garden. Plant with other penstemons and dry-loving native grasses.

WILDLIFE ATTRACTED: Hummingbirds, butterflies, bees

Sunset Crater penstemon is a choice dry-garden plant that naturalizes easily in sunny locations. The color contrast of its bright pink flowers and blue gray leaves is an eye-catcher.

Penstemon clutei

Although Sunset Crater penstemon grows in cindery soils, underneath the cinder is clay, which holds moisture available to plants despite extreme surface drought. If your garden soil is heavy, plant it on a slope to allow for adequate drainage. Leaf form is often an important characteristic to recognize and use in identifying penstemons. Like many other beardtongues, Sunset Crater penstemon has several different leaf forms on the same plant. When it is blooming, its uppermost leaves form ovate discs around the flower stem; moving down the stem, leaves are long-triangular and perfoliate (that is, clasping the stem on both sides so that the stem seems to pass through the leaves); still further down, the leaves are held away from the stems on leaf stalks, or petioles.

Penstemon eatonii

Penstemon eatonii

EATON'S FIRECRACKER
FIGWORT FAMILY (*SCROPHULARIACEAE*)
HERBACEOUS PERENNIAL
HEIGHT: 1 FOOT; FLOWER STALKS TO 3 FEET
WIDTH: 1 FOOT
ZONE 4

CHARACTERISTICS: Coarse-textured perennial forms a low clump of bright green basal leaves with smooth margins, followed by upright flower stems and tall, sometimes arching flower spikes to 3 feet tall. Upper leaves are clasping. Many tubular red flowers to 2 inches long, with a smooth staminode and stamens sometimes extended beyond the corolla; flowers dense, sometimes along one side of tall, upright stalk.

NATIVE RANGE: Southwestern United States; on the Colorado Plateau, at 2,000 to 7,500 feet on slopes, desert mesas, and in sunny, dry habitats

SEASON OF BLOOM: Early summer

OUTSTANDING FEATURES: One of the most dramatic beardtongues, with many-flowered tall spikes of thick, fire-engine-red flowers. Flowers contrast dramatically with shiny, bright green, leathery, pointed leaves. Good cut flower.

CULTURE

Soil: Well-drained; best in warm location

Exposure: Sun to light shade

Water use: Low

Propagation: Seed, cuttings, division

Care and maintenance: Very low. Cut off spent flower stalks for less dramatic second bloom.

LANDSCAPE USES: Dry garden, hummingbird plant, rockery, slope or roadside planting, container plant

WILDLIFE ATTRACTED: Hummingbirds, butterflies

Eaton's firecracker lives up to its name, with screaming red flowers atop enormous stalks. At its best when planted in full sun and reflected heat, it is a good companion to other plants with similar needs. These include scented penstemon (*Penstemon palmeri*), desert penstemon (*P. pseudospectabilis*), beargrass (*Nolina macrocarpa*), white-tufted evening primrose (*Oenothera caespitosa*), banana yucca (*Yucca baccata*), tasselbush (*Brickellia californica*), blackfoot daisy (*Melampodium leucanthum*), desert marigold (*Baileya radiata*), scrub oak (*Quercus turbinella*), Parry's agave (*Agave parryi*), New Mexico needlegrass (*Hesperostipa neomexicana*), common cliffrose (*Purshia stansburiana*), Apache plume (*Fallugia paradoxa*), and other dry-loving native plants. In warm areas, the very late-blooming cardinal penstemon (*P. cardinalis*) can be planted as a complement to Eaton's firecracker. Eaton's firecracker is similar in appearance to scarlet bugler (*P. barbatus*) but has a shorter flower tube. In cooler zones, scarlet bugler may bloom before Eaton's firecracker.

Penstemon eatonii

Penstemon linarioides

Penstemon linarioides

MAT PENSTEMON, TOADFLAX PENSTEMON
FIGWORT FAMILY (*SCROPHULARIACEAE*)
EVERGREEN SHRUB
HEIGHT: 1 FOOT
WIDTH: 3 FEET
ZONE 4

CHARACTERISTICS: Fine-textured mat of narrow gray-green leaves on spreading stems from a woody caudex, covered with many stalks of flowers just above the foliage. Lavender-blue, two-lipped, snapdragon-like flowers to three-quarter-inch long with slightly inflated white throat with yellow hairs, included stamens, and a sparsely to densely bearded staminode; all the flowers face one direction on many narrow flower stalks.

NATIVE RANGE: Colorado, Utah, Nevada, New Mexico, and Arizona, at elevations of 4,000 to 9,000 feet on dry slopes and in openings in woodlands and pine forests

SEASON OF BLOOM: Late spring through summer

OUTSTANDING FEATURES: A mat-forming native perennial with narrow leaves and lavender-blue flowers that bloom from late spring through summer. Makes an excellent drought-tolerant ground cover; attractive to bees and butterflies; generally considered rabbit resistant.

CULTURE

Soil: Will tolerate heavy soils

Exposure: Sun to light shade

Water use: Low to moderate

Propagation: Seed, cuttings

Care and maintenance: Very low

LANDSCAPE USES: Ground cover, rockery, dry garden, hummingbird garden, butterfly garden

WILDLIFE ATTRACTED: Hummingbirds, butterflies, bees

Mat penstemon makes an excellent low ground cover that can tolerate light traffic. For an all-season-long bloom of tubular lavender-purple flowers, plant it with early-blooming comb speedwell (*Veronica pectinata*) and late-blooming sweet scent (*Hedeoma hyssopifolia*), both of which are similar in appearance and habit. Other native penstemon species of similar habit include a different mat penstemon, tufted beardtongue (*P. caespitosus*), a creeping ground cover just 2 inches tall; Front Range penstemon (*P. virens*), another mat-former that bears purple flowers on upright stalks; and Crandall's penstemon (*P. crandallii*), a Colorado native that requires well-drained, coarse-textured soils. James' penstemon (*P. jamesii*) is an excellent companion for background planting with mat penstemon; it has blue-lavender flowers with white bearded staminodes on flower stalks to 2 feet tall, a slightly later blooming season, and a more upright habit.

Penstemon linarioides

Penstemon palmeri

Penstemon palmeri

SCENTED PENSTEMON, PALMER'S PENSTEMON
FIGWORT FAMILY (*SCROPHULARIACEAE*)
HERBACEOUS PERENNIAL
HEIGHT: 3 FEET; FLOWER STALKS TO 5
WIDTH: 2 FEET
ZONE 4

CHARACTERISTICS: Coarse-textured, upright perennial has clasping, grayish green leaves with a waxy blue coating, tooth-edged stem leaves, and tall flower stalks emerging from a basal clump of large, toothed leaves. Inflated, pink, two-lipped flowers with white throats, purple lines, and a showy yellow hairy staminode or beardtongue; flowers 1 ⅛ inches wide by 1 ½ inches long in a tall, narrow cluster.

NATIVE RANGE: Arizona, Utah, and California; at 3,500 to 6,800 feet, on roadsides, dry washes, and slopes and in open, dry locations

SEASON OF BLOOM: Spring to early summer

OUTSTANDING FEATURES: A tall, fragrant, early-bloomer with many large, light pink, snapdragon-like flowers on 4- to 5-foot stalks. Easy to grow; attracts hummingbirds and bees.

CULTURE

Soil: Well-drained, warm

Exposure: Full sun

Water use: Very low to low

Propagation: Seed, cuttings

Care and maintenance: Very low

LANDSCAPE USES: Roadsides, back of border, butterfly garden, hummingbird garden, naturalizing

WILDLIFE ATTRACTED: Hummingbirds, bees, butterflies

Scented penstemon is a sun-loving, giant, upright wildflower, easy to grow from seed or plant, and beautiful to see when its tall stalks of fat flowers are in full bloom. Like most penstemons, it is a rapid colonizer, establishing itself easily on disturbed sites such as road cuts and construction cuts. Scented penstemon blooms early. A later-blooming penstemon for similar microclimates is desert penstemon (*P. pseudospectabilis*), a green-leaved, 3-foot-tall beauty with many narrow, hot-pink flowers. Though shorter in stature, desert penstemon will thrive in conditions similar to those of scented penstemon, and together they will provide a continuous supply of nectar for hummingbirds.

Penstemon pinifolius

Penstemon pinifolius

PINELEAF PENSTEMON
FIGWORT FAMILY (*SCROPHULARIACEAE*)
WOODY PERENNIAL
HEIGHT: 2 FEET
WIDTH: 2 FEET
ZONE 4

CHARACTERISTICS: Upright, fine-textured, woody-stemmed perennial with bright green, narrow, pine-needle-like leaves. Many slender, orange-red, narrow tubular flowers to 1 ¼ inches long, in short panicles at branch ends.

NATIVE RANGE: Arizona, New Mexico, and Mexico, on rocky summits above 5,000 feet

SEASON OF BLOOM: Early summer into fall

OUTSTANDING FEATURES: A nonstop bloomer, heavily covered with a dense array of red-orange flowers throughout most of the summer and into the autumn. Performs well continuously under difficult growing situations and in low-maintenance areas like median strips and parkways.

CULTURE

Soil: Any; best with good drainage

Exposure: Sun to light shade

Water use: Low to moderate

Propagation: Seed, cuttings

Care and maintenance: Very low

LANDSCAPE USES: Hummingbird garden, parking strip or median planting, dry garden, low-maintenance landscape, rockery, container, foundation planting or border alongside paths or steps

WILDLIFE ATTRACTED: Hummingbirds, butterflies

The crowded, narrow, bright green leaves that look like pine needles give this penstemon its name. At the peak of bloom, the top two-thirds of this 2-foot-tall perennial are covered entirely in bright red flowers. While at its best in full sun, pineleaf penstemon will still bloom moderately in filtered light or light shade. In high-elevation gardens, it provides continuous bloom at the tail end of the growing season when many other showy species have gone to seed. Beautiful planted in combination with small-flowered white prairie aster (*Symphyotrichum falcatum*), rabbitbrush (*Chrysothamnus* spp.), and other late-season wildflowers. Named varieties available in the plant trade include 'Mersea Yellow', a yellow-blooming form, and several orange- to pink-flowering varieties.

Penstemon pinifolius

Penstemon pseudospectabilis

Penstemon pseudospectabilis

DESERT PENSTEMON
FIGWORT FAMILY (*SCROPHULARIACEAE*)
HERBACEOUS PERENNIAL
HEIGHT: 2–3 FEET
WIDTH: 2 FEET
ZONE 5

CHARACTERISTICS: Upright, open, medium texture, often multistemmed; blue-green triangular leaves. Hot-pink, tubular, 2-inch flowers in tall, rather open panicles 6 inches to 1 foot long.

NATIVE RANGE: Southwest United States, on open land and slopes at elevations to 7,000 feet

SEASON OF BLOOM: Late spring to midsummer

OUTSTANDING FEATURES: Vibrant, hot-pink, tubular flowers atop blue-green triangular leaves. Though at its best in full sun, will tolerate filtered light or morning sun.

CULTURE

Soil: Well-drained
Exposure: Full sun to partial shade
Water use: Low
Propagation: Seed, cuttings
Care and maintenance: Very low

LANDSCAPE USES: Hummingbird garden, container plant, naturalizing, rockery, slopes
WILDLIFE ATTRACTED: Hummingbirds, butterflies

The vibrant, hot-pink flowers of desert penstemon make it a sure bet for attracting hummingbirds; it grows well with other members of the hot, dry ponderosa pine forest, pinyon–juniper woodland, and desert grassland. Flower color contrasts beautifully with blue-gray and gray foliage of alligator juniper (*Juniperus deppeana*), scented penstemon (*P. palmeri*), Sonoran scrub oak (*Quercus turbinella*), sages (*Salvia* spp.), and sagebrushes (*Artemisia* spp.). An especially striking combination is achieved by planting desert penstemon in front of sand sage (*Artemisia filifolia*).

Penstemon pseudospectabilis

Penstemon rostriflorus

Penstemon rostriflorus
(Penstemon bridgesii)

BRIDGES' PENSTEMON,
BEAKED-FLOWERED BEARDTONGUE
FIGWORT FAMILY (*SCROPHULARIACEAE*)
HERBACEOUS PERENNIAL
HEIGHT: 2 FEET
WIDTH: 2 FEET
ZONE 4

CHARACTERISTICS: Many medium-textured, arching to upright, stems from a branched, woody caudex; leaf blades entire on stems, petioled and narrow; stem leaves are sessile, leaves and stem deep green. Scarlet, tubular flowers with glandular-pubescent calyxes and pedicels.

NATIVE RANGE: Southwestern United States; at 4,500 to 7,500 feet, often in canyons and in forest openings among pinyons and ponderosa pines

SEASON OF BLOOM: Midsummer

OUTSTANDING FEATURES: Nodding, scarlet, beaked flowers at the ends of many slender, upright, dark green stems with narrow green leaves. Will tolerate moderate shade; attractive to hummingbirds.

CULTURE

Soil: Well-drained

Exposure: Full sun to partial shade

Water use: Low to moderate

Propagation: Seed, cuttings

Care and maintenance: Very low

LANDSCAPE USES: Woodland garden, hummingbird garden, butterfly garden, container plant, rockery, slopes, among pinyon–juniper and chaparral plants

WILDLIFE ATTRACTED: Hummingbirds, butterflies; rabbit resistant

Bridges' penstemon will tolerate partial shade and blooms later in the season than does scarlet bugler (*Penstemon barbatus*). It also has narrower, sometimes nearly linear, leaves and a more multistemmed habit, but the two species can sometimes be confused. Scarlet bugler lacks the glandular (sticky) hairs on the calyx and pedicels (flower stalks that support individual flowers and attach to the main flower stalk) that make Bridges' penstemon easily identifiable. Like other woodland species of penstemon, Bridges' is often found in richer,

Penstemon rostriflorus

moister soils with higher organic matter than many of the sun-loving penstemons, but it is also found in dry soils of the pinyon–juniper plant community. Of similar needs and stature, it will grow well with desert penstemon (*Penstemon pseudospectabilis*).

Penstemon strictus

Penstemon strictus

ROCKY MOUNTAIN PENSTEMON
FIGWORT FAMILY (*SCROPHULARIACEAE*)
HERBACEOUS PERENNIAL
HEIGHT: 2 ½ FEET
WIDTH: 2 ½ FEET
ZONE 2

CHARACTERISTICS: Low green leaves form a compact mat of medium texture that spreads with age; upright stems hold blooms along one side. Many tubular, 2 ½ -inch-long, dark purple to brilliant blue-purple flowers in one- to four-flowered cymes attached along one side of 2- to 2 ½ -foot flowering stems.

NATIVE RANGE: Southern Wyoming to Utah, New Mexico, and Arizona at elevations of 6,000 to 10,000 feet; native in many habitats from pinyon-pine to spruce-fir communities, naturalized along roadsides and in disturbed areas.

SEASON OF BLOOM: Early to midsummer, long-blooming

OUTSTANDING FEATURES: Many tall spires of large, dark to brilliant purple-blue, tubular flowers borne above long, narrow, bright green leaves that form a low, attractive mat when the plant is not blooming. One of the easiest penstemons to grow, and very attractive to butterflies and hummingbirds.

CULTURE

Soil: Any

Exposure: Full sun

Water use: Low to moderate

Propagation: Seed, cuttings, division

Care and maintenance: Very low; remove spent blooms for second bloom.

LANDSCAPE USES: Dry garden, wildflower meadow, container plant, slopes, disturbed areas, roadsides, construction sites

WILDLIFE ATTRACTED: Butterflies, hummingbirds, bees

A familiar roadside plant often seeded by state highway departments as a roadside wildflower, this native wildflower puts on one of the most spectacular displays on the Colorado Plateau in late spring and early summer. Unlike some of its relatives from very dry climates that need baking heat and very well drained soils, Rocky Mountain penstemon is not at all fussy, and will grow quickly with regular water and in heavy soils. In dry years, encourage ample bloom by providing several deep waterings in May and early June. It can be easily grown from seed sown with the monsoons or in autumn. Seed does not require a period of cold stratification to germinate and can hold its own in a light stand of weeds. The dense mat of beautiful shiny green leaves can actually contribute to weed control once established. Try sowing Rocky Mountain penstemon with any of the globe mallows (*Sphaeralcea* spp.); they are also aggressive enough to establish in disturbed, somewhat weedy areas.

Penstemon strictus

Penstemon virgatus

Penstemon virgatus

WANDBLOOM PENSTEMON,
UPRIGHT BLUE PENSTEMON
FIGWORT FAMILY (*SCROPHULARIACEAE*)
HERBACEOUS PERENNIAL
HEIGHT: 18 INCHES
WIDTH: 1 FOOT
ZONE 3

CHARACTERISTICS: Fine-textured low mat of narrow, gray-green leaves with narrow, upright flower stalks to 18 inches tall. Tubular, 1- to 2-inch-long, pale violet to purple, two-lipped flowers, with deep purple guidelines and a smooth or sometimes bearded staminode, in one-sided spikes.

NATIVE RANGE: Arizona and New Mexico, from 5,000 to 11,000 feet, mostly in woodlands and mountain meadows

SEASON OF BLOOM: Summer, long-blooming

OUTSTANDING FEATURES: A beautiful and durable component of open meadows and native grasslands. Thrives in low spots and depressions in seasonally dry, heavy soils where it receives a long, cold saturated season, as well as in a variety of other drier and warmer conditions. Attracts hummingbirds and butterflies.

CULTURE

Soil: Will tolerate heavy soils and spring saturation

Exposure: Sun to light shade

Water use: Will tolerate little water or lots

Propagation: Seed, cuttings

Care and maintenance: Very low

LANDSCAPE USES: Naturalizing in open meadows and grasslands, openings in pine forests, wildflower meadow, rock garden, butterfly garden

WILDLIFE ATTRACTED: Butterflies

Wandbloom penstemon is an easy-to-grow penstemon often found in open areas with seasons of long freeze and a short growing season. For this reason it is a good candidate for planting at high elevations and in very cold microclimates. Compatible penstemons include Rydberg's penstemon (*P. rydbergii*), a small mountain penstemon with lavender-pink flowers in tight spherical clusters arranged in whorls around a 1-foot flowering stalk; Bridges' penstemon (*P. rostriflorus*), with many stems of tubular red flowers; scarlet bugler (*P. barbatus*); Rocky Mountain penstemon (*P. strictus*); and Whipple's penstemon (*P. whippleanus*), a low-growing, bright green-leaved beard-tongue with deep burgundy to wine-colored flowers. Other compatible mountain meadow species include Arizona and Idaho fescues (*Festuca arizonica* and *F. idahoensis*), mountain muhly (*Muhlenbergia montana*), pine dropseed (*Blepharoneuron tricholepis*), blue grama (*Bouteloua gracilis*), mountain parsley (*Pseudocymopterus montanus*), cinquefoils (*Potentilla crinita, P. hippiana,* and *P. fruticosa*), and fleabanes (*Erigeron* spp.)

Penstemon virgatus

Penstemon whippleanus

Penstemon whippleanus

WHIPPLE'S PENSTEMON,
WINE CUP PENSTEMON
FIGWORT FAMILY (*SCROPHULARIACEAE*)
HERBACEOUS PERENNIAL
HEIGHT: 2–3 FEET
WIDTH: 2 FEET
ZONE 2

CHARACTERISTICS: Medium-textured cluster of bright green leaves, heart-shaped to rounded. Whorls of nodding deep burgundy to wine-colored tubular flowers on upright stems. Flowers 2 to 3 inches long with a wide throat, conspicuously bearded with long white hairs; staminode extending beyond the wide throat, slender, white, and bearded at the end with a tuft of pale hairs. This odd appendage, which is really a sterile stamen, is what gives many penstemons the common name of "beardtongue."

NATIVE RANGE: Montana to New Mexico and Arizona at elevations of 5,000 to

12,000 feet, in many mountain plant communities and habitats ranging from alpine tundra to meadows and aspen-conifer communities

SEASON OF BLOOM: Early to late summer

OUTSTANDING FEATURES: Rich burgundy-colored, tubular flowers above bright green, rounded to heart-shaped leaves attract butterflies, hummingbirds, and bees. Extremely cold tolerant and will take light shade.

CULTURE

Soil: Any. Will tolerate both heavy soils and loose alpine screes and sands; best with regular summer water.

Exposure: Sun to light shade

Water use: Moderate

Propagation: Seed, cuttings, division

Care and maintenance: Very low

LANDSCAPE USES: Front of the border, rock garden, hummingbird garden, slope planting, container plant

WILDLIFE ATTRACTED: Hummingbirds, butterflies

In addition to burgundy, the flowers of Whipple's penstemon also occur in a variety of less dramatic colors including dusky purple to dull lavender and white. Try to purchase plants of known flower color, or buy them when they are in bloom. The rich wine-colored form is particularly beautiful in combination with yellow and gold flowers. Plant Whipple's penstemon with other members of the mixed-conifer forest including limber pine (*Pinus flexilis*), common juniper (*Juniperus communis* var. *depressa*), goldenrods (*Solidago canadensis, S. sparsiflorus,* and *S. wrightii*), Canada violet (*Viola canadensis*), golden columbine (*Aquilegia chrysantha*), coyote mint (*Monardella odoratissima*), and purple pincushion (*Phacelia sericea*). Because of its compact growth and flowering structure, place it on slopes and at eye level so that the flowers, which tend to angle downward, are most visible.

Penstemon whippleanus

Pericome caudata

Pericome caudata

TAPERLEAF, MOUNTAIN TAIL-LEAF
SUNFLOWER FAMILY (*ASTERACEAE*)
WOODY PERENNIAL
HEIGHT: 3–5 FEET
WIDTH: 3–5 FEET
ZONE 3

CHARACTERISTICS: Medium-textured, bright green, many-stemmed perennial with an upright, arching, widely spreading form. Triangular, opposite, long-petioled leaves look like arrowheads with long tails. Profuse rayless yellow disk flowers to a half-inch wide, in branched clusters 2 inches wide, cover the plant.

NATIVE RANGE: Southwest United States and Mexico; on the Colorado Plateau, at elevations of 6,000 to 9,000 feet in rich soils in coniferous forests from open ponderosa pine forest and with Douglas firs, aspens, and mixed conifers

SEASON OF BLOOM: Late summer and fall

OUTSTANDING FEATURES: Shrubby perennial with arrowhead-shaped leaves whose tips taper to long, drooping tails. Plant is entirely covered with an airy cloud of clustered yellow flowers in late summer, and leaves turn a beautiful yellow in fall. Fast-growing, beautiful as a mass planting.

CULTURE

Soil: Any; does well in rich forest soils or in mineral soil

Exposure: Sun to light shade

Water use: Low to moderate

Propagation: Seed

Care and maintenance: Very low

LANDSCAPE USES: Mass planting, filler, background, slopes, road cuts and disturbed areas, naturalizing, butterfly garden

WILDLIFE ATTRACTED: Butterflies, bees

HISTORICAL AND MODERN USES: Native American medicinal uses; found abundantly in archaeological sites in northern Arizona; root used as a remedy for arthritis.

If you've ever paused at the rest stop on the way down the hill from Flagstaff to Sedona on Highway 89A or driven up Snowbowl Road in Flagstaff and asked what the incredible show of yellow late-season blooms could be, this is the plant you've been wondering about. Taperleaf is a very fast growing perennial, dying back to the ground each winter but reaching a height of 3 to 5 feet and an equal spread by the next summer. After blooming, the plant turns a lovely yellow with fall frosts. Its heavy yellow bloom and fall color make it a wonderful candidate for mass plantings and for use along roadsides and drives. Plant taperleaf with wild rose (*Rosa woodsii*), currants and gooseberries (*Ribes* spp.), tasselflower brickellbush (*Brickellia grandiflora*), and a combination of late-blooming and early-blooming fleabanes (*Erigeron speciosus*, *E. superbus*, and *E. subtrinervis*) for a slope planting of unparalleled beauty and butterfly-attracting bloom.

Pericome caudata

Petrophyton caespitosum

Petrophyton caespitosum
(Spiraea caespitosa, Petrophytum caespitosum)

ROCK MAT, MAT ROCK SPIRAEA
ROSE FAMILY (*ROSACEAE*)
WOODY-BASED PERENNIAL
HEIGHT: 4 INCHES
WIDTH: SPREADING
ZONE 4

CHARACTERISTICS: Fine-textured, low-growing, silky silver-gray mat with dense tufts of simple leaves. Dense spikes of cream-colored flowers with five small petals, five small sepals, and many visible stamens, crowded on 1- to 4-inch upright stems; blooms similar in appearance to tiny spiraea.

NATIVE RANGE: South Dakota and Montana to New Mexico and California, on dry rocky ledges, on gravelly soils, limestone and granitic outcrops, and sandstone hanging gardens at elevations between 3,300 and 9,000 feet

SEASON OF BLOOM: Late summer and autumn

OUTSTANDING FEATURES: Low-growing, silver-leaved perennial forms a dense, tight, silky-leaved mat, with many small, creamy white flowers in dense spikes in late summer. Good rock garden plant.

CULTURE

Soil: Well-drained; prefers alkaline soil and will grow on limestone outcrops

Exposure: Sun to partial shade

Water use: Low to moderate

Propagation: Seed, cuttings, division; plant during monsoon season to ensure adequate moisture for establishment

Care and maintenance: Very low

LANDSCAPE USES: Mat form great for rockery, planting on slopes in well-drained soils, sand gardens, or establishing from seed or plugs in crevice gardens

WILDLIFE ATTRACTED: Butterflies (Spring Azure, *Celastrina ladon*)

HISTORICAL AND MODERN USES: Native American ceremonies

Rock mat can be difficult to establish in the landscape, but once established it is easy to care for and well worth the effort. It needs adequate water to become established but not so much that it will rot. Where it occurs naturally, protect it from changes in hydrology and disturbance. Rock mat transplants poorly from the wild. It is easily grown from seed, cuttings, or division of cultivated plants, which is the preferred means of obtaining it for the home garden. In the rock garden, plant rock mat side by side with native buckwheats (*Eriogonum* spp.) for complementary flower and leaf color, for compatible cultural requirements, and to attract bees and butterflies.

Pleuraphis jamesii

Pleuraphis jamesii (Hilaria jamesii)

GALLETA GRASS, CURLYGRASS, JAMES' GALLETA
GRASS FAMILY (*POACEAE*)
SOD-FORMING GRASS
HEIGHT: 1 ¹/₂ FEET
WIDTH: 2 FEET
ZONE 4

CHARACTERISTICS: Upright flower stalk above firm leaves that arch backward when dry. Medium-coarse texture with gray to straw coloration as season progresses and grass dries. Dense, fuzzy, fan-shaped spikelets arranged in zigzag fashion; spikes borne on erect culms to 2 feet tall. As spikelets fall, a fascinating zigzag stalk is revealed and remains throughout the season.

NATIVE RANGE: Southwestern United States (rare in Oklahoma and Kansas), dry hills, rocky canyons, and sandy plains; on the Colorado Plateau at elevations between 4,500 and 7,000 feet

SEASON OF BLOOM: Summer

OUTSTANDING FEATURES: A beautiful, wiry, sod-forming native grass, galleta grass spreads by runners above and below ground. It bears fuzzy clusters of spikelets in zigzag spikes on tall culms above light gray-green foliage that cures to a light straw yellow. One of the most attractive grasses for planting in dry, windswept areas; highly drought-tolerant.

CULTURE

Soil: Well-drained

Exposure: Full sun

Water use: Very low to moderate

Propagation: Seed, division

Care and maintenance: Very low

LANDSCAPE USES: Dry wildflower meadow, shortgrass prairie, butterfly garden, erosion control, slope planting, land reclamation in dry and windswept areas

WILDLIFE ATTRACTED: Butterflies, insects, large and small mammals

HISTORICAL AND MODERN USES: Traditionally used as a dietary aid and pediatric medicine. Used by some Native Americans in basketry and ceremonies. Excellent forage when green; not palatable when dry. Able to withstand close grazing and trampling.

Given sufficient water, galleta grass will establish easily in well-drained, windswept areas and can help to bind the soil, thus allowing other native plants a chance to become established in difficult situations. It is moderately competitive when planted in weedy areas and can be used to reclaim disturbed, weedy, and overgrazed lands. It has very low water needs once established. Galleta grass can take heavy foot traffic by livestock and people and can be used as an upright, naturalized turf substitute. It does best in warm locations. In zone 4, galleta grass should be planted only within the warmest microclimates and receive lots of reflected sunlight and heat. In cooler portions of zone 4, blue grama (*Bouteloua gracilis*) is a better selection, serving many of the same uses. Galleta grass can be planted as a component of shortgrass prairie and is at its best growing with other dry-loving plants of the plains, pinyon–juniper community, and desert grasslands. Compatible species include buffalo grass (*Buchloe dactyloides*), Indian ricegrass (*Achnatherum hymenoides*), saltbush (*Atriplex* spp.), globe mallows (*Sphaeralcea* spp.), rosemary mint (*Poliomintha incana*), purple sage (*Salvia dorrii* subsp. *dorrii*), prairie zinnia (*Zinnia grandiflora*), and paperflower (*Psilostrophe* spp.)

Poa fendleriana

Poa fendleriana

MUTTONGRASS
GRASS FAMILY (POACEAE)
PERENNIAL BUNCHGRASS
HEIGHT: 1–2 FEET
WIDTH: 1 FOOT
ZONE 2

CHARACTERISTICS: Upright, perennial bunchgrass of medium texture; stiff leaves upright and inrolled, usually in a basal clump. Bright green in its early season, aging to blue-gray with heat and drought. Densely arranged spikelets in an upright open panicle of pale yellow-green florets in spring, aging to straw broadly banded with lavender. Tufts of cobweblike hairs at the base of each spikelet.

NATIVE RANGE: Western United States and plains; on the Colorado Plateau, on well-drained soils in open woodland and forested areas at elevations of 5,000 to 11,000 feet.

SEASON OF BLOOM: Spring to early summer

OUTSTANDING FEATURES: Early-blooming, bright green native bunchgrass with beautiful open panicles of pale yellow-green florets in spring, drying to lavender and straw color with summer drought. Flowers are beautiful in fresh and dried arrangements.

CULTURE

Soil: Seasonally moist (spring melt), with good drainage

Exposure: Sun to shade

Water use: Low to moderate

Propagation: Seed, division

Care and maintenance: Very low. In garden, gently tease away dried foliage when new growth begins in spring.

LANDSCAPE USES: Butterfly and insect habitat, mass planting, spring and fall forage

WILDLIFE ATTRACTED: Butterflies, birds, large and small mammals

HISTORICAL AND MODERN USES: Edible seed used to make flour; fodder for sheep and horses.

This cool-season bunchgrass graces woods and meadows in the spring. Because it actively grows in cool weather, it is excellent for preventing early-season weed invasions in the landscape and can be planted as a replacement for weedy species including orchardgrass, Canada bluegrass, Kentucky bluegrass, and other alien invaders of wild gardens. Muttongrass adds a simple, elegant beauty to curbsides and parking lot planter strips while softening their appearance, and can transform a mulched median strip or make a commercial planter shine. It grows actively with the spring snow melt, and its leaves often dry to a lovely straw color during the dry windy beginning of summer, while its dried flowers impart a lavender cast to the landscape. Seeds drop to the ground to germinate with summer monsoons. The first rains resurrect the leaves, which immediately become green and actively growing again; muttongrass then remains green and productive until winter frosts. It is beautiful when planted in combination with Gambel oak (*Quercus gambelii*), prairie June grass (*Koeleria macrantha*), Arizona fescue (*Festuca arizonica*), and pine dropseed (*Blepharoneuron tricholepis*). In warm canyons, plant with chokecherry (*Prunus virginiana*), Pringle's manzanita (*Arctostaphylos pringeli*), fendlerbrush (*Fendlera rupicola*), and desert penstemon (*Penstemon pseudospectabilis*) for beautiful combinations of flower and texture.

Polemonium foliosissimum

Polemonium foliosissimum

LEAFY JACOB'S LADDER
PHLOX FAMILY (*POLEMONIACEAE*)
HERBACEOUS PERENNIAL
HEIGHT: 3 FEET
WIDTH: 3 FEET
ZONE 2

CHARACTERISTICS: Moderately coarse-textured herbaceous perennial lacks a basal rosette, has loosely upright and very leafy stalks, covered with dark green, alternately arranged, pinnately compound leaves with up to 25 lance-shaped leaflets. Five-petaled, blue to light purple flowers with yellow centers, to 1 inch across, shaped like a shallow bowl, in clusters at the tips of upright branches.

NATIVE RANGE: Colorado Plateau, in moist soil along streams and mountains at elevations of 6,000 to 9,000 feet

SEASON OF BLOOM: Summer

OUTSTANDING FEATURES: Many clear blue, bowl-shaped flowers with yellow centers borne in clusters at the top of leafy stems. Combines well with ferns and other understory plants in shade gardens or northern or eastern garden exposures.

CULTURE

Soil: Best in moist soils with organic matter

Exposure: Shade to filtered light

Water use: Moderate

Propagation: Seed, division

Care and maintenance: Regular summer water

LANDSCAPE USES: Shade garden, back of border, naturalizing on slopes and near water features

WILDLIFE ATTRACTED: Butterflies, bees

Leafy Jacob's ladder provides a lush look to shade gardens and provides pretty blue midsummer bloom. It will do well in gardens receiving regular summer water. It can be planted under aspen, ponderosa pine, Douglas fir, Gambel oak, and blue spruce trees. It grows well in combination with columbines (*Aquilegia* spp.), Fendler's meadow rue (*Thalictrum fendleri*), white-margin pussytoes (*Antennaria marginata*), Arizona and western valerian (*Valeriana arizonica* and *V. occidentalis*), New Mexican raspberry (*Rubus neomexicanus*), and New Mexico locust (*Robinia neomexicana*). A closely related variety, white Jacob's ladder (*Polemonium foliosissimum* var. *alpinum*), is found in Utah and along Oak Creek Canyon in Arizona; it has white flowers and is a robust plant to 4 feet tall. Like those of many members of the phlox family, seeds of leafy Jacob's ladder are mucilaginous when wet.

Polemonium foliosissimum

Polemonium viscosum

Polemonium viscosum

VISCID JACOB'S LADDER, SKY PILOT,
STICKY JACOB'S LADDER
PHLOX FAMILY (*POLEMONIACEAE*)
HERBACEOUS PERENNIAL
HEIGHT: 4 INCHES TO 1 FOOT
WIDTH: 1 FOOT
ZONE 2

CHARACTERISTICS: Many tiny narrow leaflets form crowded fernlike leaves from a branched caudex on this low-growing perennial. All parts of plant are sticky and fragrant. Blue, bell-shaped to funnel-shaped, five-lobed, five-petaled flowers that are longer than wide, in dense cymes.

NATIVE RANGE: Western North America, in spruce-fir and alpine tundra communities, often on talus, at elevations between 9,000 and 12,000 feet

SEASON OF BLOOM: Summer

OUTSTANDING FEATURES: Crowded clusters of bell-shaped, fragrant, bright violet-blue flowers whose petals make a vibrant contrast with the glowing orange anthers; flowers show off beautifully atop finely divided dark green leaves, seeming almost disproportionately large in comparison. Very cold-tolerant.

CULTURE

Soil: Well-drained. Will tolerate coarse, loose soils.

Exposure: Full sun

Water use: Moderate

Propagation: Seed

Care and maintenance: Low

LANDSCAPE USES: Rock garden, slope planting, butterfly garden, container, perennial border

WILDLIFE ATTRACTED: Butterflies and bees

Viscid Jacob's ladder is a striking and hauntingly beautiful plant; once seen in flower, it is not to be forgotten. Like those of many cultivated plants, its flowers seem to almost overpower its delicately divided leaves. The orange anthers contrast strikingly with the blue-purple flowers, and the entire plant is thickly fragrant, emitting a delicious odor under the warming influence of the sun (although some people find the scent strong and disagreeable and call all members of the genus "skunk leaf" or "skunk plant"). A native of alpine and subalpine habitats, it blooms best in full sun and needs good drainage and summer water. It is extremely cold hardy and can be planted in the garden with other plants of high elevations including potentillas (*Potentilla* spp.), bluebells (*Campanula parryi* and *C. rotundifolia*), purple fringe (*Phacelia sericea*), rhodiolas (*Rhodiola* spp.), and sedums (*Sedum* spp.).

Polemonium viscosum

Potentilla hippiana

Potentilla hippiana

WOOLLY CINQUEFOIL, SILVERY CINQUEFOIL
ROSE FAMILY (*ROSACEAE*)
HERBACEOUS PERENNIAL
HEIGHT: 6 INCHES
WIDTH: 2 FEET
ZONE 3

CHARACTERISTICS: Medium-textured, silky, silver-leaved leafy perennial grows close to the ground in early summer and becomes more upright and leafy-stemmed as it flowers. Many yellow, five-petaled flowers, with numerous yellow pistils and 20 yellow stamens, resembling tiny yellow roses, are held in upright open cymes.

NATIVE RANGE: Western North America, in meadows and open coniferous forests

SEASON OF BLOOM: Early summer

OUTSTANDING FEATURES: A delightful small-area ground cover that does especially well in sunny gardens. Yellow, roselike flowers appear in late summer, attracting many butterflies. Leaves that look like fat silver feathers turn wonderful shades of rust, bronze, and purple with fall frosts.

CULTURE

Soil: Will tolerate cold and seasonally saturated soils

Exposure: Sun to light shade

Water use: Low to moderate

Propagation: Seed, division

Care and maintenance: Very low. For best growth, do not overwater or overfertilize.

LANDSCAPE USES: Ground cover, wildflower meadow, butterfly plant, fall color

WILDLIFE ATTRACTED: Butterflies, bees

HISTORICAL AND MODERN USES: Native American medicinal use as a poultice and to make a lotion to treat burns

Woolly cinquefoil can be planted as a small-area ground cover, as part of a mountain meadow, or as a perennial-garden specimen. Plants grown with a lot of supplemental water or nitrogen fertilizer will be more upright, green, leafy, and rangy, so plant woolly cinquefoil in full sun and avoid pampering it. Two other potentillas make good ground covers. Partridge feather (*Potentilla anserina*), a ground-hugging silver-leaved species to 6 inches tall, bears bright yellow flowers above leaves that are bright green above and silvery white beneath; it spreads by conspicuous, red-tinged aboveground runners. Hair-tuft cinquefoil (*P. crinita*), a low-growing, gray-green leaved plant, has wider leaflets that are shallowly toothed at the apex and cheery lemon-yellow flowers; this Four Corners native grows in open pine forests between 6,000 and 8,000 feet and is hardy to zone 4. For a beautiful low-maintenance butterfly meadow in areas with cold soils and short growing seasons, plant woolly cinquefoil and hair-tuft cinquefoil with mountain parsley (*Pseudocymopterus montanus*), yarrow (*Achillea millefolium* var. *occidentalis*), Arizona fescue (*Festuca arizonica*), deergrass (*Muhlenbergia rigens*), mountain muhly (*Muhlenbergia montana*), littleleaf pussytoes (*Antennaria parvifolia*), Geyer's onion (*Allium geyeri*), old man's whiskers (*Geum triflorum*), western blue flag (*Iris missouriensis*), wild strawberry (*Fragaria ovalis*), Fendler's sandwort (*Arenaria fendleri*), and New Mexico vervain (*Verbena macdougalii*).

Potentilla hippiana

Potentilla thurberi

Potentilla thurberi

THURBER'S CINQUEFOIL, SCARLET CINQUEFOIL
ROSE FAMILY (*ROSACEAE*)
HERBACEOUS PERENNIAL
HEIGHT: 2 ½ FEET
WIDTH: 2 FEET
ZONES 4–8

CHARACTERISTICS: Medium-textured perennial with long-petioled, dark green, palmate leaves; forms a rounded, compact mound until time of bloom, when it sends up tall, leafy-stemmed, flowering stalks and develops a slightly more open habit. Many broad-petaled flowers to 1 inch wide, ranging from deep red to salmon-red, in large, showy, loose clusters on 2 ½-foot stalks.

NATIVE RANGE: Arizona, New Mexico, and northern Mexico; on the Colorado Plateau from 5,500 to 9,000 feet, mostly in rich soil of coniferous forests

SEASON OF BLOOM: Midsummer to early autumn; long-blooming

OUTSTANDING FEATURES: Deep red flowers attract bees and make a beautiful contrast in the garden with blue- and white-flowered plants. Long blooming season.

CULTURE

Soil: Moist and rich, with organic matter

Exposure: Sun to shade

Water use: Low to moderate

Propagation: Seed

Care and maintenance: Very low

LANDSCAPE USES: Shade garden, butterfly garden, bee plant

WILDLIFE ATTRACTED: Very attractive to bees

In French, cinquefoil means "five leaves," and this plant's palmately divided leaves have five to seven dark green, finely toothed leaflets. Though Thurber's cinquefoil can be planted in either sun or shade, it will bloom more heavily in sun or filtered light than in dense shade. Its deep red flowers and dark green palmate leaves show beautifully when planted in front of flowering shrubs like Utah serviceberry (*Amelanchier utahensis*), chokecherry (*Prunus virginiana*), blue elderberry (*Sambucus caerulea*), snowberries (*Symphoricarpos* spp.), or mountain spray (*Holodiscus dumosus*); it also makes a handsome companion to blue- and white-flowered native perennials like leafy Jacob's ladder (*Polemonium foliosissimum*), fleabanes (*Erigeron* spp.), and wild strawberry (*Fragaria ovalis*).

Potentilla thurberi

One woody species of potentilla, shrubby cinquefoil (*Potentilla fruticosa*), is native to mountain meadows of the Colorado Plateau. It is a 3- to 4-foot-tall, durable evergreen shrub, frequently used in regional landscapes; it has gray-green, featherlike leaves of three to seven felty, narrow leaflets and is covered with open, inch-wide yellow flowers throughout summer. Choose local ecotypes of shrubby cinquefoil for drought tolerance and best adaptation to local conditions; ensure getting the flower color you want by purchasing plants when in bloom.

Primula parryi

Primula parryi

PARRY'S PRIMROSE
PRIMROSE FAMILY (*PRIMULACEAE*)
HERBACEOUS PERENNIAL
HEIGHT: 15 INCHES
WIDTH: 15 INCHES
ZONE 1

CHARACTERISTICS: Coarse-textured, clumping, stemless perennial with basal, upright, oblong, bright green leaves to 1 foot tall; flowers atop an 18-inch stalk. Bright rose-pink flowers with a golden eye have five spreading lobes to three-quarters of an inch wide, joined into a narrow tube; flowers in an open umbel at the top of a stout stalk held above basal leaves; seed in a capsule.

NATIVE RANGE: Rocky Mountains south into mountains of Arizona and New Mexico, at elevations of 10,000 to 12,000 feet, in moist rock crevices, wet meadows, and along streams

SEASON OF BLOOM: Late summer

OUTSTANDING FEATURES: Many bright magenta-pink flowers above large, fleshy leaves.

CULTURE

Soil: Moist

Exposure: Sun to light shade

Water use: Moderate to high

Propagation: Seed, division

Care and maintenance: Low; be sure to provide ample water.

LANDSCAPE USES: Water features, moist gardens, high-elevation wet meadows

WILDLIFE ATTRACTED: Butterflies, bees

Primula parryi

Named after C. C. Parry, an important early botanical explorer of the West, this native of high-elevation meadows needs a long winter chill and regular water to bloom and grow. If you can provide these conditions in your garden, Parry's primrose will prove a delightful addition; if not, plan to enjoy this spectacular beauty in its native habitat.

Pseudocymopterus montanus, red form

Pseudocymopterus montanus

MOUNTAIN PARSLEY, ALPINE FALSE SPRINGPARSLEY
PARSLEY FAMILY (*APIACEAE*)
HERBACEOUS PERENNIAL
HEIGHT: 2 FEET
WIDTH: 2 FEET
ZONE 2

CHARACTERISTICS: Upright, green-stemmed, fine-textured native perennial from a deep taproot; leaves vary substantially in shape and from pinnately compound to finely dissected. Many, tiny, five-petaled flowers with five sepals, five stamens, and two styles, arranged in showy flat-topped umbels to 3 inches across; yellow and paprika color forms occur. Flowers are followed by winged seeds.

NATIVE RANGE: Rocky Mountains and Colorado Plateau, at elevations of 5,500 to 12,000 feet in moist meadows and dry grasslands

SEASON OF BLOOM: Late spring to autumn; long-blooming

OUTSTANDING FEATURES: Large, showy, flat-topped umbels of many tiny flowers above bright green edible leaves that look like finely divided parsley; flowers may be yellow or paprika to reddish purple, and provide nectar and a perfect perch for butterflies. Flowers can be used in fresh bouquets; dried seed heads can be used in wreaths and dried arrangements.

CULTURE

Soil: Should be wet seasonally in spring and during monsoon season

Exposure: Sun to light shade

Water use: Low to moderate

Propagation: Seed

Care and maintenance: Very low

LANDSCAPE USES: Wildflower meadow, butterfly garden, salad garden, herb garden; companion plant for native grasses in openings in ponderosa pine forest

WILDLIFE ATTRACTED: Butterflies, bees

HISTORICAL AND MODERN USES: Edible stalks and leaves used as a summer green or as flavoring in soups and salads; used in some Navajo ceremonies.

Mountain parsley is a wild beauty, with flower color and leaf forms so variable it is hard to believe that you are looking at plants of the same species. In Flagstaff, yellow-flowering forms often have green parsleylike leaves, while paprika-flowering forms have finely divided gray-green foliage. Plant mountain parsley with native grasses and other wildflowers for a long-blooming butterfly habitat, or give it a place of honor in a sunny salad garden. Members of the parsley family (*Apiaceae*) are often edible, but some, such as poison hemlock (*Conium maculatum*) and water hemlock (*Cicuta douglasii*), are deadly poisonous even in minute quantities and should not even be touched. As with gathering wild mushrooms, it is critical to make sure you know your species before indulging. Other edible members of the family include osha (*Ligusticum porteri*), mountain springparsley (*Cymopterus montanus*), bulbous springparsley (*C. bulbosus*), purple springparsley (*C. purpureus*), wild parsley (*Cymopterus* spp.), wild celery (*C. fendleri*), and sweet cicely (*Osmorhiza depauperata*).

Pseudocymopterus montanus, yellow form

Ratibida columnifera

Ratibida columnifera (Ratibida columnaris)

YELLOW CONEFLOWER, MEXICAN HAT
SUNFLOWER FAMILY (*ASTERACEAE*)
HERBACEOUS PERENNIAL
HEIGHT: 1–3 FEET
WIDTH: 3 FEET
ZONE 4

CHARACTERISTICS: Yellow coneflower and Mexican hat are two color forms of the same species. Medium-textured, upright perennial has an open mound of finely divided green leaves; flowers are borne at the tips of branched stems. Yellow coneflower has a purplish central cone and reflexed petals of yellow, yellow with a brown base, or deep brick-red to mahogany; Mexican hat has drooping brick-red ray petals and red disks.

NATIVE RANGE: Plains states to Canada and Mexico, at elevations of 5,000 to 8,500 feet, on plains and in openings in pine forests

SEASON OF BLOOM: Summer, long-blooming

OUTSTANDING FEATURES: Flower in rich, warm colors up to 3 inches across, on branched stems, top the finely divided, bright green leaves of this easy-to-grow North American wildflower. Choose brick-red Mexican hat or golden yellow coneflower, or plant both. Long and prolific blooms are sure to delight you and the butterflies.

CULTURE

    Soil: Any. Tolerant of heavy clay soils.

    Exposure: Full sun

    Water use: Low to moderate

    Propagation: Seed

    Care and maintenance: Very low

LANDSCAPE USES: Perennial garden, butterfly garden, wildflower meadow, disturbed areas

WILDLIFE ATTRACTED: Butterflies, honeybees

HISTORICAL AND MODERN USES: Many Native American uses, including snakebite remedy and reducing fevers

Ratibida columnifera

These easy-to-grow, heavy-blooming wildflowers are often included as a reliable component of packaged seed mixes for wildflower meadows and butterfly gardens. To achieve pleasing color change over time, plant yellow coneflower and Mexican hat together; each one has a different period of bloom. Great with Wheeler's wallflower (*Erysimum wheeleri*) and western wallflower (*E. capitatum* var. *capitatum*). Both yellow coneflower and Mexican hat tolerate heavy clay soils, but for best growth be sure to loosen heavy soils to a depth of a foot to allow their roots to penetrate deeply.

Rosa woodsii

Rosa woodsii (Rosa arizonica, R. fendleri)

WILD ROSE, WOODS' ROSE, ARIZONA ROSE
ROSE FAMILY (*ROSACEAE*)
WOODY PERENNIAL
HEIGHT: 3–6 FEET
WIDTH: SPREADING
ZONE 2

CHARACTERISTICS: Upright, medium-textured, multistemmed, thicket-forming deciduous shrub. Many delightfully fragrant, large, showy, pink, five-petaled roses with
numerous yellow stamens in summer, followed by glossy red hips that may persist into
winter.

NATIVE RANGE: Western North America, in ponderosa pine forests and along slopes and
streams; on the Colorado Plateau, in many diverse plant communities from
pinyon–juniper to mixed conifer forest.

SEASON OF BLOOM: Summer

OUTSTANDING FEATURES: Intensely fragrant pink flowers in clusters, plentiful rose hips, leaves that color up in fall, plus red stems and branches. Provides excellent cover for wildlife and food for birds and other animals. Bright red hips are edible and often remain on the plant throughout the winter.

CULTURE

Soil: Any

Exposure: Sun to light shade

Water use: Low to moderate

Propagation: Offsets and divisions, seeds, cuttings

Care and maintenance: Very low. Cut back to shape, thin, or shorten; remove dead canes.

LANDSCAPE USES: Barrier plant, wildlife plant, erosion control, screen, fragrance, slopes, riparian areas

WILDLIFE ATTRACTED: Birds, deer, other mammals; provides cover for nesting and roosting

HISTORICAL AND MODERN USES: Hips are high in vitamin C, used in teas, jams, jellies, and wines. Petals are dried for sachets; fresh petals are soaked to make a skin or eye wash, and candied for cake decoration.

Wild roses are easy plants for many uses; because of their thicket-forming habit, they are best in wild or informal gardens. Many prickles make them excellent as barrier plants or natural security fencing. The extensive root system and dense branches perform well for erosion control on slopes. Wild rose establishes easily on disturbed, poor, and rocky soils. Not only the flowers but also the leaves and stems are sweetly fragrant. In cool, moist areas, wild roses work well when planted in combination with aspen trees (*Populus tremuloides*), serviceberry (*Amelanchier utahensis*), red-twig dogwood (*Cornus sericea*), wild currants and goose-berries (*Ribes* spp.) and wild raspberries (*Rubus* spp.). In drier, warmer areas they can be planted with wax currant (*Ribes cereum*), three-leaf sumac (*Rhus trilobata*), pale wolfberry (*Lycium pallida*), and other dry-loving shrubs. Because they form abundant offsets, they multiply rapidly and are easy to divide; an established garden stand may be readily shared with friends and neighbors.

Rosa woodsii

Rudbeckia laciniata

Rudbeckia laciniata

CUTLEAF CONEFLOWER
SUNFLOWER FAMILY (*ASTERACEAE*)
HERBACEOUS PERENNIAL
HEIGHT: 3 FEET; FLOWER STALKS TO 8 FEET
WIDTH: 3 FEET
ZONE 3

CHARACTERISTICS: Coarse-textured mounding perennial has bright green, long-petioled leaves to 1 foot long, cut into narrow pinnate lobes or segments. As the flowering stems emerge, it takes on a more upright, wide columnar form. Large (3- to 4-inch) yellow coneflowers with long, yellow, reflexed ray flowers and cylindrical yellow-green disk flowers, in open clusters at the ends of 6- to 8-foot stalks.

NATIVE RANGE: North America, except the Pacific Southwest; on the Colorado Plateau, in rich soil along streams, in moist meadows, and in seasonally moist depressions at elevations of 5,000 to 9,200 feet.

SEASON OF BLOOM: Summer, long-blooming

OUTSTANDING FEATURES: Flowering stalks of this tall, fast-growing perennial may reach a height of 6 to 8 feet and are crowned with big bunches of large yellow flowers with yellow-green conelike centers. Long-blooming and covered with butterflies the entire bloom season.

CULTURE

Soil: Any; moist

Exposure: Full sun to light shade

Water use: Moderate to high

Propagation: Seed, division

Care and maintenance: Will achieve modest size with moderate water, needs a lot of water to achieve giant size quickly.

LANDSCAPE USES: Background plant, moist meadow, old-fashioned garden with hollyhocks and foxglove, giant garden, riparian garden, butterfly garden, accent plant

WILDLIFE ATTRACTED: Butterflies

HISTORICAL AND MODERN USES: Native American burn dressing and veterinary aid. Culinary plant with edible leaves and stems. Toxic to cattle, sheep, and swine.

A fast-growing perennial with many very large yellow flower heads, cutleaf coneflower will bloom from mid-season until autumn. It makes an impressive focal point in a sunny garden, where it will attract butterflies nonstop for weeks, or in a riparian habitat when planted with bee balm (*Monarda fistulosa* var. *menthaefolia*), alkali pink (*Sidalcea neomexicana*), yellow monkeyflower (*Mimulus guttatus*), cardinal monkeyflower (*M. cardinalis*), and cardinal flower (*Lobelia cardinalis*). It can be grown in combination with plants of moist meadows and streams including rushes (*Juncus* spp.), sedges (*Carex* spp.), purple geranium (*Geranium caespitosum*), Richardson's geranium (*G. richardsonii*), valerians (*Valeriana* spp.), American bistort (*Polygonum bistortoides*), mule's ears (*Wyethia arizonica*), little sunflower (*Helianthella quinquenervis*), water birch (*Betula occidentalis*), red-twig dogwood (*Cornus sericea*), and willows (*Salix* spp.). If you like big, structural plants, this is one for you! It's fun to plant a coneflower "house" for children: Space coneflower plants on four sides of a square about 3 feet apart to build walls, plant giant sunflowers outside the perimeter as corner posts, seed the area inside the house with yarrow or native grasses, and children can enjoy a lush green hideaway filled with butterflies and other natural wonders.

Salvia azurea, center

Salvia azurea

AZURE BLUE SAGE
MINT FAMILY (*LAMIACEAE*)
HERBACEOUS PERENNIAL
HEIGHT: 3 FEET
WIDTH: 2 FEET
ZONE 3

CHARACTERISTICS: Narrow-leaved, fine-textured, gray-green perennial; whorls of two-lipped, tubular, true-blue flowers on tall, upright spikes.

NATIVE RANGE: Central and southeastern United States

SEASON OF BLOOM: Late summer

OUTSTANDING FEATURES: A late-season display of bright blue tubular flowers on tall spikes graces this drought-tolerant, easy-care, perennial herb; attractive to butterflies.

CULTURE

Soil: Warm

Exposure: Full sun

Water use: Very low to low

Propagation: Seed, cuttings

Care and maintenance: A prolific self-seeder; remove unwanted seedlings.

LANDSCAPE USES: Butterfly garden, fragrance garden, dry border

WILDLIFE ATTRACTED: Butterflies, bees

The flowers of azure blue sage make it a special treat for the eye in autumn, when their color mirrors the clear blue skies of the mountains. Azure blue sage becomes floppy with too much water or shade, so save yourself time by siting it properly in the garden. Give it a hot, sunny spot—if you plant in early summer, be mindful of where the sun will be shining later in the season. Azure blue sage is beautiful when accompanied by other late-blooming species including the false goldenasters (*Heterotheca villosa* and *H. villosa* var. *foliosa*), native sunflowers (*Helianthella quinquenervis*, *Helianthus maximilianii*) rabbitbrush (*Chrysothamnus* spp.), groundsels (*Senecio* spp.), Richardson's goldflower (*Hymenoxys richardsonii*), hardy hummingbird trumpets (*Epilobium canum* var. *latifolium*), and globe mallows (*Sphaeralcea* spp.). It will also show off beautifully in the foreground of quaking aspen, western Virginia creeper (*Parthenocissus inserta*), golden currant (*Ribes aureum*), and other native plants with good fall color. All sages are attractive to bees and butterflies; two noteworthy woody Colorado Plateau species are rose sage (*Salvia pachyphylla*), a low-growing fragrant shrub with dense whorls of rose-pink bracted flowers (hardy to zone 5), and purple sage (*S. dorrii* subsp. *dorrii*), a low, rounded shrub with blue-purple flowers (hardy to zone 4).

Salvia azurea

Schizachyrium scoparium

Schizachyrium scoparium

LITTLE BLUESTEM, LITTLE FALSE-BLUESTEM
GRASS FAMILY (*POACEAE*)
PERENNIAL BUNCHGRASS
SIZE: 2–4 FEET
WIDTH: 2 ½ FEET
ZONE 3

CHARACTERISTICS: Upright, erect growth habit with stems and leaves closely bunched, medium texture. Leaves flat and stiff, to three-sixteenths of an inch wide, light green when young, aging to darker green and finally deepening to shades of deep orange, red, and red-violet in fall. Florets arranged in narrow branching inflorescences of wispy, long-awned seed heads. Parts of the inflorescence are covered with many long, woolly hairs that glisten, as do the twisted awns.

NATIVE RANGE: North America except Southeast; on the Colorado Plateau to 7,500 feet

SEASON OF BLOOM: Late summer; attractive seed heads persist throughout fall and early winter

OUTSTANDING FEATURES: Incredibly bright red fall color softens to brick red but remains into winter, along with long-haired inflorescences with fluffy seed heads that reflect the sunlight—two features that make this native bunchgrass a choice selection for dry gardens, slopes, and meadows. Colorful fall foliage and flower stalks are beautiful in dried arrangements.

CULTURE

Soil: Adaptable; great in rocky soils, heavy clays. Must have good drainage.

Exposure: Sun to light shade

Water use: Low to moderate

Propagation: Seed, division

Care and maintenance: Very low. To maintain neatness, tease out dried leaves once new growth begins in spring.

LANDSCAPE USES: Specimen or mass planting, perennial border, rockery, prairie or wildflower meadow, slopes, erosion control, wildlife habitat

WILDLIFE ATTRACTED: Wind-pollinated; visited by butterflies, birds, large and small mammals, insects

This beautiful native grass is a dominant species of the prairie. On the Colorado Plateau, little bluestem is at its best planted in sunny areas, where it is very tolerant of wind and rocky soils. During dry seasons, and in dry years, it will do better with occasional deep water. In cool zones or partial sun, be sure to provide plenty of reflected heat by planting it among rocks or near walls, paths, or stonework. The spectacular beauty of little bluestem shows best at the top of a slope, backlit by afternoon sun. Red fall color dulls as winter deepens, but usually lasts throughout much of the winter and contrasts nicely with snow. It also provides fine color contrast when planted with gray-leaved plants including sagebrush (*Artemisia* spp.), rubber rabbitbrush (*Ericameria nauseosa*), saltbush (*Atriplex* spp.), and winterfat (*Krascheninnikovia lanata*), and can splash color across the landscape when planted among shrubs with strong fall color like the sumacs (*Rhus trilobata* and *R. glabra*). Plant little bluestem with other prairie plants and grasses including Indian ricegrass (*Achnatherum hymenoides*), sand dropseed (*Sporobolus cryptandrus*), native lupines (*Lupinus* spp.), and other prairie legumes. Little bluestem also combines well with other members of the pinyon–juniper and dry ponderosa pine plant associations. Silver beardgrass (*Andropogon saccharoides* var. *torreyana*) has similar characteristics and is hardy in zones 4 through 9.

Senecio flaccidus

Senecio flaccidus var. *flaccidus*
(*Senecio longilobus, S. douglasii* var. *longilobus*)

THREAD-LEAF GROUNDSEL
SUNFLOWER FAMILY (*ASTERACEAE*)
WOODY-BASED PERENNIAL
HEIGHT: 3 FEET
WIDTH: 3 FEET
ZONE 4

CHARACTERISTICS: Dense, upright shrub with leaves finely divided into narrow lobes; all parts of the plant are covered with woolly white hairs. One-inch yellow daisies with woolly bracts in flat-topped clusters, with the outermost flower heads opening first; followed by woolly achenes (one-seeded fruits) with a fluffy pappus (bracts atop the achene).

NATIVE RANGE: Southwestern and central United States, in many habitats from 2,500 to 7,500 feet

SEASON OF BLOOM: Late summer into autumn; may bloom year-round in warm locations

OUTSTANDING FEATURES: This woolly perennial has upright stems covered in thread-like, silvery leaves. Every stem is topped with large, open clusters of yellow daisies from late summer until fall.

CULTURE

Soil: Any; warm

Exposure: Full sun to light shade

Water use: Very low to low

Propagation: Seed, cuttings

Care and maintenance: Very low; can be headed back to encourage dense growth habit.

LANDSCAPE USES: Dry wildflower meadow, dry garden, butterfly garden

WILDLIFE ATTRACTED: Butterflies, bees

HISTORICAL AND MODERN USES: The word "groundsel" means "pus swallower"; groundsels were historically used to treat green wounds and old ulcers, both in Europe and in the New World. Native Americans made arrows from the straight stems.

Thread-leaf groundsel is a beautiful, drought-tolerant, shrublike native plant. It does best in bright sun and warm locations, with minimal water. It is a heavy bloomer from late summer into autumn, its flowers nearly always covered with visiting butterflies. In warmer parts of its range, this groundsel has been observed to bloom every month of the year.

Senecio flaccidus

Senecio multilobatus

Senecio multilobatus
(Packera multilobata)

MANY-HEADED GROUNDSEL
SUNFLOWER FAMILY (*ASTERACEAE*)
HERBACEOUS PERENNIAL
HEIGHT: 2 FEET
WIDTH: 1 FOOT
ZONE 4

CHARACTERISTICS: Low-growing, medium-textured perennial has light gray, felty basal leaves and open clusters of small yellow daisies atop upright stalks. As in all groundsels, the green bracts that enclose the flower head consist of one row of identical, picket fencelike phyllaries of equal height and width.

NATIVE RANGE: Four Corners, Wyoming, and Texas; plains, mesas, canyons, and pine forests at elevations of 5,000 to 7,000 feet

SEASON OF BLOOM: Early summer

OUTSTANDING FEATURES: Low-growing perennial has soft, gray leaves with serrated edges and many small, yellow, daisylike flower heads in early summer that will be covered with butterflies. Once established, it thrives on natural precipitation.

CULTURE

Soil: Any

Exposure: Sun to light shade

Water use: Very low to low

Propagation: Seed

Care and maintenance: Very low; let seed fall to naturalize.

LANDSCAPE USES: Naturalizing, dry meadow, openings between ponderosa pines, dry border, ground-cover garden

WILDLIFE ATTRACTED: Butterflies, bees

HISTORICAL AND MODERN USES: Pueblo Indians made eyedrops from blossoms; Ramah Navajo used cold root extract as a childbirth aid. In times of scarcity, roast seeds were part of survival gruel. Alkaloids contained in many groundsels cause liver damage.

A general note on groundsels: Though humble in name, size, and stature, groundsels contribute a bounty of beauty to the natural garden. Two related species, Wooton's groundsel (*Senecio wootonii*) and mat groundsel (*S. actinella*), are early bloomers. Wooton's groundsel has spatula-shaped, leathery, gray-green basal leaves on a long, tapering, flattened stalk, and a flowering habit nearly identical to that of many-headed groundsel, but blooms earlier in the garden and tolerates more shade. Mat groundsel does best in full sun, where it forms a ground-hugging, dull green mat 2 to 3 feet across, punctuated by large, long-stemmed, solitary flowers. Plant these three groundsels near one another for continuous cheery yellow flowers throughout the early season and plentiful nectar for butterflies and bees. For colder, moister zones, try nodding groundsel (*S. bigelovii*), an upright, green-leaved species with many nodding yellow flowers that occurs naturally in moist soils of coniferous forests and grassy hillsides at elevations of 7,000 to 11,000 feet.

Senecio spartioides

Senecio spartioides

BROOM GROUNDSEL,
BROOMLIKE RAGWORT
SUNFLOWER FAMILY (*ASTERACEAE*)
HERBACEOUS PERENNIAL
HEIGHT: 2 ½ FEET
WIDTH: 3 FEET
ZONE 3

CHARACTERISTICS: Upright, medium-textured plant that is leafy throughout; leaves are linear or divided into long linear lobes. Large clusters of small, yellow, daisylike flowers at tips of branches.

NATIVE RANGE: From California, Nevada, Wyoming, South Dakota, south to Texas, throughout southwestern United States; on the Colorado Plateau, at elevations of 6,500 to 9,000 feet in openings in pine forests.

SEASON OF BLOOM: Late summer to early autumn

OUTSTANDING FEATURES: Many yellow daisy flowers atop broomlike green stems with long, narrow leaves provide a good hit of late-season color. Very drought-tolerant.

CULTURE

Soil: Any; tolerates poorly drained and frigid soils

Exposure: Full sun

Water use: Low

Propagation: Seed, cuttings

Care and maintenance: Very low

LANDSCAPE USES: Dry garden, border, butterfly garden

WILDLIFE ATTRACTED: Butterflies

HISTORICAL AND MODERN USES: Native American dye plant, many traditional medicinal uses. Poisonous to livestock, although they rarely eat it.

Plant broom groundsel in combination with other late-season bloomers including rabbit-brush (*Ericameria* spp. and *Chrysothamnus* spp.), Richardson's goldflower (*Hymenoxys richardsonii*), and showy goldeneye (*Heliomeris multiflora* var. *multiflora*), and with early-blooming groundsels for season-long yellow bloom throughout the landscape. Yellow flowers of broom groundsel contrast warmly with the violet-purple flowers of prairie clover (*Dalea purpurea*). The upright form of these two flowering perennials is mirrored by warm-season grasses including mountain muhly (*Muhlenbergia montana*), pine dropseed (*Blepharoneuron tricholepis*), sand dropseed (*Sporobolus cryptandrus*), and little bluestem (*Schizachyrium scoparium*).

Sidalcea neomexicana

Sidalcea neomexicana

ALKALI PINK, NEW MEXICAN CHECKERBLOOM,
SALT SPRING CHECKERBLOOM
MALLOW FAMILY (*MALVACEAE*)
HERBACEOUS PERENNIAL
HEIGHT: 1–3 FEET
WIDTH: 2 FEET
ZONE 3

CHARACTERISTICS: Medium-textured, leathery perennial; green leaves, rounded teeth on red-edged leaf margins; leaves are of two forms, the upper ones deeply palmately divided, the lower ones lobed. Grows from a deep taproot. Deep-pink to deep purple-pink, five-petaled flowers, with five green sepals and many stamens united to form a center column that surrounds the style, to 1 ½ inches wide, on 1- to 2-foot-tall spikes, followed by a "cheesewheel" that breaks into wedges of round, flat seeds.

NATIVE RANGE: Western United States and Mexico; on the Colorado Plateau, from 5,000 to 9,500 feet, along streams and in wet meadows, seeps, and ephemeral drainages

SEASON OF BLOOM: Early summer, long-blooming; sometimes repeat-blooms with late-season rains

OUTSTANDING FEATURES: Spikes of deep-pink to purple flowers much like hollyhock blossoms rise above red-edged, rounded leaves, attracting butterflies and humming-birds.

CULTURE

Soil: Moist; will tolerate alkaline soils

Exposure: Full sun

Water use: Moderate to high

Propagation: Seed, division

Care and maintenance: Very low; will self-sow given adequate moisture

LANDSCAPE USES: Hummingbird garden, perennial border, butterfly garden, moist meadow

WILDLIFE ATTRACTED: Hummingbirds, butterflies

HISTORICAL AND MODERN USES: Navajos used medicinally. Leaves can be eaten as greens.

Sidalcea neomexicana

This pretty perennial, with its many pink flowers, will grow well in seasonally saturated areas, going dormant throughout dry periods, and will thrive in damp areas with year-round moisture. Plant alkali pink in areas of spring melt, in ephemeral drainages, in ditches by roadsides, and in moist gardens and containers.

Silene laciniata

Silene laciniata

INDIAN PINK, CATCHFLY, MEXICAN CAMPION, CARDINAL CATCHFLY
PINK FAMILY (*CARYOPHYLLACEAE*)
HERBACEOUS PERENNIAL
HEIGHT: 1 FOOT
WIDTH: 1 FOOT
ZONE 3

CHARACTERISTICS: Fine-textured, low-growing, herbaceous perennial with dark green, narrow to relatively broad, lance-shaped, sticky green leaves; plants in Arizona are of a relatively broad-leafed subspecies, *Silene laciniata* subsp. *greggii*. Flowers up to 1 inch across, five-petaled, cardinal-red, the petals deeply notched with several pointed lobes, lightly fragrant, borne on slender upright stems; fruit a capsule of many tiny seeds.

NATIVE RANGE: Southwest United States and Mexico; on the Colorado Plateau, at elevations of 5,500 to 9,000 feet, often in coniferous forests

SEASON OF BLOOM: All summer

OUTSTANDING FEATURES: This relative of carnations and garden pinks has flowers like bright red starbursts with five showy, deeply slashed petals with fringed edges; flowers are attractive to hummingbirds and butterflies.

CULTURE

Soil: Well-drained

Exposure: Sun to light shade

Water use: Low to moderate

Propagation: Seed, cuttings, division

Care and maintenance: Low. Plants get scraggly with age; cut back after bloom to encourage compact growth.

LANDSCAPE USES: Hummingbird plant, perennial garden, shade garden, butterfly garden, front of border, rock garden, openings between ponderosa pines, in oak woodlands, and with other conifers

WILDLIFE ATTRACTED: Hummingbirds, butterflies

HISTORICAL AND MODERN USES: Burn dressing

The deeply spreading roots and rhizomes of Indian pink make it extremely drought-tolerant once established. "Pink," the common name for its family, comes from the petal edges that appear to have been cut by pinking shears. Flowers are borne on narrow, upright sticky stems that trap flies and small insects, giving the plant another common name catchfly. Although its flowers are very showy, its foliage is rather sparse and sprawling; to disguise this tendency, plant it to grow up through other low-growing flowering plants and between compact native grasses including blue grama (*Bouteloua gracilis*) and Idaho fescue (*Festuca idahoensis*). Use it in the foreground with other woodland perennials including scarlet bugler (*Penstemon barbatus*), Bridges' penstemon (*P. rostriflorus*), Aspen fleabane (*Erigeron speciosus*), and desert columbine (*Aquilegia desertorum*).

Silene laciniata

Sisyrinchium demissum

Sisyrinchium demissum

BLUE-EYED GRASS, STIFF BLUE-EYED GRASS
IRIS FAMILY (*IRIDACEAE*)
HERBACEOUS PERENNIAL
HEIGHT: 6 INCHES
WIDTH: CLUMPING
ZONE 3

CHARACTERISTICS: Fine-textured, clumping perennial with dark green, narrow, sword-shaped leaves to 6 inches long. Two or more six-tepaled, blue to deep purple flowers to 1 inch across with a column of three stamens forming a yellow center, on one or more stalks from a single sheath, held just above the flat leaf blades; followed by seeds in a three-chambered capsule.

NATIVE RANGE: Kansas west to Nevada; on the Colorado Plateau, in moist places and along streams at elevations of 5,000 to 10,000 feet

SEASON OF BLOOM: Summer

OUTSTANDING FEATURES: A dainty iris relative whose many six-tepaled, deep-blue flowers, centered with yellow six-pointed stars, peep just above slender, grasslike leaf blades. Self-sows; easy to divide for transplanting.

CULTURE

Soil: Moist

Exposure: Sun

Water use: Moderate to high

Propagation: Seed, division

Care and maintenance: Very low

LANDSCAPE USES: Perennial border, container garden, moist wildflower meadow

WILDLIFE ATTRACTED: Butterflies

Blue-eyed grass is not really a grass, but a member of the iris family. Unlike grass flowers, which lack petals, the six "petals" of blue-eyed grass are actually tepals (petals and sepals that are identical; collectively they are called the perianth). This sweet-looking plant brightens any meadow with its many blue eyes. Flowers open with the morning sun and close with overcast skies or darkness. New flowers appear regularly for a long blooming season. Plant blue-eyed grass with other moist meadow plants and wildflowers; it is particularly lovely paired with yellow monkeyflower (*Mimulus guttatus*). Capsules of blue-eyed grass split and disperse their many small dark seeds to self-sow; plants also increase quickly by offsets, which can easily be separated for transplant.

Sisyrinchium demissum

Solidago canadensis

Solidago canadensis

CANADA GOLDENROD
SUNFLOWER FAMILY (*ASTERACEAE*)
HERBACEOUS PERENNIAL
HEIGHT: 3–4 FEET
WIDTH: SPREADING
ZONE 2

CHARACTERISTICS: Upright, medium-textured, deep green perennial of imposing stature and arching habit; leaves crowded. Many small, yellow, radiate flowers in large, upright panicles to 4 feet tall, followed by showy plumes of white-pappused seeds.

NATIVE RANGE: North America except West Coast states, in moist places

SEASON OF BLOOM: Late summer

OUTSTANDING FEATURES: This tall, leafy perennial is an eye-catcher in the garden, with full spikes of many small yellow flowers in late summer and into autumn.

CULTURE

Soil: Seasonally moist

Exposure: Sun to shade

Water use: Low to moderate

Propagation: Seed, division

Care and maintenance: Very low

LANDSCAPE USES: Perennial garden, shade garden, butterfly garden, tall border

WILDLIFE ATTRACTED: Butterflies, bees, other insects

HISTORICAL AND MODERN USES: Dye plant; fruit and seeds edible

Canada goldenrod is a large plant of imposing stature. It is lovely when planted with other late-flowering plants including azure blue sage (*Salvia azurea*), coral bells (*Heuchera sanguinea*), Missouri evening primrose (*Oenothera macrocarpa*), and purple geranium (*Geranium caespitosum*); and its yellow flowers and dark leaves show beautifully when placed beside plants with purple and red fall color including chokeberry (*Photinia melanocarpa*), three-leaf sumac (*Rhus trilobata*), and western sand cherry (*Prunus primula* var. *besseyi*).

Solidago velutina

Solidago velutina (Solidago sparsiflora)

FEW-FLOWERED GOLDENROD, DESERT GOLDENROD,
THREE-NERVE GOLDENROD
SUNFLOWER FAMILY (*ASTERACEAE*)
HERBACEOUS PERENNIAL
HEIGHT: 2 FEET
WIDTH: SPREADING
ZONE 2

CHARACTERISTICS: Upright, medium-textured perennial has three-veined, rough-textured leaves. Two-foot-tall, one-sided, arching spikes bear many small yellow flowers with five to ten or more yellow rays and yellow disks, followed by many fluffy white seeds.

NATIVE RANGE: Southwest and plains states, in many habitats below 9,000 feet

SEASON OF BLOOM: Late summer to autumn

OUTSTANDING FEATURES: Low-growing, free-blooming, drought-tolerant perennial with arching panicles of many yellow flower heads; attracts butterflies, does well in shade. Beautiful in bloom and in seed.

CULTURE

Soil: Any

Exposure: Sun to shade

Water use: Low to moderate

Propagation: Seed, division

Care and maintenance: Very low

LANDSCAPE USES:

Butterfly garden, shade garden, perennial border, with ponderosa pines, naturalizing

WILDLIFE ATTRACTED: Butterflies, other insects

HISTORICAL AND MODERN USES: Hopi use flowers to produce yellow and gold-toned dyes; other Native Americans and settlers used as medicinal plant; range plant.

Despite its common name, few-flowered goldenrod is a prolific and showy bloomer, with many yellow flower heads on 2-foot stems. It can be distinguished from Canada goldenrod (*Solidago canadensis*) by its sparse short leaves and arching, one-sided inflorescence, as well as by its smaller growth habit. Goldenrods are great butterfly attractors in late summer to spring. Plant it with Thurber's cinquefoil (*Potentilla thurberi*), purple geranium (*Geranium caespitosum*), and Richardson's geranium (*Geranium richardsonii*), for a long-blooming, easy-care, low-growing garden border.

Sphaeralcea coccinea

Sphaeralcea coccinea

COWBOY'S DELIGHT, SCARLET GLOBE MALLOW, COPPER MALLOW
MALLOW FAMILY (*MALVACEAE*)
HERBACEOUS PERENNIAL
HEIGHT: 1 FOOT
WIDTH: 1 FOOT
ZONE 4

CHARACTERISTICS: Low-growing, gray-leaved perennial grows from a taproot, with upright stems; deeply cleft ovate to heart-shaped leaves are covered with tiny star-shaped tufts of hair. Each flower consists of five grenadine- to salmon-colored petals fused around a central pollen-bearing column; like grapes, flowers are borne on short stalks along a common axis, and bloom from the bottom upwards; followed by "cheese-wheels" of compressed, rounded fruits.

NATIVE RANGE: Great Plains to northeastern Arizona; on the Colorado Plateau, at 5,000 to 8,200 feet, in grasslands and pinyon–juniper communities

SEASON OF BLOOM: Summer and autumn

OUTSTANDING FEATURES: Large grenadine-colored blossoms atop pewter-gray foliage on this long-blooming, butterfly-attracting perennial. Easy to establish in hot, dry disturbed areas and needs no care once established.

CULTURE

Soil: Any; establishes easily in disturbed soils

Exposure: Full sun

Water use: Very low to low

Propagation: Seed, division

Care and maintenance: Very low. Water well the first season; once established, very drought-tolerant and freely self-seeding and spreading.

LANDSCAPE USES: Wildflower meadow, dry garden, butterfly garden, roadsides, disturbed areas

WILDLIFE ATTRACTED: Hummingbirds, butterflies, bees, mammals; grazed by sheep and goats

HISTORICAL AND MODERN USES: Native American food, medicinal, and dye plant; its mucilaginous quality led to its use for soothing or protecting mucous membranes, and the Hopi ground its roots into a paste for casting broken bones; it was also used to harden adobe floors. Its seeds were eaten.

Like other globe mallows, cowboy's delight establishes readily in disturbed areas and can become weedy. It is a credible choice for planting in hot, dry, unirrigated areas and combines well with other dry-loving species including Indian ricegrass (*Achnatherum hymenoides*), galleta grass (*Pleuraphis jamesii*), sagebrush (*Artemisia tridentata* and *A. nova*), evening primroses (*Oenothera caespitosa, O. pallida* subsp. *pallida,* and *O. pallida* subsp. *runcinata*), purple sage (*Salvia dorrii* subsp. *dorrii*), prince's plume (*Stanleya pinnata*), and verbenas (*Glandularia bipinnatifida* and *Verbena macdougalii*). It can also be tamed and brought into dry ornamental plantings, where it mixes nicely with other gray-leaved perennials such as fringed sagebrush (*Artemisia frigida*). Its deep orange-red flowers are effectively highlighted by purple-, blue-, and white-flowered drought-tolerant plants including blue veronica (*Veronica incana*) and Wasatch penstemon (*Penstemon cyananthus*). Most Colorado Plateau species of globe mallow are similar in appearance, and all lend themselves to naturalizing and dry gardening. Related species include small-flowered globe mallow (*Sphaeralcea parvifolia*), an extremely abundant plant in north-central and northern Arizona, with whitish or grayish herbage; gray globe mallow (*S. incana*), a tall, nearly shrubby species with numerous wandlike flowers and yellow-green foliage, commonly found in dry open areas; and Fendler's globe mallow (*S. fendleri*), the characteristic species in the ponderosa pine belt and among oaks, found at elevations between 3,000 and 8,000 feet.

Sporobolus airoides with *Lobelia cardinalis* at right and *Mimulis cardinalis* in background

Sporobolus airoides

ALKALI SACATON
GRASS FAMILY (*POACEAE*)
PERENNIAL BUNCHGRASS
HEIGHT: 2–3 FEET; FLOWER STALKS TO 5 FEET
WIDTH: 2 $^1/_2$ FEET
ZONE 4

CHARACTERISTICS: Coarse-textured perennial bunchgrass with arching leaves and an upright inflorescence 3 to 5 feet tall. The airy, open inflorescence consists of one-flowered spikelets borne on an open panicle and is pinkish, turning to straw-colored with age.

NATIVE RANGE: Western North America, Great Plains, and Mexico; on the Colorado Plateau, below 7,500 feet

SEASON OF BLOOM: Late summer

OUTSTANDING FEATURES: Seed heads of this tall native bunchgrass are quite showy, floating in large, open panicles above bluish leaves. Easy to establish from seed; tolerates dry, salty, and alkaline soils.

CULTURE

Soil: Will tolerate salty or alkaline soils

Exposure: Full sun

Water use: Low to moderate

Propagation: Seed

Care and maintenance: Very low

LANDSCAPE USES: Dry meadow or tallgrass prairie, container garden, specimen or mass planting, erosion control, land reclamation

WILDLIFE ATTRACTED: Wildlife habitat; birds and small mammals eat the seeds and use the clumps for cover.

HISTORICAL AND MODERN USES: Edible grain, forage, reclamation of disturbed or overgrazed lands

Alkali sacaton is one of the dropseeds, an interesting and useful group of grasses that have provided food for humans and animals across the ages. They require almost no maintenance and offer great beauty and durability as ornamentals. All are drought-tolerant, warm-season grasses. Alkali sacaton has light, airy seed heads borne well above bluish foliage; plants age to the color of golden straw. A naturally occurring variety, giant sacaton (*Sporobolus airoides* var. *wrightii*), is a larger grass with flowering spikelets borne in enormous upright panicles on stalks 6 feet tall. In late summer this entire inflorescence turns golden yellow, offering a vibrant color contrast to the basal clump of arching green leaves. Both alkali sacaton and giant sacaton can be planted in place of the many invasive non-native grasses currently recommended for ornamental use; these include maidenhair grass (*Miscanthus sinensis*), fountain grass, and pampas grasses. The sacatons are also useful in the reclamation of areas previously planted with South African lovegrasses (*Eragrostis curvula* and *E. lehmanniana*). Sand dropseed (*Sporobolus cryptandrus*), another ornamental species, grows best in sandy soils and provides the practical benefit of stabilizing blowing sands. Black dropseed (*S. interruptus*) is a sod-forming, low-growing northern Arizona endemic that shows great promise as a cold-hardy native turfgrass.

Stanleya pinnata

Stanleya pinnata

PRINCE'S PLUME, DESERT PLUME
MUSTARD FAMILY (*BRASSICACEAE*)
WOODY PERENNIAL
HEIGHT: 3—6 FEET
WIDTH: 3 FEET
ZONE 4

CHARACTERISTICS: Upright, coarse-textured, woody-based perennial. Entire plant a pale grayish green, with narrow leaves, to 7 inches long at base, shorter on upper stem; many are pinnately divided and look like shiny gray feathers. Four-petaled yellow flowers have conspicuous long stamens and pistils, to 1 ¼ inches, in a dense terminal raceme to 2 feet long, blooming first at base and progressing up spike, ripening from bottom up into slender, 2-inch-long, two-celled drooping seed pods.

NATIVE RANGE: Central and western North America; dry plains, mesas, stony slopes, and sagebrush areas at elevations between 2,500 and 8,000 feet

SEASON OF BLOOM: Spring to summer

OUTSTANDING FEATURES: A handsome, regal, gray-leaved plant that loves sun and heat, with long sprays of feathery, fringed-looking yellow flowers resembling cleomes or spiderflowers, on very tall stalks.

CULTURE

Soil: Well-drained

Exposure: Full sun

Water use: Very low

Propagation: Seed

Care and maintenance: Very low

LANDSCAPE USES: Accent plant, dry garden, slope planting, back of dry border

WILDLIFE ATTRACTED: Bees and butterflies

HISTORICAL AND MODERN USES: Native Americans used seeds for mush and plant as a potherb after boiling and discarding the first water. Natural occurrence indicates selenium in soils; toxic to livestock.

Plant prince's plume in hot, dry places with shrubs, grasses, cacti, succulents, and wildflowers of the high desert, chaparral, or pinyon–juniper. Suitable companions include manzanitas (*Arctostaphylos pungens* and *A. pringlei*), Parry's agave (*Agave parryi*), yuccas (*Yucca* spp.), beargrass (*Nolina macrocarpa*), blazingstars (*Mentzelia* spp.), dropseeds (*Sporobolus cryptandrus* and *S. airoides*), needlegrasses (*Hesperostipa comata* and *H. neomexicana*), sagebrush (*Artemisia tridentata*), and dry-loving tall penstemons like Eaton's firecracker (*Penstemon eatonii*) and scented penstemon (*P. palmeri*).

Symphyotrichum falcatum

Symphyotrichum falcatum
(Aster falcatus, A. commutatus,
Virgulus falcatus)

WHITE PRAIRIE ASTER, WHITE PRAIRIE DAISY, FALL WHITE ASTER
SUNFLOWER FAMILY (*ASTERACEAE*)
HERBACEOUS PERENNIAL
HEIGHT: 2 FEET
WIDTH: 2 FEET
ZONE 4

CHARACTERISTICS: Fine-textured, upright perennial with hairy stems and grayish green narrow leaves to a quarter-inch long growing all along stems. Many small white daisies with yellow centers, to a half-inch wide, cover the branches.

NATIVE RANGE: Western and Central North America, in many habitats

SEASON OF BLOOM: Late summer into autumn; long-blooming

OUTSTANDING FEATURES: A profusion of small, white, daisylike flowers with yellow centers and narrow petals entirely cover the branches of this shrubby, late-season wildflower. Great for a wildflower meadow.

CULTURE

Soil: Well-drained

Exposure: Sun to light shade

Water use: Low to moderate

Propagation: Seed

Care and maintenance: Very low

LANDSCAPE USES: Wildflower meadow, understory plant, butterfly garden, white-flower garden, mass plantings including roadsides and road cuts

WILDLIFE ATTRACTED: Butterflies

HISTORICAL AND MODERN USES: Absorbs selenium from the soil and may be toxic to wildlife.

Entirely covered with small white flowers, white prairie aster brightens up a dark spot when planted in partial shade under ponderosa pines, Gambel oaks, Douglas fir, and aspens. Under aspens, plant with columbine (*Aquilegia* spp.), bluebells (*Campanula rotundifolia* and *C. parryi*), leafy-bract aster (*Symphyotrichum foliaceum* var. *canbyi*), and native grasses including Arizona fescue (*Festuca arizonica*), pine dropseed (*Blepharoneuron tricolepis*), and mountain muhly (*Muhlenbergia montana*). When planted in full sun with hoary tansyaster (*Machaeranthera canescens*), rabbitbrush (*Chrysothamnus* spp.), Richardson's gold-flower (*Hymenoxys richardsonii*), and showy goldeneye (*Heliomeris multiflora* var. *multiflora*), white prairie aster adds to a long-blooming, butterfly-attracting wildflower meadow during late season. To provide cover and seed for birds and wildlife, add plenty of native grasses as filler in any wildflower meadow. A related species, leafy-bract aster (*Symphyotrichum foliaceum* var. *canbyi*), is a low-growing perennial with bright green leaves and pale purple flowers; its name comes from the many reflexed leafy bracts that surround the flower head.

Symphyotrichum falcatum

Thalictrum fendleri

Thalictrum fendleri

FENDLER'S MEADOW RUE, MOUNTAIN MEADOW RUE
BUTTERCUP FAMILY (*RANUNCULACEAE*)
HERBACEOUS PERENNIAL
HEIGHT: 1—3 FEET
WIDTH: 2 FEET
ZONE 3

CHARACTERISTICS: Fine- to medium-textured, fernlike perennial has delicate, stalked compound leaves divided several times into leaflets that are wider than long, forming a compact plant before bloom and elongating when flowers form. Male and female flowers borne on separate plants; flowers lack petals; male flowers have many golden stamens dangling from threadlike stalks, female flowers are tiny, rounded clusters.

NATIVE RANGE: Western United States and Mexico; on the Colorado Plateau, in pine and spruce-fir forests at elevations of 5,000 to 9,500 feet

SEASON OF BLOOM: Summer

OUTSTANDING FEATURES: Mountain meadow rue is a columbine relative grown primarily as a drought-tolerant foliage plant that resembles and can take the place of maidenhair fern in dry, shady gardens. In bloom, the tiny tasseled male flowers are a delight. Foliage is useful in cut flower bouquets.

CULTURE

Soil: Any

Exposure: Shade to sun

Water use: Low to moderate

Propagation: Seed

Care and maintenance: Very low; to maintain a compact, maidenhair fern–like habit, remove flowering stalks as they begin to elongate.

LANDSCAPE USES: Shade garden, maidenhair fern substitute, filler

WILDLIFE ATTRACTED: Wind-pollinated

Fendler's meadow rue grows well without supplemental water within the range of its natural habitats. In sun, plants will need more water than those in shade; too much water makes plants look coarse-textured and ungainly. Use mountain meadow rue as a background plant or filler in low-water gardens. In warmer places, it is an excellent choice for planting under native oaks that may be killed by fungus if understory plants receive irrigation. Other native plants that will do well in dry shade include snowberry (*Symphoricarpos rotundifolius* var. *parishii*), desert columbine (*Aquilegia desertorum*), and creeping barberry (*Mahonia repens*).

Thalictrum fendleri

Thermopsis pinetorum

Thermopsis montana
(T. rhombifolia var. montana, T. pinetorum)

BIG GOLDEN PEA, MOUNTAIN GOLDEN BANNER
PEA FAMILY (*FABACEAE*)
RHIZOMATOUS PERENNIAL
HEIGHT: 3 FEET
WIDTH: SPREADING
ZONE 3

CHARACTERISTICS: Upright, coarse-textured perennial has dark green compound leaves with three broad leaflets to 4 inches long; spreads underground by rhizomes to form large clumps that follow zones of soil moisture. Many 1-inch yellow pea flowers in upright terminal clusters at the ends of stems, followed by 4-inch-long, pealike pods.

NATIVE RANGE: Western North America, in meadows and clearings in pine forests at elevations of 6,000 to 9,500 feet

SEASON OF BLOOM: Spring

OUTSTANDING FEATURES: A lupinelike plant valuable for its early bloom of bright yellow pea flowers in large clusters at the tops of leafy, rich, dark green stems.

CULTURE

Soil: Moist

Exposure: Sun to shade

Water use: Low to moderate

Propagation: Seed, division

Care and maintenance: Very low

LANDSCAPE USES: Mass planting, butterfly planting

WILDLIFE ATTRACTED: Butterflies, including those in the gossamer wing family

HISTORICAL AND MODERN USES: Native American medicinal use

Plant big golden pea in a moist depression near an upland mass of silvery lupine (*Lupinus argenteus*), false indigo (*Amorpha fruticosa*), and New Mexico locust (*Robinia neomexicana*) for a long display of pea flowers and a contrast of dark green foliage of the golden banner with the silvery leaves of the lupine. Its bloom will be longer lasting in shade and with protection from drying spring winds. Although big golden pea resembles lupines, it has three leaflets, whereas lupines have four or more leaflets. Big golden pea is a robust rhizomatous perennial; be sure to plant it away from irrigated gardens because it will spread prolifically in moist areas.

Thlaspi montanum var. *fendleri*

Thlaspi montanum var. *fendleri* (*Thlaspi fendleri, T. alpestri*)

WILD CANDYTUFT, FENDLER'S PENNYCRESS
MUSTARD FAMILY (*BRASSICACEAE*)
HERBACEOUS PERENNIAL
HEIGHT: 3–6 INCHES
WIDTH: 4–6 INCHES
ZONE 2

CHARACTERISTICS: Small, fine-textured mound of petioled basal, dark green, oval leaves with smooth edges to a quarter-inch long; smaller, arrow-shaped, alternate leaves clasp the flower stem. Many four-petaled, white flowers with tiny yellow centers, to three-eighths of an inch, in terminal clusters, may be tinged with pink or lavender. Flowers are followed by a persistent wedge-shaped or rounded seed pod with a characteristic notch at its apex.

NATIVE RANGE: Western North America; on the Colorado Plateau, at elevations of 4,000 to 12,000 feet, mostly in coniferous forests

SEASON OF BLOOM: Spring; occasional repeat bloom with summer monsoons

OUTSTANDING FEATURES: Clusters of many four-petaled white flowers above deep green, shiny leaves cover this earliest blooming, diminutive spring ephemeral. After it blooms, its wedge-shaped shieldlike fruits persist into the summer; leaves often disappear until the next spring. Dried seed pods can be used in arrangements.

CULTURE

Soil: Any; will tolerate spring moisture and summer drought

Exposure: Sun to shade

Water use: Moderate

Propagation: Seed, division

Care and maintenance: Very low

LANDSCAPE USES: Rock garden, butterfly garden

WILDLIFE ATTRACTED: Butterflies

Among the pine forests, you know it's springtime when the wild candytuft blooms! Plant it with other early bloomers, such as crocus, Siberian squill, snowdrops, Arizona or western valerian (*Valeriana arizonica* and *V. occidentalis*), pasque flower (*Anemone multifida*), thimble flower (*Anemone cylindrica*), MacDougal's bluebells (*Mertensia macdougalii*), Oregon buttercups (*Ranunculus oreogenes*), western spring beauty (*Claytonia rosea*), Woodhouse's phlox (*Phlox woodhousei*), muttongrass (*Poa fendleriana*), creeping barberry

Thlaspi montanum var. *fendleri*

(*Mahonia repens*), bladderpods (*Lesquerella arizonica* and *L. intermedia*), Nevada bitterroot (*Lewisia nevadensis*), and dwarf lewisia (*L. pygmaea*) for hard-to-find early bloom. Wild candytuft often is found in depressions that collect snow melt or nestled in the protection of rocks that provide warmth, moisture, and protection from extremes of spring weather. It needs spring moisture to get started, but can tolerate dry periods by going dormant. Take advantage of these seasonally moist microsites in your garden to plant a host of spring ephemerals.

Townsendia exscapa

Townsendia exscapa

STEMLESS TOWNSEND DAISY
SUNFLOWER FAMILY (*ASTERACEAE*)
HERBACEOUS PERENNIAL
HEIGHT: 2 INCHES
WIDTH: 6 INCHES
ZONE 3

CHARACTERISTICS: Low, cushionlike rosette of hoary, grayish green, narrow, linear to spatula-shaped leaves with a prominent midrib, to 2 inches long. Stemless, white to light pink, 2-inch daisies with yellow centers and spreading, folded rays, nestled singly or in clusters in center of leaves.

NATIVE RANGE: Central and Western North America, on open slopes, hillsides and mesas, and in meadows and clearings in coniferous forests and oak woodlands between 4,500 and 10,000 feet

SEASON OF BLOOM: Spring

OUTSTANDING FEATURES: A delightful spring bloomer that bears large, white to light pink, yellow-centered daisies nestled among its low gray-green leaves.

CULTURE

Soil: Well-drained

Exposure: Sun

Water use: Low to moderate

Propagation: Seed, division

Care and maintenance: Very low

LANDSCAPE USES: Rock garden, dry wildflower meadow with grasses, butterfly garden

WILDLIFE ATTRACTED: Butterflies

HISTORICAL AND MODERN USES: Native American use as gynecological aid; range plant

It's always a surprise to come upon stemless Townsend daisy, growing so close to the ground that you almost have to step on it to notice it. In the native landscape, it can be grown along with native dandelions (*Agoseris* spp.) to provide early nectar to butterflies and bees. Plant it in rocky areas that hold spring snow melt for an unusual and most delightful spring show. Two companion plants with similar bloom period are old man (*Hymenoxys bigelovii*) and Woodhouse's phlox (*Phlox woodhousei*). Interspersing stemless daisy among littleleaf pussytoes (*Antennaria rosulata*) creates another intriguing plant combination. Other species of Townsendia, including silvery townsendia (*T. incana*), Easter daisy (*T. eximia*), and mountain townsendia (*T. montana*), have pink to lavender flowers; all are worthy of a trial in a dry or rocky butterfly garden.

Tradescantia occidentalis

Tradescantia occidentalis

WESTERN SPIDERWORT, PRAIRIE SPIDERWORT
SPIDERWORT FAMILY (*COMMELINACEAE*)
HERBACEOUS PERENNIAL
HEIGHT: 1–2 FEET
WIDTH: 1 FEET
ZONE 4

CHARACTERISTICS: Medium-textured, grasslike perennial has drooping, bluish-green, narrow, folded leaves, to 12 inches long, that clasp stems with sheathing bases and stick out at awkward angles. Violet-pink to purple-blue color forms; flowers, with three equal-sized petals, six yellow stamens, and hairy filaments, are borne in umbellate clusters at stem tips; each flower lasts for one day.

NATIVE RANGE: Central and southwest United States; on the Colorado Plateau, on slopes and in sandy soils at elevations to 7,000 feet

SEASON OF BLOOM: Early summer to midsummer

OUTSTANDING FEATURES: Drought-tolerant perennial has violet-pink to purple-blue flowers in terminal clusters. Flowers last only a day and are best seen in the early morning, but the plant produces blooms continuously through the season.

CULTURE

Soil: Best in well-drained or sandy soil

Exposure: Sun to light shade

Water use: Low to moderate

Propagation: Easy to grow from seed (sown in spring) or cuttings (in summer)

Care and maintenance: Let leaves die back to ground after bloom. Will self-sow.

LANDSCAPE USES: Slope planting, mixed planting with other native perennials

WILDLIFE ATTRACTED: Bees

HISTORICAL AND MODERN USES: Used by Native Americans as a potherb.

The hairy filaments on the flowers of western spiderwort are said to be the reason for its common name. It can grow in full sun, but it also does well in partial shade, filtered light, or part-day sun. Plant in sandy soils or on a slope, with butterfly milkweed (*Asclepias tuberosa*), bee balm (*Monarda fistulosa* var. *menthaefolia*), Arizona thistle (*Cirsium arizonicum*), bracken (*Pteridium aquilinum*), ageratina (*Eupatorium herbaceum*), tassel-flower brickellbush (*Brickellia grandiflora*), California brickellbush (*B. californica*), taper-leaf (*Pericome caudata*), and Fendler's meadow rue (*Thalictrum fendleri*) for a beautiful, natural-looking butterfly habitat. A closely related species found among pines of Arizona and New Mexico is pinewoods spiderwort (*Tradescantia pinetorum*); it has smaller flowers and tubers on the roots, which were used by Native Americans for food.

Tradescantia occidentalis

Valeriana arizonica

Valeriana arizonica

ARIZONA VALERIAN
VALERIAN FAMILY (*VALERIANACEAE*)
HERBACEOUS PERENNIAL
HEIGHT: 14 INCHES
WIDTH: 14 INCHES
ZONE 4

CHARACTERISTICS: Low-growing, medium-textured perennial grows from slender rhizomes, has smooth, bright green, broadly elliptic leaves, mostly in a basal rosette; stem leaves are opposite, clasping, arrow shaped, sometimes pinnately lobed. Lavender-pink, five-lobed, tubular-funnel form flowers borne just above leaves in rounded clusters; clusters spread and open to 2 inches wide as they mature; white stamens and anthers of flowers extend beyond lobes.

NATIVE RANGE: Colorado, Utah, and Arizona, at elevations of 4,500 to 8,000 feet, mostly in moist soil of coniferous forests in pinyon–juniper and ponderosa pine communities

SEASON OF BLOOM: Spring through early summer

OUTSTANDING FEATURES: Blooms very early, often when snow is still on the ground, with clusters of many small, pink, tubelike flowers in a low, bright green mat.

CULTURE

Soil: Moist

Exposure: Full sun to light shade

Water use: Moderate

Propagation: Seed, division

Care and maintenance: Divide to increase

LANDSCAPE USES: Mountain meadow, shade garden

WILDLIFE ATTRACTED: Butterflies

HISTORICAL AND MODERN USES: As sedative. Taproot cooked and eaten by aboriginal Native Americans; it is said to be foul-tasting and poisonous unless cooked, and pressed specimens are described by Stanley L. Welsh in *A Utah Flora* (1993) as smelling "not unlike a wet bed or an old foot locker."

Calyx lobes of the valerians are modified into plumose bristles that "unroll as the seeds ripen and act as parachutes to aid their dispersal," according to botanist Ruth Ashton Nelson. Valerians do well in moist, shady gardens and go well with fleabanes (*Erigeron* spp.), columbines (*Aquilegia* spp.), geranium-leaf larkspur (*Delphinium geraniifolium*), pussytoes (*Antennaria* spp.), and Indian pinks (*Silene laciniata*). Western valerian (*Valeriana occidentalis*) is an early bloomer, very similar to Arizona valerian but with smaller flowers and more pronounced pinnate lobing of the leaves. Tall, or edible, valerian (*V. edulis*) is an upright plant to 4 feet tall with a thick taproot; it grows from a woody caudex, with basal leaves and a tall stalk with small white flowers in a very open, branched inflorescence in summer.

Verbena macdougalii

Verbena macdougalii

NEW MEXICO VERVAIN
VERBENA FAMILY (*VERBENACEAE*)
HERBACEOUS PERENNIAL
HEIGHT: 3 FEET
WIDTH: 2 FEET
ZONE 3

CHARACTERISTICS: Upright, medium-textured perennial has gray-green, lance-shaped, irregularly toothed, opposite leaves to 4 inches long, and hairy square stems. Lavender to purple, five-lobed flowers with three lobes bent downward, two lobes bent upward, to a quarter-inch wide, on erect, candelabra-like panicled spikes; flowers open first at bottom of spike and progress upwards; dry fruit separates into four nutlets.

NATIVE RANGE: Wyoming to southwest United States; on the Colorado Plateau, at elevations between 5,000 and 8,000 feet, often in pine forests, in open flats, and along roadsides

SEASON OF BLOOM: Late summer

OUTSTANDING FEATURES: Many purple flowers in distinctive candelabra-like arrangement in late summer. Drought- and cold-tolerant; naturalizes easily; attractive to butterflies.

CULTURE

Soil: Any

Exposure: Sun

Water use: Low to moderate

Propagation: Seed

Care and maintenance: Very low. In drought years a few deep waterings will promote plant vigor and growth, plant will be stunted with extreme drought.

LANDSCAPE USES: Wildflower meadow, butterfly garden, naturalizing, dry garden, roadsides and disturbed areas

WILDLIFE ATTRACTED: Butterflies, bees

HISTORICAL AND MODERN USES: Native American medicinal and ceremonial uses. Aerial parts used as a sedative or nervine tea to soothe teething babies.

Verbena macdougalii

Distinctive New Mexico vervain is easy to identify because of its upright form, candelabra-like erect panicles of many five-lobed flowers, square stems, and opposite leaves. It needs very little care and naturalizes easily. Water New Mexico vervain regularly to establish it in disturbed sites such as road and construction cuts. Plant with silvery lupine (*Lupinus argenteus*), western sneezeweed (*Hymenoxys hoopesii*), geranium-leaf larkspur (*Delphinium geraniifolium*), showy goldeneye (*Heliomeris multiflora* var. *multiflora*), Arizona fescue (*Festuca arizonica*), and other wildflowers of the open ponderosa pine forest to create an easy-to-establish flower meadow.

Viola canadensis

Viola canadensis

CANADA VIOLET, CANADIAN WHITE VIOLET
VIOLET FAMILY (*VIOLACEAE*)
HERBACEOUS PERENNIAL
HEIGHT: 6 INCHES TO 1 FOOT
WIDTH: 1 FOOT
ZONE 3

CHARACTERISTICS: Clumping, medium-textured, bright green perennial with heart-shaped leaves with toothed margins, to 3 inches long; flowers grow from the axils of upper leaves. Many white flowers with yellow throats and purple veins, to three-quarters of an inch wide, growing from axils of upper leaves; flowers irregular with five petals, four arranged in pairs, the lower petal larger and spurred; fruit a three-celled, many-seeded capsule.

NATIVE RANGE: North America; on the Colorado Plateau, at elevations between 5,400 and 11,500 feet, mostly in rich moist soil in coniferous forests

SEASON OF BLOOM: Early summer, repeat bloom with monsoons

OUTSTANDING FEATURES: Many charming white flowers above heart-shaped leaves on this early-blooming, shade-loving native perennial. Flowers are edible.

CULTURE

Soil: Moist, will grow in soils with organic matter or in lean, loose soils

Exposure: Shade to sun

Water use: Moderate to high

Propagation: Seed, division; will naturalize

Care and maintenance: Very low; protect from slugs and deer

LANDSCAPE USES: Shade garden, perennial border, mass planting, naturalizing under trees, container plant, butterfly plant

WILDLIFE ATTRACTED: Butterflies; deer like to eat flowers

HISTORICAL AND MODERN USES: Flowers are edible.

Feature Canada violet in a low garden border or in a mass planting where its bright green leaves and sweet white flowers can be easily seen. Like many other violets, Canada violet does best in moist locations. Western dog violet (*Viola adunca*) is found at elevations of 4,500 to 11,500 feet in moist mountain meadows in mountain brush, aspen, ponderosa pine, lodgepole pine, spruce-fir, meadow, and alpine tundra communities. Only 4 inches tall, it bears blue-violet 1-inch flowers with a whitish lower petal lined with purple, vertical veins and a prominent backward spur extending beyond the upper petals. Another violet that needs regular moisture is meadow violet (*V. nephrophylla*); it has blue-violet flowers with white markings on the lower three petals and kidney-shaped basal leaves with rounded teeth. One violet that is tolerant of sun, heat, and drought is prairie violet (*V. pedatifida*), a dark purple flowering species with very finely palmately dissected leaves; it is an early bloomer, and will bloom through summer if given regular water.

Viola canadensis

Wyethia arizonica

Wyethia arizonica

ARIZONA MULE'S EARS
SUNFLOWER FAMILY (*ASTERACEAE*)
HERBACEOUS PERENNIAL
HEIGHT: 2 FEET
WIDTH: 2 FEET
ZONE 4

CHARACTERISTICS: Upright native perennial with velvety rosette of large, dark green, hairy basal leaves 3 inches wide, to 18 inches long, with a white, coarse midrib and nearly horizontal veins; smaller stem leaves; large taproot. Bright yellow sunflowers with ten to fifteen rays, yellow disks, heads to 2 ½ inches wide; solitary at tips of stems, sometimes borne down among the basal leaves.

NATIVE RANGE: Four Corners states, in forest openings and moist meadows at 6,400 to 9,500 feet

SEASON OF BLOOM: Late spring to early summer, long-blooming

OUTSTANDING FEATURES: Low-growing perennial with big, soft, velvety basal leaves shaped like mule's ears and large, cheerful, clear yellow sunflowers.

CULTURE

Soil: All moist soils; does well in heavy clays or fine sands

Exposure: Sun

Water use: Moderate

Propagation: Seed

Care and maintenance: Very low. Remove spent flower stalks in spring.

LANDSCAPE USES: Perennial garden, butterfly garden, meadow

WILDLIFE ATTRACTED: Butterflies, birds

HISTORICAL AND MODERN USES: Has been used medicinally by Native Americans. The thick taproot is said to be edible when cooked.

Arizona mule's ears is beautiful when planted with little sunflower (*Helianthella quinquenervis*); also grows well with Arizona fescue (*Festuca arizonica*), golden columbine (*Aquilegia chrysantha*), and native larkspurs and geraniums. A related species, badlands mule's ears (*Wyethia scabra*), has a rosette of smaller basal leaves and is found in sandy soils from Wyoming to Arizona and New Mexico. It is a better choice than Arizona mule's ears for planting in hot dry areas with loose, rocky, or very well drained soils.

Yucca baccata

Yucca baccata

BANANA YUCCA
AGAVE FAMILY (*AGAVACEAE*)
SUCCULENT PERENNIAL
HEIGHT: 2–2 ¹/₂ FEET; FLOWER STALK TO 5 FEET
WIDTH: 3 FEET
ZONE 4

CHARACTERISTICS: Evergreen succulent with thick, upright flowering stalk to 5 feet tall above basal rosette of long, swordlike leaves. Many creamy-white flowers, with six petal-like tepals, to 3 inches long, followed by edible banana-shaped fruits to 5 inches long.

NATIVE RANGE: Southwestern United States, on dry plains and slopes, at elevations of 3,000 to 8,000 feet elevation

SEASON OF BLOOM: Early summer

OUTSTANDING FEATURES: Armed, swordlike leaves; waxy, bell-shaped, ivory flowers that are followed by edible banana-shaped fruits. A dramatic plant that remains green throughout the winter; very drought-tolerant.

CULTURE

Soil: Warm, well-drained

Exposure: Sun

Water use: Very low to low

Propagation: Seed, offsets

Care and maintenance: Very low

LANDSCAPE USES: Accent plant, succulent garden, dry garden, container plant, night garden, ethnobotanic garden

WILDLIFE ATTRACTED: Yucca moths

HISTORICAL AND MODERN USES: Edible flowers, fruits, and seeds; soapy lather made from roots; leaves used to make sandals, woven goods, and baskets.

Unlike plants in the genus *Agave*, which are monocarpic (blooming once and dying after setting seed), yuccas begin to produce flowering stalks and fruits at maturity and continue to do so in alternating years thereafter. They enjoy a fascinating symbiotic relationship with their pollinator, the yucca moth. The banana yucca traditionally supplied many needs of native people and continues to do so today. Flowers, fruits, and seeds are edible. Plant with members of the dry ponderosa pine forest including

Yucca baccata

Parry's agave (*Agave parryi* subsp. *parryi*); cacti including prickly pear, beavertail, claret cup, and hedgehog; Fremont barberry (*Berberis fremontii*); mountain mahogany (*Cercocarpus montanus*); alligator juniper (*Juniperus deppeana*); Apache plume (*Fallugia paradoxa*); common cliffrose (*Purshia stansburiana*); and fernbush (*Chamabatiaria millefolium*), and with plants of the pinyon–juniper woodland including Utah juniper (*Juniperus osteosperma*), one-seed juniper (*J. monosperma*), wolfberry (*Lycium* spp.), and New Mexico olive (*Forestiera neomexicana*). Banana yucca can also be planted as part of a succulent garden. Cobweb yucca (*Yucca harrimaniae*) is a smaller, stemless, architecturally interesting plant; its gray leaves are edged with curling fibers that add to its striking appearance.

Zinnia grandiflora

Zinnia grandiflora

PRAIRIE ZINNIA, LITTLE GOLDEN ZINNIA,
ROCKY MOUNTAIN ZINNIA
SUNFLOWER FAMILY (*ASTERACEAE*)
HERBACEOUS PERENNIAL
HEIGHT: 6–12 INCHES
WIDTH: 6–12 INCHES
ZONE 5

CHARACTERISTICS: Fine-textured low mound with narrow, three-ribbed opposite leaves; covered in many large yellow-orange daisies with three to six rounded ray flowers surrounding reddish disk flowers, in showy heads borne singly on the tips of branches.

NATIVE RANGE: Southwest United States, plains, and Mexico; on the Colorado Plateau, on dry slopes and mesas at elevations up to 6,500 feet

SEASON OF BLOOM: May to October

OUTSTANDING FEATURES: This small, mounding perennial thrives in sunny, windswept locations and is covered with showy yellow-orange flowers in summer. An easy-care plant that is attractive to butterflies and hummingbirds.

CULTURE

Soil: Warm, well-drained

Exposure: Full sun

Water use: Very low to low

Propagation: Seed

Care and maintenance: Very low

LANDSCAPE USES: Dry border, dry wildflower meadow, rock garden, butterfly garden

WILDLIFE ATTRACTED: Hummingbirds, butterflies

Prairie zinnia needs warmth and good drainage to survive. Plant it among rocks for reflected heat, with other dry-loving wildflowers and grasses of the windswept Southwest. Some useful species for similar conditions are Indian ricegrass (*Achnatherum hymenoides*), buffalo grass (*Buchloe dactyloides*), woolly paperflower (*Psilostrophe tagetina*), greenstem paperflower (*P. sparsiflora*), galleta grass (*Pleuraphis jamesii*), showy four-o'clock (*Mirabilis multiflora*), four-wing saltbush (*Atriplex canescens*), alkali sacaton (*Sporobolus airoides*), purple three-awn (*Aristida purpurea* var. *purpurea*), spreading three-awn (*A. divaricata*), whitestem blazing star (*Mentzelia albicaulis*), rose heath (*Chaetopappa ericoides*), cutleaf wild heliotrope (*Phacelia crenulata*), pale evening primrose (*Oenothera pallida* subsp. *pallida*), creeping evening primrose (*O. pallida* subsp. *runcinata*), stemless evening primrose (*O. caespitosa*), southwestern prickly poppy (*Argemone pleiacantha*), small-flowered globe mallow (*Sphaeralcea parvifolia*), scarlet globe mallow (*S. coccinea*), and purplemat (*Nama hispidum*).

USEFUL REFERENCES

Brenzel, Kathleen Norris, ed. *Sunset Western Garden Book*. Menlo Park, Calif.: Sunset Publishing Corp., 2001.

Cronquist, Arthur, et al. *Intermountain Flora: Vascular Plants of the Intermountain West*. New York: Hafner Publishing Co., 1972.

Cullina, William. *New England Wild Flower Society Guide to Growing and Propagating Wildflowers of the United States and Canada*. Boston: Houghton Mifflin Co., 2000.

Davis, Ray J., and collaborators. Dubuque, Iowa: W. C. Brown, 1952.

Hickman, James C., ed. *The Jepson Manual: Higher Plants of California*. Berkeley: University of California Press, 1993.

Kearny, Thomas H., and Robert H. Peebles. *Arizona Flora*. Berkeley: University of California Press, 1964.

Marinelli, Janet, general ed. *The Brooklyn Botanic Garden Gardener's Desk Reference*. New York: Henry Holt and Co., 1998.

Martin, William C., and Charles R. Hutchins. *A Flora of New Mexico*. Vaduz, Germany: J. Cramer, 1980.

Moerman, Daniel E. *Native American Ethnobotany*. Portland, Oreg.: Timber Press, 1998.

Phillips, Harry R. *Growing and Propagating Wild Flowers*. Chapel Hill: University of North Carolina Press, 1985.

Weber, William A. *Colorado Flora: Eastern Slope*. Boulder: University Press of Colorado, 1996.

————. *Colorado Flora: Western Slope*. Boulder: University Press of Colorado, 1996.

Young, James A., and Cheryl G. Young. *Collecting, Processing, and Germinating Seeds of Wildland Plants*. Portland, Oreg.: Timber Press, 1985.

NATIVE PLANT SOURCES

ARIZONA
Biddle's Nursery
1259 Highway 89A
Sedona, AZ 863336-5739
928-282-5078

**Flagstaff Native Plant
and Seed**
400 East Butler Avenue
Flagstaff, AZ 86001
928-773-9406
www.nativeplantandseed.com

Nature's Rewards
2654 East Route 66
Flagstaff, AZ 86004
928-714-9492

**Northern Arizona Tree
Farms**
884 North Highway 89
Chino Valley, AZ 86323-5912
928-636-2663

**Warner's Nursery and
Landscaping**
1101 East Butler Avenue
Flagstaff, AZ 86001
928-774-1983

CALIFORNIA
Las Pilitas Nursery
3232 Las Pilitas Road
Santa Margarita, CA 93453
805-438-5992
www.laspilitas.com

Northwest Native Seed
17595 Vierra Canyon Road
#172
Prunedale, CA 93907
831-663-6031

**Theodore Payne
Foundation**
10459 Tuxford Street
Sun Valley, CA 91352
818-768-1802
www.theodorepayne.org

COLORADO
Alplains Seeds
P.O. Box 489
Kiowa, CO 80117
303-621-2247

Arapahoe Acres Nursery
9010 South Santa Fe Drive
Littleton, CO 80125
303-791-1660
www.arapahoeacres.com

Arkansas Valley Seed
P. O. Box 270
Rocky Ford, CO 81067
719-254-7469
www.seedsolutions.com

Bear Mountain Alpines
P. O. Box 2407
Evergreen, CO 80439
303-674-1209

Chelsea Nursery
3347 G Road
Clifton, CO 81520-8143
970-434-8434

Harlequin's Gardens
4795 North 26th Street
Boulder, CO 80301
303-939-9403
www.harlequinsgardens.com

Laporte Avenue Nursery
1950 Laporte Avenue
Fort Collins, CO 80521
970-472-0017

**Pleasant Avenue
Nursery**
506 South Pleasant Avenue
Buena Vista, CO 81211
719-395-6955

**Rocky Mountain Native
Plants Co.**
3780 Silt Mesa Road
Rifle, CO 81650
970-625-4769

**Rocky Mountain
Rare Plants**
1706 Deerpath Road
Franktown, CO 80116-9462
www.rmrp.com

**Sunscapes Rare
Plant Nursery**
330 Carlile Avenue
Pueblo, CO 81004
719-546-0047
www.sunscapes.net

Timberline Gardens
11700 West 58th Avenue
Arvada, CO 80004
303-420-4060
www.timberlinegardens.com

Western Native Seed
P. O. Box 188
Coaldale, CO 81222
719-942-3935
www.westernnativeseed.com

IDAHO
**Seeds Trust (High
Altitude Gardens)**
4150 B Black Oak Drive
Hailey, ID 83333-8447
208-788-4363
www.seedstrust.com

MONTANA
Bitterroot Restoration
445 Quast Lane
Corvallis, MT 59828
406-961-4991
www.bitterrootrestoration.com

NEVADA
Comstock Seed
917 Highway 88
Gardnerville, NV 89410
775-746-3681
www.comstockseed.com

NEW MEXICO
Agua Fria Nursery
1409 Agua Fria Street
Santa Fe, NM 87505
505-983-4831

**Bernardo Beach Native
Plant Nursery**
3729 Arno Street NW
Albuquerque, NM 87107
505-345-6248

Go Native
P. O. Box 3631
Las Cruces, NM 88003
800-880-4698
www.gonative.com

High Country Gardens
2902 Rufina Street
Santa Fe, NM 87507-2929
800-925-9387
www.highcountrygardens.com

Plants of the Southwest
3095 Agua Fria Road
Santa Fe, NM 87501
800-788-7333, 505-438-8888
www.plantsofthesouthwest.com

Santa Ana Garden Center
157 Jemez Dam Road
Bernalillo, NM 87004
505-867-1322
www.santaana.org/garden.htm

Santa Fe Greenhouses
2902 Rufina Street
Santa Fe, NM 87507
505-473-2700
www.santafegreenhouses.com

Sierra Vista Growers
2800 NM Highway 28
Anthony, NM 88021
505-874-2415

UTAH
Granite Seed
1697 West 2100 North
Lehi, UT 84043
801-768-4422
www.graniteseed.com

Great Basin Native Plants
75 West 300 South
Holden, UT 84636
435-795-2303

High Desert Gardens
2971 South Highway 191
Moab, UT 84532
435-259-4531

Wildland Nursery
550 North Highway 89
Joseph, UT 84739
435-527-1234
www.wildlandnursery.com

WYOMING
Wind River Seed
3075 Lane 51$^1/_2$
Manderson, WY 82401
307-568-3361
www.windriverseed.com

INDEX